001

003

This unusual and multifaceted book evades summary description as an architectural history, a work of urban theory, a sociological, ideological or psychological study, or a text placed within the ambit of cultural studies. The author James Madge was both a professional and academic architect, teaching, lecturing, writing and running his own practice while employed for many years at the Polytechnic of Central London (latterly the University of Westminster). His attachment to architecture as a discipline remained constant (and emphatic in what he identified as properly constituting 'research in architecture'), yet his own education and wide-ranging historical and theoretical knowledge propelled him, later in his career particularly, into territory beyond that conventionally identified with a strictly 'architectural' agenda.

It is this inquisitiveness that informs the posthumous publication of Sabbioneta: Cryptic City and which prompted James to devote, on his retirement from teaching, the final years of his career to researching and writing this book. Undoubtedly it was also motivated by a certain critical dissatisfaction with received opinion on the subject (Vespasiano Gonzaga and Sabbioneta), which he modestly discovered had also been voiced in the available literature, a discourse otherwise secure in its adherence to the institutional canons of Renaissance scholarship (whether of art, economic or social history).

One may speculate to what extent James' family background and classical humanist education grounded this book, his final work. His parents were Kathleen Raine and Charles Madge (William Blake scholar and sociologist respectively) and his mentor at Cambridge Colin Rowe - perhaps the leading architectural theorist of his generation. Cryptic City is focused on the urban culture of the Renaissance, which had preoccupied James at intervals for much of his working life, and its thematic may be related to the unstable mix of pragmatism and idealism that characterized the later phase of post-war reconstruction which he experienced as a young architect. This resurfaces in his preoccupation with the ambivalent proto-modern psyche of Gonzaga, to be construed in the form and meaning of his ideal city Sabbioneta. Throughout his career James established, in the form and content of his lectures, occasional papers and reviews, a trajectory of interest in the emergence of modern architecture; in investigations of material culture laced with social critique; in Phenomenology, and the credentials of the newfound Rationalism developed in the Italian architecture of the 60's and 70's. These interests were mediated by his longstanding knowledge of Renaissance culture, and variously impact on the make-up of Cryptic City.

There is a specific debt to the Italian architects Aldo Rossi and Giorgio Grassi, which is associated with the urban imperatives and revival of classicism explicit in the architecture and thinking of the Italian Neo-Rationalist movement. James recalls his initial experience of Sabbioneta: the city enveloped in fog loses the commonplace charm admired by the visiting tourist. Instead, he observes an urban landscape transformed in an image of uncanny typological cogency. The fog becomes in his description a metaphor for a deeper psychological and architectural intent. In obscuring incidental qualities it ironically serves to clarify the stable architectural form (and spatiality) of Sabbioneta's own set of urban typologies. In this, James' first encounter with his cryptic city, the distinct qualities of Rossi's rationalism are held in imaginative suspension. He neatly deconstructs Rossi's incipient romanticism which viewed the fog entering Sant' Andrea in Mantua as 'the unforeseen element that modifies and alters'. For James at Sabbioneta the fog also reveals a contrary paradigm: Rossi's 'rational construction of the city over time'.

The implications of this observation encapsulate the range of investigation that follows in Cryptic City. From a focus on the social and architectural we move on to the ideological and technical. Building on discussion of cultural exigencies, two 'conversations' at the heart of the book act as precursors to a final dénouement or descent into mythological and psychological aspects of Gonzaga's relationship with his own city (in the final chapters).

As for Rossi, it is the idea of the city in the mind of its 'architect' that is the extended focus of James study, something pursued in considerable depth and which required the literary licence to explore enigmas surrounding Gonzaga, his city and psyche. This content lends a certain gravitas to the book, but also substantiates its cross-disciplinary resonance and value, which is thoroughly embedded in the text. Both Gonzaga's city and James Madge's writing are marked by their respective eras, material culture and protagonist/author/architect's life. To read historically is necessarily a valedictory process, yet an essential one to architects in their practice. While this study may lack the nuanced and stringent perspective of the professional Renaissance scholar, it gains from inhabiting discursive territory at the periphery of architectural discourse. This develops and expands both our architectural comprehension of the city of Sabbioneta and our understanding of the vicissitudes experienced by Vespasiano Gonzaga, its central protagonist (not unrelated, perhaps, to those induced by the habitual idealism of the prototypical modern architect).

Andrew Peckham

Today we tend to think of the culture of 16th century Italy under the rubric Mannerism; in this study of the small, Northern Italian city of Sabbioneta that rubric is pushed to one side and the inert subject of Mannerism is brought to life in a story focused on the activity of building. James Madge approaches the problem of Sabbioneta by conceiving the city as a work of architecture, in other words as a form conditioned by the circumstances of its production. Influenced, but by no means persuaded, by the arguments of the rationalist architects Giorgio Grassi and Aldo Rossi, Madge uses the case of Sabionetta as a means of testing their thinking about the relationship between form and reality. What he discovers is that the most pressing reality factor in the production of Sabbioneta is the mind of Vespasiano Gonzaga. Vespasiano was a cadet prince of the aristocratic Mantuan family of the same name; but Vespasiano actually worked as an agent for the king of Spain, serving as a soldier and a governor of various provinces.

What is interesting about Vespasiano is that he lived at the historical moment when architecture, in the disciplinary sense that we know it today, had only just begun to emerge and was by no means stable. Vespasiano's reflections upon architecture, as expressed in Sabbioneta, of course offer insights into the changing social environment that was the basis of his world; however – and this is what interests Madge - in doing so they, perhaps inadvertently, tell us something about the history of modern architecture that is often left out of more seminal accounts.

Dr Victoria Watson

Bibliotheque McLean
19 Portfleet Place
De Beauvoir Road
London
N1 5SZ

bibliothequemclean.com
mail@bibliothequemclean.com

*The publishers gratefully acknowledge the generous support
of Nicholas Deakin, Anna Hopewell, Andrew Roberts
and Victoria Watson toward the publication of this book.
The publishers would additionally like to thank John Naylor
and Andrew Peckham for help and contributions and
Andrew Roberts for his deft copy-editing and invaluable
editorial advice.*

ISBN 978-0-9558868-1-2

Designed by Mark Boyce

Printed in the United Kingdom by
Butler Tanner and Dennis

Contents

~

Introduction

If the image of Italy, formed in the English mind from holidays in Tuscany, is of a landscape of arid hills hatched by vineyards, softened by the silvery foliage of olive groves, accented by the dark figure of cypress trees and crowned, now and then, by the disorderly cluster of a small town, then the plain of Lombardy is hardly, in this sense, 'Italian' at all. Lombardy, on the contrary, is as flat as any landscape can be, the only elevation being the huge earth embankments which contain the flooding of the Po and its tributaries. Most of the time, even when one is close to them, the Alps are invisible in a fine haze and when, on an unusually clear day, they do appear it is as a ghostly whiteness almost indistinguishable from cloud. The Apennines, to the south, present their shaded side to the Po valley and can usually be made out as dark outlines of indeterminate distance. Between these ranges, expanding in width from West to East, lies some of the most fertile and productive land in Europe, constantly supplied with water from the alpine snows, an intricate and entirely man-made network of irrigation channels and waterways and a mosaic of immaculately tended fields, orchards and plantations, trees in straight rows and irregular clumps in which, for all the vastness of the sky, one feels always enclosed. It is a landscape which has been continuously ordered and managed since Roman times and which has supported a population, both urban and rural, of greater density than would be found elsewhere in southern Europe.

Traditional rural architecture in Lombardy is almost entirely of brick and roman tile, with the un-dressed trunks of poplar trees for main beams; farms (cascine) are huge agglomerations, built to accommodate numerous families, with open-sided barns of enormous scale and uncompromising structural clarity. In the towns, a similar architecture has the added decorum of a plaster coating which translates the constructional forms of rural building into an urbane but understated classicism. Because the 'architecture' which one sees in Lombardy resides, so frequently, in the buildings' plaster veneer which needs to be renewed on a regular basis, it is more difficult than elsewhere to date it with accuracy or to identify subsequent modifications; the cycle of renewal provides, on the other hand, an opportunity to see the architecture in a marvellously pristine condition, un-mellowed by the action of time. Many of the small towns in Lombardy retain the imprint of a roman castrum, with regular street layout and at least a trace of walls or gateways. They tend to have a strongly defined centre, marked by a constituted public open space, in, or adjacent to which it is not uncommon to find stretches of arcading at street level.

The experience of being in a small town in Lombardy is, in many respects, encapsulated in the experience of being in Sabbioneta; one has the sensation that here, in a complete form, is the town which all the others have not quite managed to be. Only in a few instances, at first sight, does its architecture suggest an ambition beyond that to be found elsewhere; only in a few places does the regularity of its order suggest an origin unlike that of many towns nearby. It is easy not to notice that the sequence of Sabbioneta's spaces and the scale of its elements have been 'managed' to increase the sensation of closure, density or extent; these things become apparent only later. And yet one has a very distinct impression, at Sabbioneta, that one is intruding in another person's world. That other person is, of course, Vespasiano Gonzaga (1531-1591), by whom Sabbioneta was invented.

Of tall stature, fair complexion, blue eyes; his limbs graceful and well-formed ~
with a long neck: accustomed through habit to the rigours of military life,
indifferent to heat or cold, he was never heard to complain of such afflictions;
often he would stand three or four hours in the scorching sun or dress in the
winter frost as others would in the summer. Content, if necessary, to eat along
with his soldiers, he dressed unobtrusively, was abstemious and took little
sleep. He had an air of authority and to feel his look could inspire either fear 012
or love; the tone of his voice was firm and clear: even in anger - astonishing,
but true - he never said what he might later regret; he entertained no mean
thoughts. [1]

So, in Alessandro Lisca's 'official' biography published in Latin a year after his death, was Vespasiano Gonzaga consigned to historical record. The qualities of stoical self-control which are here stressed are those which, by the conventions of his day, might sufficiently have accounted for the personal prestige which he enjoyed and for the admiration (much of it, evidently, genuine) which he seems to have commanded during his lifetime. From a twenty-first century standpoint, however, these qualities are likely to be understood as more specifically negative: what he did not feel, what he did not say, what inner state he did not reveal. It might appear that the picture of a believable human being, in the full complexity of his interaction with the circumstances of his life, is being deliberately withheld from us. In particular, this catalogue of repressions is clearly inadequate to explain the thing for which Vespasiano is, today, best remembered: the creation of the diminutive, 'ideal' city of Sabbioneta. It offers no clue as to why Vespasiano might have wanted to establish his own city and what, in its architecture, he was trying to achieve - hardly any of his contemporaries, possessing or not possessing comparable personal qualities, did anything remotely similar - but it is precisely these questions which seem, now as much as ever, to demand some sort of answer.

By 1878, when Attilio Carli's *Vespasiano Gonzaga Duca di Sabbioneta* was published in Florence, Vespasiano had accumulated no less than five biographies, the first two written very shortly after his death, one dating from the middle of the eighteenth century and two from the second half of the nineteenth. Reflecting, as each of these does, the proprieties, the priorities and the prejudices of the times in which they were written, these works can still be said to have in common an essentially didactic intention: to hold up the example of Vespasiano for the purpose of moral instruction. His actions, even though they may be, to a greater or less extent, embellished, censored or excused, are nevertheless to be taken at their face value, unambiguous and intentional, the life and person of Vespasiano being the sum of these actions. More modern biographical writing has wanted, increasingly, to shift its focus towards the experience of its subjects, the unfolding of their emotional and social relationships, and their political, cultural or physical environment. The only full-length biography of Vespasiano Gonzaga written during the twentieth century, that of Luca Sarzi Amadè, *Il Duca di Sabbioneta - Guerre e amori di un Europeo del XVI Secolo* (Milan 1990), reflects this changed focus of interest. Constructed like an historical travelogue, it offers a remarkably vivid account of the places and the situations in which Vespasiano found himself and it is as the sum of these experiences that Vespasiano is now seen to emerge.

1. *Alessandro Lisca: Vita di Vespasiano Gonzaga (in Latin) Verona, 1592. quoted in Irene Affò: Vita di Vespasiano Gonzaga, Parma, 1780, p.64.*

While, in the major biographies of Vespasiano Gonzaga, the construction of Sabbioneta remains a significant but secondary component of his life, the increasing volume of writing on the subject of Sabbioneta itself has tended, reciprocally, to cast Vespasiano in an instrumental but still a subsidiary role. Whilst the last fifty or so years have seen an impressive advance in the historical and interpretive study of Sabbioneta to the point that this is now a minor but significant branch of Renaissance scholarship, and while Sabbioneta's innovations, derivations and thematic transformations have come to be expounded with ever-increasing subtlety and erudition, the figure of Vespasiano himself seems to remain as two-dimensional as Alessandro Lisca left him in 1592. The 'enigma' of Sabbioneta, to which more than one writer[2] has wanted to draw attention is still, in these cases, an enigma whose solution is to be extracted from a study of the object itself and of comparable objects, rather than by seeking a deeper understanding of the man. There is an obvious reason for this, namely the lack of any direct evidence which can, with the degree of historical certainty expected in a work of scholarship, offer a view of the inner mental life of Vespasiano Gonzaga. The generally formal reticence of his correspondence, even where it touches matters of deep personal concern, the seemingly conventional - even derivative - tone of his poetry, the obviously 'staged' presentation of the extant portraits, all of these, like the record of his actions and the comments of his contemporaries (valuable though the insights which can be gained from all of them may be) might well discourage further investigation of Vespasiano's true state of mind. Still more, the sensational fabrications of A. Racheli[3], though they continue to infect the work of some more modern writers, should stand as a warning not to invent that which available evidence cannot supply.

It is, nevertheless, the purpose of this book to illuminate the architecture of Sabbioneta as, precisely, the architecture of a state of mind. Vespasiano Gonzaga was free, as 'professional' architects of his (or other) times could hardly be, to explore his own existential condition through the medium of architecture and he was not obliged to explain himself to anyone else. Had he done so in terms which could, in his day, have been understood, both his explanation and its representation in architectural form - the possibility of what architecture could do - must have remained trapped within the conventions of that time. It is intended, however, in what follows, to show that Vespasiano did explain himself with remarkable clarity, even if the conventions of his time would not have allowed him - let alone his contemporaries - to understand that he was doing so.

The major piece of 'evidence' is, of course, Sabbioneta itself. Sabbioneta has survived four hundred years of turbulent history very largely unscathed, its fortified perimeter still almost intact, all but one of its principal monuments in place, its street layout unchanged and only a handful of more modern buildings testifying to the economic stagnation in which, during most of these years, it has been suspended. So emphatically material a fact cannot as easily be reduced to an abstraction as the hearsay existence of its creator can. The character of Sabbioneta is complex and contradictory, unpredictable and elusive; it is also palpably saturated with the personality of Vespasiano Gonzaga so that to speak of one is also, in a sense, to speak of the other. Only in a sense, however: in creating Sabbioneta, Vespasiano had still to work within the limits of what a city, in that place and time, could be; he could adapt, but he could not invent its cultural meaning. In the same way, though it might be possible to describe Sabbioneta in such a way as, at the same time, to describe the state of mind in which Vespasiano conceived it, such a description could not stand as a sufficient or complete account of the mental life which he led. Neither Sabbioneta nor its creator can be reduced, in this way, to the other.

2. e.g. L. Puppi, in his Preface to P.Carpeggiani, Sabbioneta Mantua, 1972, p.III: "it. presents an enigma which seems to demand interrogation" and H-W Kruft, Städte in Utopia, Munich, 1989, p.50: "As a visitor one is like a spectator in a scenery store, trying to reconstruct the play"
3. A. Racheli, Memorie Storiche del dottor A.R., Casalmaggiore, 1849.

In seeking to identify the particular and special, as opposed to the ~
generic or typical qualities which render Vespasiano and his city significant as objects
for investigation, it is necessary, in a sense, to create an artificial space in which they
may appear as distinct from the material and cultural conditions in and by which they
were, in another sense, undoubtedly formed. A legitimate aim of historical writing can
be, of course, to subsume specific detail within a wider explanatory framework and
much of the literature concerning Sabbioneta has been directed towards this end. The
city and its creator become representatives of historical types: the type, for instance,
of a patrician class seeking to assert its power and prestige through forms which bore
conventional meanings: the type of an out-dated humanism nostalgically resuscitated
in an attempt to shut out the realities of a world in transformation: the type of an early,
uncertain step towards a new concept of urban planning, of a practical demonstration
of contemporary architectural theory or of a coded reconstruction of Antiquity. All of
these, as well as others and variations upon them, have been put forward as ways by
which Sabbioneta and Vespasiano Gonzaga could be given a relevant and secure place
in history, but all entail the risk that, drawn and superimposed upon a predetermined
pattern, Sabbioneta and Vespasiano will simply merge into their background and
disappear again from view. In the necessarily artificial space of hindsight which
this work has sought to allow him, Vespasiano may, indeed, be seen to emerge as
representative of a type - a type constructed retrospectively in the writing of the culture
of sixteenth-century Europe, hardly perceptible as a distinct entity but which, in the
writings, for instance, of Machiavelli, Montaigne or Shakespeare, can be detected in
its first efforts to define itself: the type of an 'early modern man'. The architecture
of Sabbioneta, if it has a place anywhere, has a place within some such narrative as
this.

It would be an impertinence to suppose that Vespasiano lived his life
in order to satisfy the curiosity of readers yet unborn, just as it is certain (whatever
other reasons he may have had), that he did not build Sabbioneta for the purpose
of filling a page in the history of art. There can be little doubt, on the other hand,
that Vespasiano, (not untypical in this respect) was deeply concerned with his image
in the eyes of his contemporaries and almost obsessively so with the perpetuation
of his name and memory after his death. It is also clear that he was able to exercise
very tight control over the presentation of his image and actions while he was alive
as well as over the record that might be available to posterity. One might almost say
that the dominant project of his life was, precisely, the construction of this image and
this record. In constructing himself as an historical figure, however, Vespasiano had
a very different idea of history from that which we assume today; for him, actions
and statements as well as buildings were, indeed, things expected to be taken at face
value. But this is only to say that those values are not, for us, 'face' values any more;
we cannot participate in them even if we should wish to. The questions we now ask
preclude, by their nature, answers which lie visibly on the surface which Vespasiano
presented.

Because the purpose of this study is to illuminate a state of mind
rather than to tell a story, the biographical material which it contains is not presented
chronologically but works, generally, from the end backwards (or inwards) from the
completed forms of the city and the man through the various layers or strands of their
formation. To put it another way, the investigation will start with that which can be
clearly seen (and was intended to be seen) by the outside world, searching always for
the fissures in this surface through which it may be possible to open up and explore
those more shadowy areas which might, in the public picture, appear only fleetingly
or as absences.

In Part One, then, Sabbioneta is considered first as a human and social reality in which the lives of numerous people were bound together; then, as an architectural event whose significance would have been evaluated, by Vespasiano's contemporaries, in terms of current ideas about what a city was or might be expected to be. In Part Two, Vespasiano becomes the central focus in relation to his 'working' life as a soldier and a participant in the political affairs of his time, while Part Three looks at him in the context of the intellectual world, the affinities, the influences and the enthusiasms which formed his cultural outlook. Part Four is concerned with the more personal agendas which can be discovered in Vespasiano's literary production, in the iconography and in the architectural imagery of Sabbioneta. Such a procedure as this brings with it inevitable risks in that it moves progressively away from the safe confines of verifiable evidence; beginning firmly upon solid ground, we can push boulders and ballast out from the shore until the water becomes too deep and then, at a certain point, it becomes necessary to construct a jetty of planks held in place by posts driven into the sea's floor. Eventually, there is no choice but to step into a small craft, taking care not to capsize, unfasten its moorings and move away, at the mercy of currents and tides, to navigate according to bearings of uncertain distance. The reward of a good catch is not available to those who remain on dry land.

My own first experience of Sabbioneta was in early January, 1988, when the whole of Lombardy was, as it tends to be in the winter, enveloped in fog. It was impossible, in these circumstances, to form an impression of the city as a whole or to enjoy the sensation of intimate and relaxed charm which a visitor is likely to receive on a fine summer's day. Instead, each incident of its architecture appeared in succession as an isolated and memorably insistent presence. The half-submerged bulk of the octagonal Incoronata, the disappearing perspective of arcaded streets, the ducal palace crowned by a floating central altana, the seemingly endless Corridor Grande over its empty portico and its miniature reproduction in a fragment of elevated corridor, each entirely absorbed in its own recollection of architectural type and presenting, collectively, an atmosphere distinctly uncanny if not bordering on the insane. This first, ghost-like encounter has, no doubt, left me pre-disposed to read into Sabbioneta something more than the conventional historical categories which many writers seem to have found sufficient. Sabbioneta, seen in the light of this intuition, continues, on every subsequent visit, to reveal further clues pointing away from facile interpretation.

It has heartened me to discover that I am not alone in my belief that there is more to Vespasiano Gonzaga and his city than has, in general, met the eye of their commentators. Marzio Dall'Acqua has put it perfectly:

> ....it would already be a success if we were able to instil a degree of doubt, if we could raise some questions to clear away the mire of the self-evident and the already written, that might indicate a new line for investigation. Vespasiano Gonzaga deserves it.[4]

4. Marzio Dall'Acqua, "Il Principe e la sua Primogenita" in Atti del Convegno, p.34. This is an unusually thoughtful paper, though of limited scope. Certainly, in the author's terms, it can be counted 'a success'.

Pt 1

~1)

The Human Phenomenon. Modern aspirations and contingent limitations.

020

Philosophy endowed states with souls when she made human laws on earth reflect the divine laws of heaven. She brought forth the body of the state and made it grow by providing agriculture, architecture, medicine, military skill and every other art that gives nourishment, elegance, or protection to a state.[5]

For the few thousand human beings[6] who lived in and immediately around it during the last quarter of the sixteenth century, Sabbioneta was not just a political abstraction or an architectural idea; it was a material fact. The lives that were lived there and the social and physical circumstances in which they were lived represented, or must, at least, have seemed to represent, for the most part, a normal state of affairs of more immediate significance than the unusual historical circumstances which had caused them to be living there. By good fortune, we can piece together a fairly accurate picture of what everyday life in Sabbioneta was like and of how the city, at that time, was perceived by its inhabitants from a contemporary diary, of which large extracts have survived and in which the view of a distinctly 'common' man is unselfconsciously presented.

"At the time of the carnival [March, 1590] for fifteen days there was great happiness in Sabbioneta"[7]. There was dancing in the Salon de Cavalli, where, eight months earlier, duke Vespasiano Gonzaga had installed ten equestrian statues in colourfully painted wood, his ancestors and himself, lined up along the walls. Niccolo de Dondi, our informant of these events, together with five other junior functionaries, performed their speciality, a two-sword morris-dance while groups of young men from Sabbioneta, Bozzolo and Guastalla played comedies after dinner in the same salon. On the special days of the carnival there were two plays, as the professional troupe of actors from Ferrara, the 'Confidenti', retained by Vespasiano to perform regularly at Sabbioneta, put on 'pastorals and comedies' in the newly completed Teatro al'Antico[8]. Other highlights included tilting at the ring, but tilting at the quintain had to be abandoned on account of the very bad weather.

The inauguration of the theatre with a performance of *Oedipus Rex* was, however, more than a local, seasonal celebration; attended by a glittering array of princes, noblemen and their consorts, it was a cultural event of national significance comparable to the opening, six years earlier, of Palladio's Teatro Olimpico at Vicenza (at which, also, *Oedipus Rex* had been performed). Dondi (whose principal concerns: murders, weddings, the price of food and the weather correspond more closely to those of a tabloid reader than of a present-day art historian) was evidently not aware that a Greek tragedy was being presented and he was probably not alone in this. The visual effect of the presentation must, in any case, have been stunning; many of those present had probably never before experienced a theatrical production in a purpose-made interior al'Antico; and the theatre at Sabbioneta, whose sculptures and colonnaded crescent above the cavea merged, almost imperceptibly into the fictive space of painted galleries, revealing through archways the landscape and monuments of Rome, would still have been an impressive novelty. The glittering spectacle of theatrical productions seems to have been as important to audiences in sixteenth-century Italy as their dramatic themes; Ariosto captures some of the excitement:

> *As when the curtain falls to show a scene*
> *Illumined by a thousand brilliant lights,*
> *Where archways, statues, monuments are seen,*
> *Where paint and gilding add to the delights*[9]

5. M.Ficino, *Meditations on the Soul: Selected Letters of Marsilio Ficino*, (tr. Members of the Language Department, School of Economic Science, London) Rochester, Vermont, 1996, p.106.
6. I have been unable to discover any firm indication of Sabbioneta's population during the last quarter of the sixteenth century and it seems unlikely, given the constant migrations in and out of a community such as this, that anyone would, at the time, have possessed accurate information about it. B.Arrighi, *Storia Di Mantova*, Milan 1859, p.492., gives a total population for Sabbioneta of 7106, for Bozzolo, 4240, Rivarolo, 3578 and Commessaggio, 1568. Since, in the mid-nineteenth century, none of these towns had expanded significantly beyond their walls (nor, indeed, have they since) one might guess that Vespasiano's subjects in Lombardy might have numbered between 15,000 and 20,000 souls.
7. N. de Dondi, *Estratti del Diario delle cose avvenute in Sabbioneta dal 1580 al 1600*, in G. Müller, *Raccolta di Cronisti e Documenti Storici Lombardi Inediti*, Milan,1856, p. 359.
8. It seems to have been these same 'Confidenti' who left Michel de Montaigne 'well satisfied' when he attended their performance at Bologna ten years previously, on 19th. November 1580. See Michel de Montaigne, *Viaggio in Italia*, Milan, 2003, p.214.
9. Lodovico Ariosto, *Orlando Furioso*, (first published 1516) Canto XXXII, verse 80. Translation by Barbara Reynolds, London, 1997.

With the completion of the theatre, a building programme which had started in 1554, when Vespasiano Gonzaga was twenty-three years old, came virtually to an end. A house belonging to a certain Pietro Giacomo Lombardi Orsolini was demolished (with some compensation) so that a chapel could be built on the site; a pergola of oak columns and beams was put up in the garden; a marble coat of arms fixed on the galleria facing the castello; and a pointed roof recently added to one of the towers of the castello was taken down and rebuilt lower. But these were no more than minor corrections and afterthoughts to a project which was now as complete as it would ever be. The conversion to firewood in 1590 of what scaffolding remained in the city added symbolic force to this finality[10].

The festivity of the theatre's inauguration belied a mood at Sabbioneta not only melancholic but deeply apprehensive. Vespasiano, though not yet sixty years of age, was failing rapidly in health and spirit. No longer able to walk or to ride, he had to be carried in a litter. For twelve years he had been without a male heir, following the tragic (and not fully explained) death of his fifteen-year-old son, Luigi, while Vespasiano's last, desperate attempt (if such it was) to beget a male heir with his (third) marriage in 1583 to Margherita Gonzaga had been unsuccessful. A few weeks before the carnival, nine mules had arrived from Rome with a load of marble ordered for Vespasiano's funeral monument.[11]

In these circumstances, the future of Sabbioneta, subsequent to Vespasiano's expected death, was problematic. Sabbioneta, together with nearby San Martino dall'Argine and Bozzolo were in a reciprocal feudal arrangement whereby, if any were without a male heir, it would automatically revert to whichever other could claim seniority[12]. The Gonzaga of San Martino, as well as the duke of Mantua, were already manoevering to get their hands on Sabbioneta. Vespasiano was determined, however, that his daughter Isabella, with her husband, Luigi Carrafa della Marra, Prince of Stigliano, might inherit the dukedom (though it seems that this young prince was a far from popular prospect to the inhabitants of Sabbioneta and rumors were circulating, still worse, that the city might be 'sold' to Philip II of Spain or even to France[13]). For the first time since the city's foundation, it appeared that its elaborate fortifications might be put to the test.

In the event, following Vespasiano's death in February, 1591, a settlement was negotiated through imperial notaries, whereby Isabella and her husband bought the dukedom of Sabbioneta for 180,000 scudi[14], more, it seems, from a sense of duty than through any wish to perpetuate Vespasiano's vision of courtly magnificence there. Although their annual income from Carrafa's rents was in the order of 200,000 scudi, they lived frugally.[15] Apart from the prestige of the title, it is hard to see exactly what it was that they were buying; the city had little in the way of economic life, and the cost of a garrison to defend it would probably exceed the income which it could generate. Sabbioneta had always been a project into which Vespasiano poured the wealth which came to him from other sources; in no conventional way could it be described as an investment. Neither could it have provided, had there been an heir driven by such ambition, any significant power-base from which to operate in the political arena. But if Sabbioneta made sense only in relation to the person of Vespasiano Gonzaga, what is surprising is that Vespasiano's local cousins as well as the dukes of Mantua should have been so easily taken in, seeing Sabbioneta not for what, in itself, it was but for what Vespasiano had made it seem to be: an important asset militarily, politically and artistically.

10. de Dondi, op.cit. p.374. 150 cartloads of timber from the streets were taken to the brickworks outside Sabbioneta.
11. Ibid., p.358.
12. Attilio Carli, Vespasiano Gonzaga Duca di Sabbioneta, Florence, 1878, p. 229. Carli's 'framed portrait' was written with the benefit of documentary material (including architectural drawings by Vespasiano) which were subsequently destroyed 'as being of no historical interest'.
13. L. S. Amadè, Il Duca di Sabbioneta - Guerre e amori di un Europeo del XVI Secolo, Milan, 1990, p. 285.
14. Money equivalents are difficult to establish in an economy still to a considerable extent based upon payments in kind. The schoolmaster at Sabbioneta was paid 300 scudi p.a.; 2,500 scudi was specified in Vespasiano's will to pay for the internal decoration of the church of the Incoronata. 400 scudi secured the troupe of actors from Ferrara for sixty days a year and the same sum purchased six antique sculptures from Mantua. The estates of Trajetto, Ostiano, Rodigo and Fondi inherited by Vespasiano from his mother, each with a population of 3-5000 but inefficiently managed, yielded 12,500 p.a.
15. Carli, Op. Cit. p.237.

That the phenomenon of Sabbioneta, as distinct from the illustrious person of its ruler, should have appeared convincing in the eyes of Vespasiano's contemporaries is evidence of the single-minded persistence with which he set about constructing its identity. Initially, the process was one of consolidation: a decree of 27th September, 1562 required that all citizens 'and other persons' having previously lived within the confines of Sabbioneta return within the walls with the whole of their families within the next month upon pain of losing all exemptions, immunities and privileges, either of their persons or their possessions[16]. All trading in grain and livestock was restricted to the piazza. Already, in 1557, the monastery outside the castello (St Nicholas?) had been demolished and re-located within the city[17] where were also established the houses of San Rocco and the 'Sisters of Sabbioneta'. Absentee clergy were constrained to occupy their livings. Measures such as these were by no means exceptional at the time but it required more than written edicts to make them stick.

Prior to Vespasiano's re-foundation of Sabbioneta, a small but significant Jewish community was established there, operating the 'third' bank of the principality of Mantua (founded in 1436) as well as the Hebrew printing establishment founded in 1551 and run with considerable success until the year of Vespasiano's death in 1591[18]. Although they seem to have been under continual pressure to convert to Christianity (during Lent of 1589, a Capuchin father who was preaching in the city threw in a couple of sermons for the Jews[19] and the baptism, in 1593, of a Jewish child was the occasion of some allegrezza[20]) the degree of toleration and protection afforded to the Jews in Sabbioneta compared favorably with contemporary practices in many (though not all) other parts of Italy[21]. Like the illustrious founder of Rome, Vespasiano also accepted persons who had been outlawed in other states, provided they were able to put down a deposit of 200 scudi[22].

Such, then, was the basic nucleus around which Vespasiano had constructed a population for his city; to the extent that it was made up of people who might, credibly, have been there in any case, people who had something to do within the established pattern of economic and social affairs, it provided an identity for Sabbioneta as a township comparable to many others in the district. But the structure of Sabbioneta's population was progressively transformed with the superimposition of extraneous elements by whose presence it acquired the status of civitas[23]: soldiers, intellectuals and artists.

16. Carli, Op. Cit. p.92.
17. Giancarlo Malacarne, "Gli Stemmi di Vespasiano Gonzaga del Ramo Cadetto di Sabbioneta" in Atti del Convegno, cit.. p.86.
18. By Tobias ben Eliezer Foa until, in 1567, Foa having fallen foul of church authorities (Vespasiano seems to have protected him as far as he was able) it was taken over by his gentile pupil, Vicenzo Conte. See The Jewish Encyclopedia, 1900, p. 608.
19. de Dondi, Op. Cit., p.346.
20. Ibid. p.432.
21. I know of no precise figure for the size of the Jewish community at Sabbioneta. In Arrighi's time (see note 2) out of 1080 families in Sabbioneta, some 200 were said to be Jewish, but this section of the population had been growing.
22. M. Dall'Acqua, "Il Principe e la sua Primogenita" in Atti del Convegno, p.40.
23. See Kurt W. Forster, "From Rocca to Civitas: Urban Planning at Sabbioneta" in L'Arte Fasc. 5, March 1959. Vespasiano began to call Sabbioneta a città from 1558.

Sabbioneta's permanent military establishment was substantial in relation to the city's population: when, in 1563, Vespasiano had attended the sumptuous wedding of Alfonso II d'Este, duke of Ferrara, to Barbara of Austria, sister of the emperor, he was attended by a hundred and fifty cavalry, twenty German foot-soldiers and fourteen mounted auxiliaries as well as a number of pages. Of the cavalry, more than a hundred were young members of the lesser nobility, an indication of the number of such families that had been induced to take up residence at Sabbioneta. The splendour of Vespasiano's retinue on this occasion was said to outshine that of the dukes of Mantua[24]. On Sunday, 1st October, 1589, Vespasiano paraded his troops outside the Porta Vittoria; Dondi ennumerates the contingents[25]:

From Sabbioneta: Fifty-three, dressed in jackets of crimson tan with green buttons.
From Ostiano: Forty, in variegated leaf colours.
From Rodigo: Thirty-eight in yellow cloth
From Bozzolo: Fifty, dressed in crimson.
From Rivarolo: Forty-one in deep blue.

These soldiers were 'sforzati', conscripted sons of the local gentry; in addition, there were forty-nine paid soldiers:

Arquebusiers: Seventeen dressed in green cloth with sleeves in three colours, red, white and green.
Cavalry: Thirty-two, armed and wearing green cloth jackets with velvet sleeves of red and white.

It seems that bombardiers were not included as objects of display, but to man Vespasiano's substantial arsenal of cannon (ninety-seven pieces were founded in 1586[26], bringing the total to more than a hundred and twenty) there must have been a sizeable number of these.

By comparison with the numbers of troops often to be found in neighbouring Casalmaggiore, regularly used as a staging-post for troops in the service of Philip II (twelve companies stopped there, for instance, in 1582, on their way from Naples to Flanders to fight the 'Ugonotti'), Vespasiano's 'army' could hardly have counted as a formidable fighting force, its function apparently more symbolic - and, it seems, decorative - than operational. Largely recruited from local families, the soldiers in Sabbioneta do not appear to have been disruptive of civil life; for two murders reported by Dondi in Sabbioneta between 1580 and 1591, there were ten in Casalmaggiore.

024

24. See Irene Affò, Vita di Vespasiano Gonzaga, Parma, 1780, p.35. Affò, archivist at the papal library at Parma, was a prolific writer of biography (including Vespasiano's father, Luigi Gonzaga and his aunt Giulia) and other antiquarian subjects. Despite the prominence of moral, religious and political attitudes which reflect the times in which he wrote, his research is remarkably thorough and his interpretation generally shrewd and unbiassed.
25. de Dondi, Op. Cit.,p.354.
26. L.S.Amadè, Op. Cit. p.275.

Intellectuals

If the male offspring of respectable families had the opportunity to advance themselves by means of military instruction, Vespasiano had also provided that they could follow the other 'road by which to become useful and achieve nobility'[27] appointing Mario Nizolio from Brescello to organise 'free' instruction in Latin, Greek, Law and Medicine. Of the 300 scudi which he was to receive, 100 was to be provided directly by Vespasiano 'for the love and care which he has for his subjects' and the rest to be raised by a levy on these same subjects 'whether exempt or not' with residents of Sabbioneta paying more than those of the other towns on account of the greater convenience of having the school on their doorstep. By the same Statute, and on pain of a fine of 200 scudi, his subjects were forbidden to send their sons to school anywhere else. Unlike the famous school set up at Mantua by Vespasiano's great-great-great-grandfather, Gianfrancesco Gonzaga, where Vittorino da Feltre was responsible for the education of a generation of brilliant humanist aristocrats - as well as some of their wives[28] - it seems that Vespasiano's Academy at Sabbioneta had little lasting impact. In 1584, nevertheless, the emperor Rudolf II conferred upon Vespasiano the right to award doctorates (along with the right to legitimise bastards).

Nizolio was aged seventy-four when he took up his appointment at Sabbioneta. Best known, in his day, as the author of the *Observationes*, a lexicon of ciceronian language and usage (versions of which have been part of the apparatus of Latin instruction even down to our own times[29]) he was by no means the conventional and outmoded humanist that this might suggest. Drawn into controversy in defence of Cicero's right to be taken seriously as a philosopher, he believed that he had hit upon a fundamental objection to Aristotelian dialectics as conventionally employed in schools of the sixteenth century.[30] Leibnitz, who discovered and republished Nizolio's *De Veris Principiis* in 1670, was inclined to agree:

> There have been many who have advised, counselled and declaimed for abolishing barbarous terms from philosophy: but few have done what Nizolius did, for it is easier to censure than to correct. [....] Nevertheless there has not yet been found one who so cut to the quick the terminology of the schools in the other branches of philosophy as our Nizolius did in Logic.[31]

We do not know precisely what 'our Nizolius' taught to the youth of Sabbioneta, but of the five principles which he set out in De Veris Principiis, the fourth, the unrestrained liberty of philosophy, suggests an intellectual climate which could in no way be described as *retardataire*:

> To speak more plainly, in the quest for truth one should hold oneself to follow as masters and teachers not so much Plato or Aristotle or any other ancient or modern writer, but rather the five senses, perception, reflection, memory, use, and experience.[32]

27. In the Statute by which the Academy was instituted at Sabbioneta in 1562. Quoted in full by Affò, Op. Cit., p. 31.
28. See W.H.Woodward, Vittorino da Feltre and other Humanist Educators, Cambridge, 1897. Lodovico II Marquis of Mantua met his future spouse, Barbara of Brandenburg, at La Gioiosa.
29. Arnold Toynbee is reported to have said that he was brought up on the Observationes in Latin school: see Marius Nizolius, De Veris Principiis, ed. Quirinus Breen, Rome, 1956, Introduction, p.XVII.
30. Rejecting the distinction between syllogism and enthymeme, where the former is 'pure' and the latter 'imperfect', figurative and suitable only for the purposes of rhetoric, Nizolio showed that this arose from a grammatical misunderstanding whereby universal concepts were expressed in the singular form. "One fish stands for all fishes ..... But when one uses the plural, or joins it to the name of the genus, it is not figurative but literal speech." Nizolio believed that this 'discovery' could free philosophy from a confusion which had prevailed over two thousand years.
31. Ibid., p.LV.
32. Ibid., p.LXIX.

A regular visitor at the Sabbioneta court, though not a salaried member of it, was Bernardino Baldi, Abbot of Guastalla, poet and polymath, who spoke twelve languages and was among the first to take an interest in Etruscan antiquities. His 'head-hunting', recorded by Affò[33], is indicative of his precocious reputation. In 1580, when Baldi was twenty-six years old, he was appointed as court mathematician to Ferrante Gonzaga II, duke of Guastalla and brother-in law to Vespasiano on the latter's marriage to Margherita Gonzaga; but he was also under heavy pressure to take up a post at the ducal court at Mantua as instructor to the young prince Vincenzo, causing a voluminous correspondence between various intermediaries, threats, cajolements and appeals to natural justice. Though Affò is at pains to dismiss claims that Vespasiano was also trying to lure Baldi to Sabbioneta on a permanent basis, it is clear that something of the sort was in the offing. With increasing insistence, Margherita wrote to him in Vespasiano's name, during 1583 and 1584, pressing him "to stay eight or ten days, not to study, but to pass the time agreeably".

As well as treatises and commentaries on a wide range of subjects and his *Lives of the Mathematicians* (ancient, arabic, medieval and modern), of whose more than two thousand manuscript pages only a small fraction has ever been published, Baldi wrote a number of works concerning architecture, evidently related to conversations between himself and Vespasiano, to which we shall return[34]. Also on the prompting of Vespasiano, Baldi devised a large-scale solar timepiece which was evidently intended to be set up at Sabbioneta:

> *My excellent and very dear friend.*
>
> *The Duchess my wife has given me the drawing for the clock, and the gnomon. I am pleased to see that the obelisc can be fifteen feet high and the base able to receive shadow up to 23 hours, and that if Signor Don Ferrante doesn't go to Genoa accompanying Her Excellency, that you will be able to get over here when I send for you at a time when we can expect suitable weather, dry and clear with plenty of sunshine and the ground not sodden, so that we can set it out at our pleasure. Since nothing else occurs to me, I commend myself to you,*
>
> *From Sabbioneta, 22nd March 1583,*
> *Vespasiano Gonzaga[35].*

Carlo Magnanimi, among the musicians salaried at Sabbioneta, was also in demand at more powerful courts, including that of Guglielmo, duke of Mantua, whose otherwise lack-lustre cultural establishment was in the forefront of musical development[36]. In more or less permanent residence at the court of Sabbioneta, there was an assorted company of intellectuals; Attilio Carli's reconstruction[37] includes the following:

There were two legal experts and a writer of Latin texts.

There was a thirty-year-old, self-taught mathematician, astronomer, doctor and philosopher (presumably the 'Giuseppe Scala Siciliano Matematico' who received 100 scudi in Vespasiano's will[38]) who made astronomical observations from a tower at the back of the ducal palace.

There was a scholar of Greek with a special interest in Greek music; he is said to have believed that art could improve upon nature in respect of young peoples' ears, which could be made receptive to harmony by pulling them.

33. I. Affò, Vita di Monsignore Bernardino Baldi, Primo Abate di Guastalla, Parma, 1783, p.29ff..
34. See Guido Zaccagnini, Bernardino Baldi nella Vita e nelle Opere, Pistoia, 1908, p.16.
35. Ibid. p.40.
36. I. Affò, Vita di Vespasiano Gonzaga, Op. Cit. p.50. See also Ian Fenlon, "The Gonzaga and Music" in D.Chambers and J.Martineau, Splendours of the Gonzaga, London, 1981.
37. A. Carli, Op. Cit. Pp.167-178.

Marcello Donati started a botanical garden, still a rarity at the time. (There was also a collection of rare animals[39]).

Two historians were attached to Vespasiano's intellectual circle: Scipione Ammirato and Gianmichele Bruto, both - interestingly, perhaps, in view of Vespasiano's association with the Spanish court of Philip II - committed to a nascent Italian nationalism, the expulsion of foreigners and the establishment of some sort of federal state.

Literature was represented in the persons of Bernardino Marliani, who wrote a life of Castiglione, Bernardo Tasso, father of the more famous poet and 'several other poets'.

There was a genealogist at court, and 'Messer Antonio delli Amici', barber and surgeon (who also got 100 scudi in the will), but, Carli insists, no astrologer and no court jester.

It is clear from a list such as this, which reads more like the cast of a comic opera than the brilliant entourage of Cosimo de' Medici, Giangaleazzo Maria Sforza or Federigo da Montefeltre, that Sabbioneta, for all that some writers have wanted to call it a 'little Athens'[40], represented something other than the perfect flowering of humanist culture. Aside from its limited power as a magnet for exceptional talent (it was not, by the standards of its time, a wealthy court), by the time that Sabbioneta was established the times had moved on and humanists of the old style were in short supply. Intellectuals were more likely to be found in the freer ambience of the Venetian Republic than in the courts of princes where, under the pressures of the counter-reformation and the formality of imported Spanish manners, protocol was coming increasingly to outweigh innovation.

In the view of P. Carpeggiani and a number of other authors, Vespasiano's intellectual circle is to be seen as a nostalgic attempt to reinstate humanistic values no longer relevant in the new climate of Mannerism and the counter-reformation[41]; it is unnecessary, however, to impose historical stereotypes of this sort upon the group of people with whom Vespasiano chose to surround himself. By education and, evidently, by inclination, the classical world was deeply embedded in the culture which Vespasiano personally inhabited, but it is equally clear that he was not simply attempting a re-enactment of courtly patronage as it had flourished in the previous century. Rather, the intellectual life of Sabbioneta seems to have reflected a new, empirical interest in natural, cultural and and historical phenomena which anticipates ways of thinking not fully developed until the following century. We have noted the radical position adopted by Nizolio in terms of authority and truth, in which Quirinius Breen, Nizolio's modern editor, has detected 'a Baconian ring'[42] These issues will be examined later in more detail but there is, in any case, no reason to suppose that Vespasiano's contemporaries would have seen his intellectual circle as anachronistic.

38. Quoted in full by Affò, Op. Cit. Pp.58-63
39. Susanne Grötz, "La Saletta di Enea e il Mite della Città Ideale" in Atti del Convegno, Cit. p.173.
40. e.g. C.Yriarte, "Sabbioneta, la petite Athènes" in Gazette des Beaux Arts XL t.19, 1898.
41. See P. Carpeggiani, Sabbioneta, Mantua, 1972, p. 45.
42. Marius Nizolius, Op. Cit., note 269, p.LXIX.

In his patronage of painting, Vespasiano seems to have chosen, deliberately, not to employ artists with established reputations but to promote undiscovered talent: "That which is not praiseworthy is soon erased, what does that do for me? But if I can bring it about that those gifted by nature become famous by the spur of emulation, people will say that my Sabbioneta is an academy, a school"[43]. Bernardino Campi, one of a family of painters from Cremona who, for a time, set up a studio in Sabbioneta, was an artist of considerable standing in his day. The brothers Alessandro and Giovanni Alberti seem to have produced cartoons for the decoration of the Corridor Grande but to have left rather abruptly before the work was finally executed[44]. Vespasiano is said to have remarked on this occasion: "Let them go; with artists, people of fantasy, you must always expect that one fine day their brains will be turned"[45]. Less fortunate was the young Flemish painter, Joanni a Villa Brabanto, who drowned in the Oglio before reaching Sabbioneta where - who knows? - he might indeed have achieved renown.

Antonio Cavalli, whose foundry at Sabbioneta produced not only coins and medals (Vespasiano is said, himself, to have worked on the dies for a number of these) but also medium-sized artillery pieces and architectural ornaments, was widely admired for the technical quality, though not for the artistic originality, of his work. For his own portrait in bronze, however, Vespasiano took no chances, commissioning Michelangelo's most distinguished successor, Leone Leoni whose seated figure of the duke, in the guise of a Roman Emperor, is the outstanding art treasure still remaining at Sabbioneta. Despite the endeavours of many writers to attach the names of supposed designers to the various works of architecture at Sabbioneta, there is little, if any evidence that anyone who would have been described as an 'architect' - aside from Vincenzo Scamozzi, whose involvement in the design of the theatre and its fixed scene is well documented - worked for any length of time at Sabbioneta during Vespasiano's lifetime.

Vespasiano was a collector, not only of people but also of antiquities, works of art, books and curiosities. Of the works of sculpture which he assembled (some inherited, some purchased and some excavated and sent over from Cartagena in Spain, where he was constructing fortifications), we know only that they formed an important component of the collection later displayed in Mantua under the Habsburgs and rated by a French traveller in 1826 fourth in the whole of Italy, after Rome, Florence and Naples[46]. Some are still to be seen at Mantua, including the amorino by Michelangelo. According to Vasari, Vespasiano possessed three paintings by Giulio Romano, a Birth of Christ featuring the portrait of Isabella Boschetti (mistress of Federigo Gonzaga, first duke of Mantua), 'a beautiful St. Jerome' and a rather strange painting (now in the Hermitage Museum, St. Petersburg) in which two lovers on a couch are secretly watched by an old woman concealed behind the door[47].

028

43. A.Carli, Op. Cit. p.201.
44. U. Bazzotti, "La Galleria degli Antichi di Sabbioneta: Questioni cronologiche, attributative e iconografiche" in Atti del Convegno, Op. Cit. p. 384
45. Quoted (in French) by C. Yriarte, Op. Cit., p.212.
46. A.Carli, Op. Cit. p.183.
47. Giorgio Vasari, Lives of the Artists, trans. G.Bull, London, 1987, Vol. II, p.226. If the 'Petersburg Lovers' was, indeed, as Vasari claims, a gift to Vespasiano from Duke Federigo, it was a curiously inappropriate thing to give to a boy who cannot have been more than nine years old (Federigo died in 1540) and, in the event, prophetically tactless.
48. A.Racheli, Memorie Storiche di Sabbioneta, (first published Casalmaggiore, 1849) Bologna, 1979. p.682. In this case, Racheli can probably be trusted, as he is quoting decrees of 1586 and 1587. The arrangements described here are markedly superior to those which prevail at the public library at Sabbioneta today.
49. Quoted in I.Affò, Op.Cit., p.50.

There were two libraries at Sabbioneta: Vespasiano's private collection which was kept in his own studiolo and the other, accessible to the public, in the care of the Servite monks. This library was open on Tuesdays, Thursdays and Saturdays during normal office hours, subject to permission of the librarian, for those properly dressed in doublet and 'cappa da corte'; those who attempted to get in by bribing the custodian were banned thereafter[48]. The contents of neither library is now known but a Cremonese bookseller, Tommaso Vachelli (not, admittedly, an altogether disinterested witness) praised Vespasiano's collection in 1581 as 'far ahead of those of other princes in number, variety of authors, antiquity and elegance'[49]. Affò, writing in 1780, had seen, still extant, a great number of letters in which, throughout his life, Vespasiano engaged his 'dependants' to search out books for him.

Two years before his death, Vespasiano had the portraits of famous generals removed from his galleria to make room for deers' antlers and other naturalia which he had sent from Prague. One wonders whether the eleven large and eleven small buffalos that arrived from Fondi (Vespasiano's birthplace and, after his mother's death, his property on the coast between Rome and Naples) on 22nd October[50] 1589 were intended as an addition to Vespasiano's live collection of rare species or as part of some abortive agricultural project. In either case, we have further evidence of a somewhat eccentric foray into a nascently 'modern' and empirical interest in natural phenomena.

Without wishing, on the one hand, to smother the life and culture of Vespasiano's Sabbioneta (as some writers have done) beneath a blanket of superlatives or, on the other, to marginalise it within a broader synoptic account of the progress of European civilization, one might, nevertheless, allow that Sabbioneta, in the last year of Vespasiano's life, convincingly represented ideas which were cherished by other Italians of the time. It was an independent duchy subject only to the Holy Roman Emperor. It was a place where civil and military values were upheld and cultivated, where the arts and scholarship could be seen to flourish, and it was a peaceful, disciplined and, on the whole, well-governed state. It could be said to have represented, in microcosm, the Italian ideal which had haunted the Renaisance from its very inception[51]. One should not be surprised, therefore, that other rulers might have wished to appropriate it - if only as a prestigious ornament. The extent to which it was, in reality, the personal achievement of a single individual was effectively disguised in the skill of its presentation but it was a matter only of weeks after Vespasiano's death that the reality became evident. The collapse, not only of Sabbioneta's cultural life but also of civil authority, was immediate and dramatic.

Understandably, perhaps, Vespasiano's son-in-law, Luigi Carrafa, seems to have taken seriously the possibility of a military attack at a time of uncertainty over the succession of power in Sabbioneta. Already, while Vespasiano was terminally ill, he had blocked the canal system so as to maintain the water-level of Sabbioneta's moat, because, as Dondi tells us, 'of his suspicions'[52] On 8th March, Carrafa dismissed the majority of Sabbioneta's troops, keeping only a hundred and eight Italians and sixty Germans, having already moved in sixty of his own (Neapolitan) swordsmen and four hundred mercenaries from Pontremolo, Parma and Bologna. Persistent rain which, during the carnival of March, 1590, had forced the abandonment of tilting at the quintain, continued through April and May, leading to a failed harvest and a food crisis across much of Europe worse than any since 1556/7[53]. Grain prices at Sabbioneta rose, in 1591, to more than twice their level of 1589 (never again, during that century, did they return to earlier levels). The presence of so large a garrison, increasing inflationary pressure upon an already insufficient food supply, seems to have brought to a head a mounting atmosphere of tension.

50. de Dondi, Op. Cit., p.355.
51. For a lucid account of the nationalism of Dante and Petrarch, and of the attempted 'unification' in 1347 by Cola di Rienzo, Tribune of Rome, see Denys Hay, The Italian Renaissance in its historical background, Cambridge, 1989, pp. 98-100.
52. De Dondi, Op. Cit.. p.379.
53. See Massimo Montanari, La Fame e L'abbondanza, Roma-Bari, 1997, p. 127.

On 10th March, as Dondi recounts the episode[54], a meeting of the
Council of the Rurali took place, as it did regularly, in the Palazzo della Ragione.
Already dubious of the significance of a number of German troops scattered around
the piazza, they moved on to the matter of a widespread dissatisfaction with the
behaviour of Niccolò de Oldi, then Captain of the militia and of the city gates. With
one voice, they shouted that they were aggrieved, leapt up in a fury and, brandishing
their arms, rushed into the piazza shouting "to arms, to arms, ring the bells". Two
strokes on the church bell and the word passed from one to another brought a crowd
of armed citizens into the piazza. Hearing of this commotion, Niccola Zanichelli (a
member of one of Sabbioneta's leading families) went to the Porta Vittoria to warn
Captain Bartolomeo Mezzoco that people were armed against him in the piazza:
before Mezzoco could decide what to do, the prince, Luigi Carrafa, with another of
his captains, arrived in his carriage. All of them then proceeded to the piazza in the
carriage where the crowd had increased further. A certain don Giacomo Antonio
Zovanelli, holding a pistol, approached the carriage and said to the prince: "Sir, we
don't want him here" and pointed at Mezzoco but was unable to say more because he
was so angry. As the crowd surged more densely round the carriage, the prince and
Mezzoco jumped out, Mezzoco taking hold of the prince and sheltering behind him
from the fury of these men who would certainly, otherwise, have killed him; in this
way, the prince got him into the palace. Zanichelli and Ludovico Mesirotti, another
leading nobleman of the city, were sent out to get a clear account of the cause of
the trouble, since, when they were in the carriage, it had been impossible to speak
coherently. Unanimously, the people demanded that Mezzoco, along with his nephew,
an ensign of cavalry, be expelled from Sabbioneta, and that Niccolò de Oldi be put in
prison as they did not wish to be governed by such people; these things they wanted
done straight away (it was eleven o'clock at night). Having conferred with the prince,
these noblemen attempted to prevaricate, promising full satisfaction the following day,
but they were shouted down: "we want him out now, now, now!" Carrafa gave way;
Niccolò de Oldi was imprisoned in the Castello while Mezzoco and his nephew, under
escort to ensure their safety (Mezzoco so confused that he hardly knew where he was),
left by the Porta Vittoria, arriving four hours later at the Angel Inn at Casalmaggiore.
Members of the Council immediately apologised to the prince, on behalf of the
people, for their disrespectful behaviour, were let off with a warning not to do it again
and delivered 'un bel sermoncino' to the populace from the stair in the Piazza della
Colonna (outside the Castello) and so, shouting "long live the lord prince of Stigliano
and the princess his consort", the population went home to bed.

Though much condensed, I have tried to retain something of
the breathless tone of Dondi's narrative whose headlong confusion conveys with
remarkable force the pace of events and the inability of Carrafa to control them. It
is worth noting that it was Mesirotti and Zanichelli, two of Vespasiano's principal
lieutenants, who were able to re-establish a coherent dialogue and reach a solution.
Another point is worth noting: during the time that the prince and his captains had
reached the comparative safety of the Palazzo Ducale, and were deciding what to
do next, almost the entire population had arrived armed in the piazza, had sealed
off the streets and kept out all the mercenary troops except for the few who were
already posted at the steps of the palazzo. Their defensive posts had been so efficiently
organised that if any of the troops had made a move they would have been cut to pieces,
and these experienced veterans were astonished at the good order and discipline of the
insurgents, a thing they had never seen elsewhere[55]. The legacy of Vespasiano's military
instruction and civic discipline at Sabbioneta could still prove its effectiveness in the
face of a sizeable mercenary presence.

54. De Dondi, Op. Cit., pp.383-
387.
55. Ibid., p.385.

Early in April, Carrafa moved his household into the Castello; and, suspicious again, he had large quantities of artillery mounted on its towers[56] It was in the Palazzo ducale, a structure entirely without defensive capability, that Vespasiano had died six weeks previously and this appears to have been his principal residence during his lifetime; here, he had kept his personal library in a room where he would have been an easy target from the piazza. From the greater safety of the Castello, Carrafa set out to reassert his authority. The appearance of a comet 'with important signs'[57] was conveniently interpreted as a portent of treachery; a 'conspiracy' against Caraffa and Isabella was duly discovered. In a rapid swoop under the command of the German officer Magella, many arrests were made and a 'leader' in whose cellar was found a cask full of weapons was killed in the scuffle. Arrests, including women, continued for several days while members of the Mesirotti, Zanichelli and other leading families were subjected to harassment and forced to move elsewhere with heavy payments of security. In early May, lawyers arrived in preparation for the trial and, on the twelfth, a torturer from Cremona. All citizens were made to hand in their arms and even soldiers forbidden to carry arms except on specific duty. Large rewards were announced for the delivery, dead or alive, of suspects who had escaped. Following a trial in June, a number of 'conspirators' were executed while others, including Antonio Zovanelli (he whose anger during the insurrection had rendered him speechless) were released with payment of a heavy fine, or banished.

While all this was going on, Margherita Gonzaga, Vespasiano's widow, left Sabbioneta and went back to live in Guastalla 'to the great sorrow of all'. Other noted residents also began to leave but the arrival of fresh troops continued on a regular basis. It can, of course, be no more than a matter of conjecture that the conspiracy discovered and ruthlessly put down in Sabbioneta during the early summer of 1591 was a cynical fabrication of the prince, intended to demonstrate his command of events. While it is unclear what the alleged conspirators might, if successful, have hoped to achieve in the face of the inevitable hostility of neighbouring powers, the duke of Mantua, the emperor and king Philip of Spain, it is nevertheless probable that the threat of such uprisings was regarded as real. A popular revolt took place at Udine in 1511, in which almost the entire feudal and urban nobility had been blasted and burned out of their houses, massacred, stripped and cut in pieces by the mob (who then proceeded with the carnival, dressing in the clothes of their victims and "calling each other by the names of those whose clothes they wore")[58]. Such eruptions of repressed class animosity, though less frequent in Italy than in Germany or France, were a reminder of the increasingly insecure foundations upon which political power rested. As J.R.Hale has observed[59], "none [of the rulers] had anything like the sort of standing army that could impose their will on reluctant subjects".

A standing army of mercenaries could, in any case, turn out to be a liability, as Carrafa was shortly to discover: on 24th June a squabble broke out between Guglielmo Cernio, the German commander of cavalry, and some Bolognese troops led by Alessandro Legnani. Five Germans were wounded (three mortally) and one of the Bolognese; the two sides then barricaded themselves in various palaces and in the upper part of the Porta Vittoria and it was only after three days of street fighting, with heavy artillery moved in to demolish, if necessary, the palace from which Legnano refused to come out, that the two sides were separated, their leaders sequestered in the Castello 'e qui cessò il rumore'[60].

56. Ibid. p.391.
57. Ibid., p.391.
58. Furio Bianco, "Mihi vindicatem: aristocratic clans and rural communities in a feud in Friuli in the late fifteenth and early sixteenth centuries" in Dean, T., and Lowe, K.J.P., Crime, Society and the Law in Renaissance Italy, Cambridge, 1994, p. 249.
59. J.R.Hale, The Civilization of Europe in the Renaissance, London, 1994, p.86.
60. 'and here the disturbance ended' Dondi, Op. Cit., pp 404-407.

During the following weeks, Carrafa vacillated between measures of appeasement (some prisoners released, Mesirotti allowed to return) and increasingly restrictive measures: the expulsion of non-resident families unless they had official employment, the walling up of the Porta Imperiale 'because of his great suspicion'. The reward for capture of escaped suspects was raised. But it seems that, by this time, he had had enough: on 14th July, he made a relative, Lelio Carrafa, Governor of Sabbioneta (though he, also, left at the beginning of September). On 19th October, Carrafa and Isabella set off for Caravaggio, near Milan, on the pretext that they were unwell and needed the change of air. Two months later, fourteen cart-loads of clothes, silver, tapestries, bedding and household equipment set off from Sabbioneta to furnish a house in Milan where the prince intended to live for a while[61].

When, on 28th March of the following year, news came from Milan that the Emperor had confirmed Carrafa's investiture as the new duke of Sabbioneta, the people of Sabbioneta started preparations for a huge celebration; there were to be two triumphal arches made, decorated with paintings and arms; there were to be gifts of clothing, singing and instrumental music. Word came from the prince, however, that they should not waste money which could be used for other things; since one of the arches was almost finished, they finished it; but if it was not already clear, it must have become very clear in this moment that Sabbioneta had no longer any special relationship with its ruler: that it would be, from now on, no more than any other small town, governed by appointees on behalf of an absent feudatory. The remaining movable possessions of Carrafa and Isabella were despatched to the kingdom of Naples on 22nd May[62].

This account, largely recovered from the contemporary record of a generally unreflective participant, should serve to establish that Vespasiano, in the creation and in the political direction of his minute city-state, was not pursuing a nostalgic or a utopian fantasy, inexplicable to his subjects; that he was, on the contrary deeply serious in his attempt to rise to the historical challenge of his time. In this chapter, three points should have been established:

1.　　　Sabbioneta, as an idea, belonged not only to Vespasiano, its creator, but also, in a significant degree, to his subjects. To see it as nothing more than the whim of an eccentric nobleman imposed, once and for all, over the heads of a sullenly acquiescent populace is to overlook the extent to which the life and the institutions of Sabbioneta were sustained in a continuous and interactive development, paternalist and, on occasion, coercive, no doubt, but explicable to all concerned in terms of the thoughts which drove it. It was Luigi Carrafa who attempted to govern solely in his own personal interest, dispensing with the basis of mutual trust and confidence which Vespasiano had established, and the traumatic events of his first year as ruler of Sabbioneta testify to the strength of the bond which his actions repudiated.

2.　　　At Sabbioneta, Vespasiano demonstrated, albeit on a very small scale, the possibility of a form of government and culture which many Italians of his day would have considered highly desirable: independent, subject only to the supreme authority of the Holy Roman Emperor; peaceful within its own boundaries and defended by a largely local militia whose good discipline, as well as its colourful presence, was a source, not of fear and resentment but of pride. These are themes recurrent in Italian writing of this time:

61. Ibid., pp. 410-419.
62. Ibid., pp. 419-421.

Therefore, if your illustrious house desires to follow these excellent men who redeemed their lands, it is necessary before all else, as a true basis for every undertaking, to provide yourself with your own native troops, for one cannot have either more faithful, more loyal, or better troops. And although each one separately may be brave, all of them united will become even braver when they find themselves commanded, honoured, and well treated by their own prince[63].

Sabbioneta might, indeed, be seen in this respect as the representation, in microcosm, of an Italian ideal (we have already noted an interest of this sort among intellectuals patronised at Vespasiano's court). Carrafa's betrayal of this ideal might, equally, be considered emblematic of its subversion by selfish and thoughtless individuals which many writers both then and subsequently, have seen as a tragedy of Italy's national history.

3.

The atmosphere of festivity which characterized the last years of Vespasiano's rule at Sabbioneta cannot easily be dismissed as the imposition from above of a preconceived form. In many of its manifestations, on the contrary, it might appear to have been at variance with the mood and the circumstances of Vespasiano's own life. That there existed, amongst the ordinary citizens of Sabbioneta, a spontaneous inclination to celebrate the special identity of their city, to take pleasure in the honours achieved by its ruler and to embellish the forms of everyday life with ornament and style, is a perception which emerges clearly from the pages of Dondi's diary but one which, in the name of agendas belonging more to the twentieth than to the sixteenth century, many writers[64] have not wanted to believe. It was the frustration of this desire to celebrate, when Luigi Carrafa made clear his lack of interest in it, which marked the inception of a systematically oppressive regime. Quoting Machiavelli again:

A prince also should demonstrate that he is a lover of talent by giving recognition to men of ability and by honouring those who excel in a particular field. [....] He should, besides this, at the appropriate times of the year, keep the populace occupied with festivals and spectacles. And because each city is divided into guilds or clans, he should take account of these groups, meet with them on occasion, offer himself as an example of humanity and munificence, always, nevertheless, maintaining firmly the dignity of his position, for this should never be lacking in any way[65].

The single characteristic which distinguishes the thought of writers such as Machiavelli in the sixteenth century from that of the fifteenth is, precisely, that it is an attempt (often, indeed, dismissed as cynical) at practical realism. To see Vespasiano's project at Sabbioneta as a nostalgic flight back into the idealistic dreams of an obsolete humanism is a distortion possible only at a distance of four hundred years; in the eyes of a thinking contemporary, Sabbioneta might well have appeared politically relevant and institutionally advanced.

63. Niccolò Machiavelli, The Prince, trans. P. Bondanella and M. Musa, Oxford, 1984, p.86.
64. e.g. H.W. Kruft, Städte in Utopia, Munich, 1989, p.50: "The city is a monologue on the nature of an ideal state in which the ruler, the chief player is: Vespasiano Gonzaga. The piece ends logically with the death of the ruler who, both as a person and as an institution, leaves the scene. The town, as it now remains, is an empty set. The inhabitants are film extras. Sabbioneta demonstrates... that a city, conceived with a single intent, is not, in the long run, viable."
65. Machiavelli, Op. Cit., p.76.

Vespasiano's idea of the sort of society which he wanted to institute at Sabbioneta provides, already, an indication of the 'style' of thinking which he brought to all of his varied enterprises and which will form a recurrent theme of this book. We discover an engagement with the most recent and up-to-date formulations held in dialectic tension with a deeply informed consciousness of history. We find a determination to think independently and to act experimentally but constrained by an often startling objectivity. Hardly, as one writer would have it, "Typical to the point of caricature of his class and period"[66] unless, by this, one were to mean that, in the person of Vespasiano Gonzaga, one is able to study many of the decisive transformations through which, during the sixteenth century, a 'modern' personality may be seen to emerge.

66. John Fleming, "History of Sabbioneta" in Architectural Review, Vol.131 No.784 (1962) p.444. The 'caricature' is of this writer's own making.

035

~2)

The Architectural Event. The contemporary discourse of the city and Vespasiano Gonzaga's critical reformulations.

The building is conceived in this manner. Since no one can conceive by himself without a woman, by another simile, the building cannot be conceived by one man alone. As it cannot be done without a woman, so he who wishes to build needs an architect. He conceives it with him and then the architect carries it. When the architect has given birth, he becomes the mother of the building. Before the architect gives birth, he should dream about his conception, think about it, and turn it over in his mind in many ways for seven to nine months, just as a woman carries her child in her body for seven to nine months.

[....]

Building is nothing more than a voluptuous pleasure, like that of a man in love. Anyone who has experienced it knows that there is so much pleasure and desire in building that however much a man does, he wants to do more. Sometimes he is never concerned with the expense: examples of this are seen every day. When a man is in love, he gladly goes to see his beloved. When she is in a place where he can see her, he is not sorry for the time spent nor is he bored. So he who builds goes gladly to see his building, and as often as he sees it the more he wants to see it and the more his heart swells. [....] There is no half way for him; he loves it. [67]

Filarete's account of the respective activities of patron and architect (written about 1461-64) is undoubtedly the expression of a desire rather than a reality; it was part of a vigorous campaign conducted by a small number of individuals for whom it was important to identify themselves as 'professional' designers in the field of architecture as distinct from the manual tradesmen traditionally entrusted with the physical production of buildings. The writing of a treatise (addressed, it should be noted, to a potential patron, not to others who might wish to learn how to be architects) though it could hardly demonstrate the author's ability as a designer (the writers of treatises were not necessarily able designers) was intended to demonstrate, more specifically, that the author was privy to a specialised architectural discourse, the possessor of an intellectual qualification. Paradoxically, of course, the intellectual property and the discourse specific to architectural activity could only come into existence through the repeated production and dissemination of an architectural literature and its application in practical design by a community of professionals, so that the early treatises, starting from a clean slate, must needs be cobbled together from what was immediately available. Common to all of the treatises written during the Renaissance was, for this reason if for no other, a heavy and frequently pedantic reliance upon Vitruvius, whose *Ten Books on Architecture* was the only substantial text on the subject to have survived from antiquity. Knowledge of this and of other classical sources was central to the notion of a specialised architectural discourse and a large part of the early treatises is given over to the exhibition of such knowledge, even though the scope for any practical application of this arcane learning was strictly limited in the prevailing circumstances of building patronage.

A century later, when the architectural project of Sabbioneta was getting under way, the emergence of an architectural 'profession' had undoubtedly progressed; sufficiently so, that architectural historians writing of this period are often inclined to see their work as incomplete if they are not able supply the name of a 'professional' person in relation to the production even of quite modest buildings. One may detect, here, a predisposition to solidarity amongst members of the bourgeoisie in celebration of the early emergence of that class.

67. Antonio Averlino (known as Filarete), Treatise on Architecture, trans. J. R. Spencer, Newhaven and London, 1965, p. 15.

The case of Sabbioneta, however, has not proved rewarding in terms of such a desire to 'name' an architect. It is known that Domenico Giunti (who did draw the plan for Ferrante Gonzaga's new city of Guastalla, but was not responsible for the buildings there) was approached by Vespasiano at the outset of the project but declined the commission because he was too busy[68]. It is known that Giovan Pietro Bottaccio was responsible for site supervision from 1557 till 1584 when he was succeeded in this role by Paolo Tusardi[69]. It is known that Gerolamo Cataneo was consulted in 1560, possibly in connection with the walls or gates[70]. It is known that Vincenzo Scamozzi was employed for the design of the theatre and fixed scene (his autograph drawing is in the Gabinetto Disegni e Stampi of the Uffizi in Florence[71]). The name of Jacopo Strada, who knew and published some works of Sebastiano Serlio and who may have designed the 'antiquarium' in Munich, a possible precedent for the Corridor Grande at Sabbioneta, is raised speculatively by some writers[72]. But it is also known that Vespasiano Gonzaga had a passionate interest in architecture and it is reported that drawings by him of the fortifications and other structures at Sabbioneta were extant during the nineteenth century (though subsequently 'lost') as well as drawings for the Corridor Grande sent by him from Spain to his cousin and agent in Sabbioneta, Ercole Visconti[73].

With varying degrees of emphasis, the consensus of recent scholarship has moved towards the view that Vespasiano did, in fact, design, rather than merely ordain the buildings of Sabbioneta[74].How or when he might have learned the necessary skill of architectural drawing (not, generally a part of the education of a prince and certainly not a thing that could be extracted from any treatise available in his day) is not known. According to Carli[75], courtiers and gossipers thought it absurd, in Vespasiano's position, to try to do architecture but his military employment was, as we shall see later, very largely concerned with the design of fortifications, and the few drawings from his hand to have survived sufficiently demonstrate his understanding of spatial and geometrical relationships and his familiarity with the graphic conventions of architectural representation.(Fig.1.1) Unless, then, by 'architecture' one were to mean minor constructional details, profiles or ornaments (which may, to a greater or less extent, have been delegated to his site supervisors) there seems reason enough to believe that the architecture of Sabbioneta is the work of Vespasiano Gonzaga. Sabbioneta may be considered, then, as a unitary mental and artistic production ordered in the mind of the same man who populated and ruled it. Historically, it is probably unique in this respect.

Vespasiano, we are told, 'not only studied avidly the works of modern writers but continually studied the works of Vitruvius, which he had in his hand all the time'[76]. We need not take too literally the implication that Vitruvius' text was, to Vespasiano, some sort of 'comfort object' without which he would have been incapable of making an architectural decision. Such a reference would, in Vespasiano's time, have been understood metaphorically: knowledge of architecture's primary text was the fundamental knowledge by which the credentials of an architect were established. Vespasiano's friend Bernardino Baldi provided him with a glossary of the obscure technical Latin terms used by Vitruvius[77], suggesting not only that Vespasiano read Vitruvius in the original Latin but also that he took seriously the authority which such knowledge implied.

Pt 1 ~2

040

68. I.Affò, Op. Cit., note 36, quotes Faroldi MS Life of Vespasiano. Giunti's employment as architect, engineer and guardaroba to Ferrante Gonzaga was evidently more than adequately rewarded: according to Vasari (life of Niccolò Soggi) Giunti was able to buy premises in Rome for 2,000 scudi, and others later on.
69. Marani, E. and Perina, C., Mantova: le Arti, Vol. III. Mantua, 1965, p. 133.
70. I.Affò, Op. Cit., p.27.
71. Paolucci, A. and Maffezzoli, U., Sabbioneta; il Teatro all'Antica, Modena, 1993, p.13.
72. e.g. Sanvito, P., "Collezionismo Imperialregio e Collezionismo a Sabbioneta: L'influenza del Modello Asburgico" in Atti del Convegno, Cit., p.192.
73. A.Carli, Op. Cit., pp 89 & 178.
74. Mary Hollingsworth, Patronage in Sixteenth Century Italy, London, 1996, p.102, has no problem attributing the whole of the work to Giunti (Giunti was dead during most of the time that Sabbioneta was under construction) while Nikolaus Pevsner, History of Building Types, London, 1979, p.112, strikes out on his own with the suggestion that not only the theatre at Sabbioneta but also the Corridor Grande was the work of Scamozzi. However, Kurt Forster, "From 'Rocca' to 'Civitas': Urban Planning at Sabbioneta" in L'Arte, Fasc.5, March, 1959, Hanno-Walter Kruft, Op. Cit., p.37 and P. Carpeggiani, Sabbioneta, Mantua, 1972, p.41, seem to be in broad agreement that Vespasiano was the architect.
75. A.Carli, Op. Cit., p.88.
76. I. Affò, Op Cit., p.27.
77. Bernardinus Baldus de verbor. Vitruvian.

When he returned to Sabbioneta in 1578, after ten years' absence in the service of Philip II in Spain, rather than going immediately to see his daughter, Isabella, who was confined there in a convent, Vespasiano chose first to make an inspection of his primogenita, his city "which he had conceived entirely by himself, without copulating with anyone"[78]. This remark, on the face of it not only tasteless but also unnatural in a father, becomes, at least, explicable if it is understood as referring to the passage in Filarete's *Treatise on Architecture* quoted at the beginning of this chapter. That Vespasiano should have picked out a sexual metaphor for the affective bond between himself and his city is revealing in relation to issues considered later in this book. For the present, it corroborates our supposition that Vespasiano considered himself to be the designer of Sabbioneta and indicates an engagement with (as well as a characteristically ironic detachment from) the nascent discourse of architecture as it was developed in the treatises.

'Modern' writers whose work Vespasiano might also have read, if they included the four major treatises on the subject of architecture written before the design of Sabbioneta was established, would have included, in addition to Filarete, quoted above: L.B.Alberti, *On the Art of Building in Ten Books*[79] (about 1450), Francesco di Giorgio Martini's *Architettura civile e militare*[80] (two redactions, c. 1470 and 1492) and Pietro Cataneo's I *Quattro Primi Libri di Architettura*[81] (1554). One cannot take it for granted that he read all (or any) of them (only Alberti and Cataneo were available in print during the sixteenth century) but our interest, here, is in Vspasiano's relation, as a designer, with the discourse as a whole rather than with the prescriptive origin of any particular design decision. We are not concerned, for the present, with the derivation or associative resonance of specific architectural forms or motifs to be found at Sabbioneta as these will figure in later chapters, when we know more about the particular world which Vespasiano inhabited. In what follows, it is our aim to discover what sort of thing it was possible to say about the design of cities: what were the parameters and the imperatives in relation to which a theoretical consideration of the architecture of the city was beginning to take shape.

Though the categories are not greatly evident in the treatises, it will be convenient to look at their various accounts of the city under two aspects: a) its content, distributive order and the implied narrative, b) its abstract formal configuration. To conclude this chapter, we can then turn to the architectural effect, the experience which Vespasiano seems to have intended.

Significatione. See Note 201 to Affò, Op. Cit. p.55.
78. *Quoted in Luca Sarzi Amadè, Il Duca di Sabbioneta-Guerre e amori di un Europeo del XVI Secolo, Milan, 1990, p.245.*
79. *The edition used here is L.B.Alberti, On the Art of Building in Ten Books, trans. J.Rykwert, N.Leach, R.Tavernor, Cambridge Mass. and London, 1988.*
80. *Edition used here is F. Di Giorgio Martini, Trattato di Architettura civile e militare, ed. Corrado Maltese, Milan, 1967.*
81. *Edition used here is Pietro Cataneo (Senese), I Quattro Primi Libri di Architettura, New Jersey, 1964.*

Content, distributive order
and narrative

In Vitruvius' account, the distributive arrangement of cities was derived and held within a codified relationship between the gods, the human attributes which they represented and the human activities which expressed those attributes. Observing that the forum should, in maritime cities, be close to the harbour, otherwise, in the middle (basilicas, treasury, prison and senate house were to adjoin the forum; theatres, baths and palaestri sited upon the basis of climate and health[82]), Vitruvius continues:

> For the temples, the sites for those gods under whose particular protection the state is thought to rest, and for Jupiter, Juno and Minerva, should be at the very highest point, commanding a view of the greater part of the city. Mercury should be in the forum, or, like Isis and Serapis, in the emporium; Apollo and Father Bacchus near the theatre; Hercules at the circus in communities which have no gymnasia nor amphitheatres; Mars outside the city but at the training ground, and so Venus, but at the harbour. It is moreover shown by the Etruscan diviners in treatises on their science that the fanes of Venus, Vulcan, and Mars should be situated outside the walls, in order that the young men and married women may not become habituated in the city to the temptations incident to the worship of Venus, and that the buildings may be free from the terror of fires through the religious rites and sacrifices which call the power of Vulcan beyond the walls. As for Mars, when that divinity is enshrined outside the walls, the citizens will never take up arms against each other, and he will defend the city from its enemies and save it from danger in war[83].

Combined with a similarly codified relationship of appropriate ornament and orders in the case of each deity, the architecture of a vitruvian city became entirely legible and fully transparent to collective ideology. This is how Francesco di Giorgio set out twenty-two principles for the planning of a city:

1) The main piazza should be as near the middle as possible because, like the navel, it is from this that the city draws all nourishment and perfection. Also, because it is equally accessible from all extremities. Round it should be fine shops and honourable professions.
2) If one piazza isn't enough for the size of the city, more may be needed, as central to each district as the main one is to the whole city.
3) The market forum should have porticos or loggias so that it can function in all sorts of weather.
4) The precinct of the cathedral should be close to the main piazza.
5) Parochial churches should be as accessible within each district as the cathedral is within the whole city.
6) The Palazzo Signorile should be raised above its surroundings, freestanding and as close to the piazza as possible, for the convenience of audiences and civic gatherings.
7) Beside this should be a loggia where, in all weather, merchants and citizens can go at their pleasure.
8) If the area is large, there should be more of these, conveniently distributed.
9) The official offices, prison, customs house, salt magazine and other communal facilities should be as near the main piazza as possible.
10) Taverns, eating houses and brothels should be in a hidden place but not far away, to avoid the problems which often occur in such places.

82. Ibid., Book V.
83. Vitruvius, Op. Cit., p.31.

11)	Banks and shops should be close to the main piazza.
12)	The silk workers' guild should be all together, not split up, in the street most common to citizens and foreigners, both for its ornament and so that the producers can easily trade amongst themselves.
13)	The wool workers' guild should be in one place, slightly removed from public places and sources of noise, for the convenience of the workers, and situated, subject to other considerations, where water is available.
14)	Dyers should be close to the above, for their mutual convenience, and near, also, to the tanners and toolers of various sorts of leather. Close to these the makers of lime and the shops of the vellum and chamois makers, so that each can work in the way that suits them.
15)	Grocers, dressmakers and haberdashers should be distributed in the main streets for general convenience.
16)	Blacksmiths and woodworkers, because of the noise, and lime makers because of the dirt which they produce, should be off the main streets but close by.
17)	Butchers should be in four or five places, spread around and covered as far as possible on account of the stench which is inevitable in these places.
18)	Slaughter-houses should be at the extremities of the city.
19)	In general, the crafts which have intrinsic beauty and decorum shall be in the principal streets and most public places, while those which are dirty or pollutant shall be segregated.
20)	Baths and steam rooms should be in various inconspicuous places according to the pleasure of the inhabitants.
21)	For the greater ornament and perfection of the city and avoidance of the pernicious effects of idleness, make a theatre or amphitheatre in which comedy, tragedy and other fables or histories can be recited and, also, so that the young men and adolescents can practise various athletic exercises. These should, in my opinion, be remote from the frequented areas, as though by accident and extraordinary, inviting those who see them to participate.
22)	All these parts should have correspondence and should be proportional to the city as a whole as the parts are to the human body[84].

For the treatise writers of the early Renaissance (and Francesco di Giorgio's twenty-two points, though more succinctly stated, are close in their prescriptive content to the provisions of the other three), there was no way that the vitruvian way of thinking about cities could be mapped onto their own conception of urban life or urban form; although Filarete wanted to place a figure of the goddess Copia on top of the church in the food-sellers' piazza and Cataneo suggests that the church adjacent to the piazza for merchants should be dedicated to Saint Matthew 'who was a banker'[85], such propositions remain marginal to their functional understanding of urban space. (Alberti does make some attempt to reinterpret the vitruvian building types in terms of fifteenth-century institutions: the military camp becomes a model for monasteries, the palaestra for schools, the basilica for legal administration but, in the case of baths and theatres, he abandons the attempt and offers a reworking of Vitruvius' text amplified with his own observation of surviving structures.[86])

84. Ibid., pp.363-365.
85. Filarete, Op. Cit., p.128 and Pietro Cataneo, Op. Cit., p.12V.
86. Alberti, Op. Cit., p.127ff.

In proposing distributive arrangements appropriate to the life of a renaissance city, these writers had little choice but to describe, to a greater or less extent, what they knew, so that one can detect, behind the general prescription, some of the actuality of Florence, Milan, Siena or Urbino. Francesco di Giorgio (like Filarete and Cataneo; Alberti, less so), adapts a vitruvian theme (but a theme by no means restricted to Vitruvius either in ancient or in renaissance writing), and takes as his starting point the metaphor of the human body:

> *Imagine a human body lying down, put a piece of string from the navel and draw a circle, square or polygon. All parts must be perfect in the same way. [Where there isn't a fortress, the cathedral takes its place with its corresponding piazza where the palazzo signorile has contact. And in the opposite quadrant the principal piazza.] The hands and feet are to constitute other temples and piazze. And just as the eyes, ears, nose and mouth, the internal arteries and organs are arranged within or around the body for its needs and purposes, so should the same order be observed, showing each form in its right place[87].*

But what he describes in his twenty-two points is a city frenetically dedicated to manufacture and trade; a city almost completely devoid of what we might today describe as cultural institutions. To him, the theatre is an oddity rather than an integral component in the city's daily life and it is the same for Cataneo (a place for staging naval games and tournaments[88]) while Filarete, whose capacity to invent unprecedented cultural institutions seems often inexhaustible, is nevertheless puzzled by the idea of amphitheatres: "Perhaps also women or others danced up there to make merry while the plays were going on."[89] and "....even though such magnificence is not usual today. Maybe I will do one [theatre] in memory of those ancients."[90]

Though absent from Francesco di Giorgio's typology, schools are recognised in the other treatises: Filarete, though he does not comment on their location, has much to say about their design and operation (as we shall discover later); Cataneo does not describe schools in detail but suggests, following Alberti, that they should be situated remote from the noise and distraction of the city centre, where the air is healthy and where there would be space for a delightful garden, shaded places to walk and beautiful running streams[91]. Alberti recognises the existence of hospitals as a specialised development of religious institutions, suggesting that those for contagious disease should be segregated outside the city and away from public roads: "Suffice it to say that every building of this type should be laid out according to the requirements of a private house."[92] Filarete, who had designed the Ospedale Maggiore in Milan, describes its planning and equipment in extraordinary detail[93]. Only in Alberti's text is there any reference to libraries[94]

If, then, the 'renaissance city' of the treatises, in terms of its institutional content was, essentially, the medieval city which these writers knew but given, as far as possible, a vitruvian 'spin' so as to locate it within a theoretical discourse, the symbolic structure which underpinned it bore little or no relation to the ancient model. Instead of a network of signification and expectation founded in the 'human' attributes of the classical deities, the city of Alberti, Filarete, Francesco di Giorgio or Cataneo was sustained within the metaphor of an 'organic' society whose parts, hierarchically ordered and interdependent, mirrored the ideal order of the human body. Writing on the structure of reciprocal duties implicit in the social order, Marsilio Ficino expresses the same thought:

87. *Francesco di Giorgio, Op. Cit., p.20.*
88. *Cataneo, Op. Cit., p.12R.*
89. *Filarete, Op. Cit., p.157.*
90. *Ibid., p.27.*
91. *Cataneo, Op. Cit., p.12R.*
92. *Alberti, Op. Cit., p130.*
93. *Filarete, Op. Cit., p.137ff.*
94. *Alberti, Op. Cit., p.286.*

The duty of the prince is to watch over all; mercy in justice, humility in greatness and greatness in humility. The duty of the magistrate is to remember that he is not the master but the servant of the law [....] The duty of the citizen, whether he be a magistrate or a private individual, is to care as greatly for the public interest as he greatly cherishes his own. The duty of the knight is bravery in war and noble action in peace; of the merchant, with true faith and diligence to nourish both the state and himself with good things from abroad; of the tradesman, honestly to distribute the provisions received from the merchant to each member of the state[95].

And elsewhere:

It is the duty of a citizen to consider the state as a single being formed of its citizens who are the parts; [....] nothing good or bad can touch one limb of the state, without affecting the others and indeed the state as a whole. And again, nothing can happen to the whole body of the state without soon affecting each limb[96].

Or, as Vespasiano's friend Torquato Tasso put it:

Oh, make but one body of your cooperating limbs; make but one head that may direct and restrain the others[97].

It should hardly be necessary to add that an ideology such as this, whose maintenance was so greatly to the advantage of the ruling classes, was likely to be found represented in the physical form of the cities in which those ruling classes were the principal building patrons. The ideological construct of the 'organic' society is perfectly mirrored in the urban form and distribution of Sabbioneta, but in a way which not only departs from current practice but also goes beyond the consensus of the treatises.

Kurt Forster has demonstrated[98], convincingly enough to have been followed without question by numerous other writers[99], that Vespasiano organised the plan of Sabbioneta as an overlapping of three conceptual zones: the private ducal functions, Castello and Palazzo Giardino, the public ducal presence, Palazzo Ducale and Palazzo della Ragione along with the principal church and, finally, the area of habitation. The overlap of these three zones then locates the main piazza, while the theatre (by this interpretation, the 'key' to the whole ensemble) is at the intersection of the duke's private and public realm. This model, which is, aside from the location of the theatre, implicit in all the treatises which we have been considering, is nevertheless complicated, in the case of Sabbioneta, by the way in which Vespasiano's 'private' quarters would subsume the city's most conspicuously military institution juxtaposed (and also linked) to the most evidently 'intimate' of his private buildings, the Palazzo del Giardino. Equally, it is provocative to find Vespasiano's studiolo, the place where his private library was kept and the place where, according to de Dondi, he died[100], located in what should represent his public and administrative persona. What is, indeed, striking about Sabbioneta, is the extent to which the boundary between 'ducal' structures, communal or 'cultural' structures and the general residential fabric seems to have been deliberately blurred. Though the city's representative institutions are, on the whole, clustered in its north-western part of the city, they are, with the exception of the ducal palace, spread out and arranged so as to define public space or to form components of, or edges to, blocks of otherwise private occupation. (Fig. 2.2)

95. Ficino, Op. Cit., p.191.
96. Ibid., p.193.
97. Torquato Tasso, Gerusalemme Liberata, first published 1581, English prose version by R. Nash, Detroit, 1987, Canto 1, 31.
98. Kurt W. Forster, From 'Rocca' to 'Civitas', cit.,p.25.
99. E.g., Chiara Tellini Perina, Op. Cit., pp.17-19.
100. De Dondi, Op. Cit., p.380.

It seems that Vespasiano wanted to create, within the limited scope Pt 1 ~2 of a small community, the impression of the greatest possible variety of public and cultural institutions and to play down the extent to which these were, in reality, extensions of his own private household. "A vulgar ambition," writes Carli[101], "would have wanted to lump all the monuments into a single building, which would have resulted in a monstrosity". Such 'monstrosities' were by no means rare; the clinker-like agglomerations which formed the ducal palaces of Milan, Mantua, Parma or Ferrara 046 (to quote only local examples) might or might not contain cultural facilities: theatre, picture or sculpture gallery, library or orchestra (nothing in any of the treatises would suggest that such things should belong within a signorial palace) but the representation of such spaces as integral to the public domain was largely unforeseen either in written theory or in aristocratic practice.

In terms of its implicit narrative, then, Sabbioneta cannot be reduced to any of its possible sources in the literature of architectural discourse; as Prince and ruler of the city which he built, Vespasiano's motivation differed from that of any of the trattatisti as much as these writers differed amongst themselves and these differences are reflected in the implicit narratives of the cities they describe.

Alberti views the city from an aristocratic standpoint: allowing that 'respectable' trade could add charm to the forum while:

> anything foul or offensive (especially the stinking tanners) should be kept
> well away in the outskirts to the north [....] Some might prefer the residential
> quarters of the gentry to be quite free of any contamination from the common
> people. Others [could accept] common retailers and other shops mixed in with
> the houses of the most important citizens. [....] Clearly utility demands one
> thing, and dignity another.[102]

Dignity was high among Alberti's priorities but it is seen as the desirable attribute of an essentially leisured way of life:

> Plato recommended that at every crossroad there be a space where nurses with
> children could meet occasionally and be together. I believe that the purpose
> behind this was not only to strengthen the children in the fresh air, but also
> to encourage the nurses to be neat by exposing them to the eyes of so many
> curious observers, and to make them less sloppy, since they are eager for praise.
> The presence of an elegant portico, under which the elders may [stroll] or sit,
> take a nap or negotiate business, will be an undoubted ornament to both
> crossroad and forum. Furthermore, the presence of the elders will restrain
> the youth, as they play and sport in the open, and curb any misbehaviour or
> buffoonery resulting from the immaturity of their years.[103]

101. A.Carli, Op. Cit., p.190.
102. Alberti, Op. Cit., p.192.
103. Ibid., p.263.

In Filarete's Sforzinda, as Hanno-Walter Kruft has put it, "architecture becomes the external representation of an educational idea."[104] Neither in a state of dignified idleness nor conspicuously occupied in trade or manufacture, its inhabitants are almost always to be found receiving instruction, exhortation, correction or inspiration. Filarete devotes several pages to the design of schools[105] (though he does not suggest any particular location within the plan of the city). His description of the curriculum and daily régime of the school for boys (aged six up to thirty) is strikingly close to the school run in Mantua by Vittorino da Feltre[106], although the latter was coeducational. For girls (up to seventeen), where reading, cooking, embroidery and weaving, "in sum, all the skills that pertain to a woman", Filarete proposes a building "like a convent" but with windows protected by iron bars, so that the girls could be seen from outside and selected for marriage. The four 'sinister and harsh' prisons: Senza Speranza, Male Albergho, Tenebrosa and Dolorosa[107], the Casa di Venere above which was to be an office "where the craft that is practised here will be controlled"[108] and, of course, most spectacularly, the House of Vice and Virtue are all conceived as didactic institutions. The House of Vice and Virtue is almost impossible, in spite of Filarete's attempted perspective section, to reconstruct as an architectural proposal but its educational programme is explicit and comprehensive; set on a plain reached by seven bridges so that "everyone will be obliged to cross over them to a very pleasant, beautiful and delightful place", the structure is to be "round and square". The steep stair without treads signifies "difficulty with joy" and "pleasure with pain". At the lowest level are places for Venus (her invitation in Latin, Italian, Greek, Hungarian, German, Spanish, French and many other languages) and Bacchus, "beautiful in an effeminate way". Seven segments, for the seven liberal arts, surround a theatre which is used for fighting. Examination was to be followed by a form of 'oral' in the main piazza and those failing were humiliated by having their laurel wreath hung up in the faculty with their name under it; only three repeats were to be allowed.[109] In this extraordinary institution is condensed the prevailing narrative of the whole city. Filarete is imagining a city in which his own, somewhat idiosyncratic notion of Florentine culture and of which, in Milan, he felt himself to be the representative, would prevail in every aspect of public and private life:

> There were letters everywhere that told the things that he had composed or rather that he had imposed.[110]

We have noted already the frenetically mercantile and productive tone of Francesco di Giorgio's urban narrative. Introducing his section on cities, he argues that man's superiority to the beasts resides in the fact that he, unlike other animals, doesn't just do the single thing for which he is adapted but uses his intellect and his hands, "the organ of organs and instrument of all the other instruments" so as to clothe and arm himself as he desires. This leads to specialization and from this, in turn, urban culture develops[111]. Unlike Alberti, he is fascinated by the complex interactions amongst various groups of producers: he describes in detail the planning of kitchens and latrines in various sorts of palace[112]. He is concerned with the practicalities of artisans' houses, and that women should be kept away from the disturbance of customers; that merchants should have a room on the ground floor where foreign visitors could be put up. His point of view is that of an upwardly mobile bourgeois with an appetite for the variety of urban culture.

104. Hanno-Walter Kruft, A History of Architectural Theory, London and New York, 1994, p.55.
105. Ibid., pp.228-244.
106. Woodward, Op. Cit., pp31-35.
107. Filarete, Op. Cit., p.125.
108. Ibid., p.128.
109. Ibid., pp.246-252.
110. Ibid., p.76.
111. Francesco di Giorgio, Op. Cit., p.360.
112. Ibid., pp.347 & 347, respectively.

By contrast, there is a touch of counter-reformation moralism in Pietro Cataneo's narrative of the city; while proposing that the city "where people can multiply and prosper"[113] is the most beautiful part of architecture, and approving the idea that merchants would "buy cheap and sell dear"[114] his principal concerns are hygiene (an important concern of all four writers, but with Cataneo quite obsessively so) and convenient circulation. In this respect, he is bluntly critical of the builders of ancient Rome:

> But speaking of Rome, [....] of which at its inception Romulus only made a small part, building on the Campidoglio and the Palatine hill where he was raised, as it subsequently grew, as new parts and public buildings were added, they could, in my opinion, have arranged it much better than what we see to have been done. Quite aside from the tangled and irregular arrangement of these, the squares and many of the buildings which were sited far from the Forum Romanum should have been placed round this square or close by, and the ones most frequented: basilicas, for instance, where magistrates handed out justice: similarly, curias and Rostri were remote from the forum when they should have been adjacent. [....] at these and many other places and temples remote from the principal square and centre of the city, the people and Senate used to assemble, moved, perhaps, by the auguries of the deities to whom these places were sacred. And we can see today St. Peter's, the principal cathedral of Rome, sited at the very edge of the city. [....] However, leaving aside these and many other errors which can be shown in Rome and elsewhere, and following in every respect the rules of Vitruvius, we shall contrive, with the help of Jesus Christ, within the limits of this brief discourse, to set out the details and divisions of our city according to the form of a beautiful and well-proportioned human body[115].

If Alberti had left rhetorically open the choice between utility and dignity, the priorities in Cataneo's mind are clear: it is in its efficient layout that a city mirrors the perfection of the human body while the organic interdependence of its inhabitants, so powerfully present in Francesco di Giorgio's text, is no longer a part of Cataneo's thinking. He is, however, explicitly concerned with the reputation of the city and is, for this reason, in favour of having a 'studio' (an academy) for the honour which it would bestow but also because of the cash which it would bring in, "many noble and honourable people, coming there to study from near and far"[116] and, for the same reason, sees monuments and works of art as an asset since, like Rome, such a city will be continually visited "besides Architects, Painters and Sculptors, by many fine gentlemen and noble spirits."[117] By 1554, the city could be imagined as a tourist destination. But in Cataneo's highly respectable city there is neither the leisurely occupation of public space evoked by Alberti, the headlong re-education of humanity portrayed in Filarete's treatise nor the bustle of industry and commerce which Francesco di Giorgio sees as the natural state of things; writing of houses for the nobility, Cataneo wants them "healthy, well planned and impressive" since the work of notable people often keeps them indoors[118]. Not for him the idle flâneur, the unexpected view or chance encounter. Cataneo sees the city, not through the eyes of its rulers nor through those of its industrious populace; rather, through the eyes of a city official, an agent in the exercise of power.

113. Pietro Cataneo, Op. Cit., Prologue.
114. Ibid., p.21.
115. Ibid., p.8V.
116. Ibid., p.13V.
117. Ibid., Loc. Cit.
118. Pietro Cataneo, Op. Cit., p.47.

While there are undoubtedly traces or echoes of all the four treatises in the urban narrative of Sabbioneta, there is nothing like a close fit with any of them. Like Alberti's, Vespasiano's outlook was aristocratic and, in a sense, contemplative; like Filarete's Sforzinda, Sabbioneta had a clearly didactic purpose; although far from the mercantilism of Francesco di Giorgio, the form of Sabbioneta exhibits a similarly pragmatic recognition (even celebration) of human diversity within an organic representation of the whole and, in common with Cataneo, Vespasiano has evidently wanted to achieve both the respectability and the renown of his city. But a contemporary would have noticed an element in the narrative of Sabbioneta which is almost absent in the treatises. In the 'mission statement' with which Vespasiano launched his Academy in 1562, he says:

> And bearing in mind that there are two routes by which men can achieve usefulness and nobility, either by arms or by letters, for which purpose states and dominions, large and small, acquire them, foster them and establish them; and not having, as far as our modest efforts could take us, neglected to guide our subjects in the former route: now we intend to set them off upon the route of letters, as a proper calling in peacetime which, by the grace of God and the wisdom of our Great Ones, we are enjoying at present. And taking into account, above all, the healthiness of the air, the fertility and the security of the location, we have decided to set up a public school of Humanities where our subjects will send their sons to learn, so that on leaving this school they can make their way amongst the famous in Italy for Law, or Medicine.[119]

By the time that the Academy came to be set up, Sabbioneta was, it seems, already up and running as a school for soldiers, and the extent to which Vespasiano's resident 'army' was conceived by him as a major component as well as an ornament of the city's life we have seen already in the first chapter.

The abstract formal configuration

Vitruvius invests the circle and the square with cosmological significance by tracing their derivation to the proportions of the human body:

> For if a man be placed flat on his back, with his hands and feet extended, and a pair of compasses centred at his navel, the fingers and toes of his two hands and feet will touch the circumference of a circle described therefrom. And just as the human body yields a circular outline, so too a square figure may be found from it[120].

119. Quoted in Affò, Op. Cit., p.31.
120. Ibid. p.73.

In the eyes of his renaissance readers, this added the force of principle to Vitruvius' casually pragmatic observation that a city of circular form would "give a view of the enemy from many points"[121]. Whilst Alberti remains judiciously non-committal, seeing the shape of a city as a matter to be determined entirely on the basis defensive military considerations, Francesco di Giorgio is happy to assert that the plan of a city should be set out on the vitruvian system of a circle (or square or polygon) centred on the navel of a recumbent figure[122]. His treatise, unlike that of Alberti, was illustrated with numerous sketches, filling up the margins of his manuscript, and it is these, together with Filarete's city form derived from two overlaid squares rotated at forty-five degrees (a geometrical construction much favoured during the Middle Ages)[123], which have been taken as evidence that, to a renaissance mind, an ideal defensive configuration had its source in a more general notion of ideal urban form. It is this assumption which seems to lie behind the unwillingness of so many writers to concede that the trace of Sabbioneta's walls is far from being a geometrically perfect figure. If it is correct to describe Sabbioneta as an example of the 'ideal' renaissance city as it was evoked in the works of Filarete, Francesco di Giorgio or Cataneo, it must also be admitted that its ideality does not reside in the geometry of its shape.

J.R.Hale[124] is firmly dismissive of claims that Francesco di Giorgio had based his ideal city designs upon modern principles of military science:

> These works are fascinatingly idiosyncratic, but when they are compared with the works we have been discussing [prototypical bastionated fortification] they appear quite irrelevant to the answers already proposed to the problem of fortifying against artillery. Towering and under-armed, they represent the massive doodling of a genius who is not prepared to sacrifice fantasy to logic…

Francesco di Giorgio acknowledges that the 'fury' of modern warfare was of a different order from anything known in the ancient world[125]. Experiments beginning as early as the mid-fourteenth century had meanwhile culminated, in the last years of that century, with the production by Giuliano and the elder Antonio da Sangallo of the first systematic designs for fortress and city defences based upon the construction of low, angled gun platforms (bastions) arranged so that every face could be covered by fire from the adjoining platform. Practice, during this period, had outstripped theory. After the invasion of Naples by the French in 1494, the 'fury' of heavy artillery could no longer figure as a mere rhetorical device to justify departure from the advice of Vitruvius; it rapidly became a major determinant of urban form and it is as such that it appears in the treatise of Pietro Cataneo. This work, the first in the series which we are considering to be conceived and illustrated as a printed document and aimed at a comparatively wide audience, sets out controlling dimensions for the fortification of cities of various sizes. Since the distance from a gun emplacement to the furthest tip of the adjoining bastion must be within the effective range of available artillery (Cataneo suggests a distance of four hundred and twelve braccie), the only way in which the size of a city could be increased was to increase the number of sides of its polygonal frame. Any departure from the regularity of the walls' geometry represented a reduction in the 'efficiency' with which the bastions were deployed. In this respect, the defensive circuit of Sabbioneta is by no means an efficient one: the longest range required is 325 metres and the shortest 270.

121. Vitruvius, Op. Cit., p.22.
122. Francesco di Giorgio, Op. Cit., p.20.
123. See, for instance, Otto von Simson, The Gothic Cathedral, London, 1956,, p15.
124. J.R.Hale, Renaissance War Studies, London, 1983, p.20.
125. Op. Cit., p.6. Chapter 1 of J.R.Hale, Op. Cit., provides an extremely thorough account of the early development of the bastion upon which much of the present text has depended.

It seems unlikely, in any case, that Cataneo's treatise was a source for the design of Sabbioneta's walls. Already, in 1549, Domenico Giunti had projected the seven-sided bastionated defences of Guastalla (although these were not completed until the following century) with which Vespasiano would have been familiar. The principles of the 'Italian Trace' were well established in military circles by that time and if Cataneo's contribution is of any importance, it is that he placed this knowledge within the specific discourse of architecture. As a soldier, Vespasiano could have known how to lay out fortifications without the need to consult any architectural work. One might, however, see in the design of the walls of Sabbioneta, Vespasiano's 'reply' to Cataneo: in his treatise, Cataneo illustrates fortified city plans ranging from four to ten-sided and in each of these the configuration of the bastions is varied. There are 'royal' bastions, acutely pointed with square shoulders, bastions *a cuore*, with heart-shaped lobes, bastions with a reentrant neck and flattened shoulders, bastions composed with three right-angles and others obtusely pointed; Cataneo's choice, in each case, appears to be largely aesthetic. At Sabbioneta, Vespasiano has used every one of these variants; having only six points at his disposal, three of them are, in themselves, designed a-symmetrically. Vespasiano was evidently a collector of bastions. (Fig. 2.3)

Sabbioneta's 'modern' defences were interrupted (and, to a certain extent, compromised) where the pre-existing castello looked out of the city across a widened expanse of moat. Alberti, distinguishing between cities in which a 'king' ruled with the consent of his subjects and those held down against their will by a tyrant, recommends, in the latter case, that the fortress should be 'neither inside nor outside the city'[126] and the layout of the fortifications 'must allow him to receive outside reinforcements, even some of his own men against their fellow citizens'[127]:

> *But if one wanted to give a concise description, one might not go wrong in describing [the fortress] as a well-guarded back door of the town.*[128]

In practice, such an arrangement was not always possible, particularly as cities grew and their walls extended to enclose an increasing area of habitation. At Mantua, the ducal fortress is still visible, on the edge of the lake, 'neither inside nor outside' the main body of the city but this was exceptional. At Ferrara, the ducal fortress was, by the sixteenth century, completely absorbed within the fabric of the city. The construction, in 1534, of the Fortezza da Basso, straddling the walls of Florence, was seen as a powerful (and, to most, unwelcome) symbol of the ending of the city's republican history[129]. At Vigevano, the concept of a 'well-guarded back door' was taken to bizarre lengths when the ducal fortress was linked to a guarded military back door by an enclosed and covered 'street' flying above the roads and houses of the city[130]. But aside from its political overtones, the idea that the fortezza should, visibly to the outside world, represent the forceful presence of a city (its 'head', in Francesco di Giorgio's anthropomorphic language[131], 'robust, haughty and menacing' in Cataneo's account[132]) retained its imaginative hold throughout the sixteenth century. As the walls and bastions, presenting a minimum target for modern artillery, sank nearer to the ground, the image of a militarily obsolete fortezza remained as an aesthetic necessity. But there is no way that Vespasiano's fortress could function as a 'well-guarded back door'; it had no contact with the outside world other than through the streets and public gates of the city and it is likely that contemporaries would have understood from this that Vespasiano did not regard himself as a tyrant.

126. Alberti, Op. Cit., p.121.
127. Ibid. p.117.
128. Ibid. p.123.
129. See J.R.Hale, Op. Cit., Cap. 2.
130. See Wolfgang Lotz, Studies in Italian Renaissance Architecture, Cambridge Mass. and London, 1990, pp.117-133.
131. Francesco di Giorgio, Op. Cit., p.3.
132. Pietro Cataneo, Op. Cit., p.18.

Within its circuit of bastions and curtains, the rectilinear grid of Sabbioneta's street layout is suspended, uninflected in relation to the geometry of the enclosure. The collision of two incompatible geometries is absorbed in the free space of the pomerio. This has been taken as evidence that Vespasiano followed (or, at least, took the side of) Cataneo, whose illustrations show a similar disjuncture between street layout and fortified perimeter, as against Filarete, Francesco di Giorgio and others who wanted the main streets to run radially from each gateway to a central piazza[133]. The rectangular geometry of the streets at Sabbioneta has been invested, in much of what has been written about it, with a special significance. For example:

> *Whether from the theoretical models of the trattatisti or from the concrete example of the Herculanean extension of Ferrara, Vespasiano adopted the orthogonal pattern, responding to the demands of order and rationality [….] the orthogonal grid of Sabbioneta draws inspiration from the layout of the Roman castrum: the decumanus is identified with the principal axis marked by Via Giulia (now via Vespasiano). The cardus is, however, absent so that the city seems to lack a definite centre. The crossing was, in reality, emphasised by the column of Pallas [….] set up in 1584 to mark the median of the axis and of the whole urban composition[134].*

This reading of Sabbioneta is both an elaboration and an oversimplification of the paper by Kurt Forster to which we have already referred, in which the placing of the column at an intersection of two conceptual axes is seen as marking the "fulcrum of ducal power and protective focus of the city"[135] The idea that an orthogonal street grid might represent 'order and rationality' is not a conspicuous one in the treatises but belongs to more modern urban theory and it cannot be taken for granted, in any case, that there is any special significance in Sabbioneta's rectilinear plan *per se*. There are three considerations which might point in another direction:

1) In the mid-sixteenth century, there existed no precedent, outside of theoretical works, for a planned city that was not ordered on a rectilinear grid; even in the Middle Ages, cities which were built as new foundations on reasonably regular sites, such as the Bastide towns of south-west France, were at least as rigorously orthogonal as Sabbioneta. The scenographic experiments of Baroque planning , like the fictively 'natural' space of the picturesque and romantic, were not available options to Vespasiano.

2) The majority of small towns in Lombardy show traces of a rectilinear street pattern, in some cases, very pronounced. Rivarolo Mantovano, for instance, whose road system was in place by 1460[136], is very perfectly orthogonal. The area is also strongly marked with traces of the Roman *centuriatio* still visible in minor roads, drainage patterns and field boundaries[137]. Such traces are less pronounced in the area, bounded by the Oglio and the Po, where Rivarolo and Sabbioneta are located, though they are strong in the immediate vicinity of Rivarolo itself. We have already noted, however, that Sabbioneta was settled in late Roman times and it is probable that the Roman system of land division was employed here, even if it was over a very restricted area[138]. It would not be entirely fanciful, then, to suggest that the pattern of streets visible today in Sabbioneta does not merely reproduce the idea, but quite simply is the consequence, of Roman spatial organization.

133. See Maria Rosa Palvarini and Carlo Perogalli, *Castelli dei Gonzaga*, Milan, 1983, p.181 ff.
134. Chiara Tellini Perina, *Sabbioneta*, Milan, 1983, p.17.
135. Kurt Forster, "From Rocca to Civitas: Urban Planning at Sabbioneta" in *L'Arte*, Fasc. 5, 1969, p.19.
136. The tower on the axis of the main piazza is recorded in 1462. B.M.Bologni, *Memorie Storiche dei comune di Rivarolo Fuori, Piadena, Calvatone o Città di Vegna e del Vico Bebriaco*, reprinted Cremona, 1986, p.5. Vespasiano had the streets paved with dressed stone (Ibid. p.6.)
137. See V.E.Ghisi Mutti, "La Centurazione del Territorio di Mantova" in *Civiltà Mantovana* VIII, 46, (1974).
138. Enrico Rossi and R.Marchini, "La Corte della "Grangia" a Villa Pasquali: Residenza suburbana di Vespasiano Gonzaga" in *Civiltà Mantovana*, N.107, 1998, p.54, refers to cardus and decumanus as surviving at Villa Pasquali, less than a kilometre from Sabbioneta.

3)

We need not take entirely at face value the much quoted evocation, by the newly appointed academic Mario Nizolio, of the condition of Sabbioneta before the transformation effected by his patron, Vespasiano:

It was nothing but an old castle built by Ludovico Gonzaga, surrounded by a big ditch of foul and stagnant water: at its base, cottages in the mud, some made of thatch, some of crude brick; a barren country around it and the hovels of fishermen[139].

Lodovico Gonzaga, Vespasiano's uncle, had not only built (or repaired) the castello but also initiated a programme of improvements at Sabbioneta including work on the naviglio by which the moat would receive an increased flow of water[140]. Already, in 1551, four years before the start of Vespasiano's building programme, Tobias Foà had set up his Hebrew printing establishment there while the bank founded by the brothers Azariah and Meshullam, sons of Joab of Pisa, had been there since 1436[141]. It seems that Nizolio flattered his patron by exaggerating the squalor of the pre-existing township; that, in reality, Vespasiano was not working upon an entirely clean slate. The orthogonal planning of Sabbioneta is, in fact, not nearly as perfect as many accounts would lead one to believe and it seems that, in many, instances, existing structures or boundaries had to be allowed for. It appears that the realization of Sabbioneta as we can see it today was not an immediate process followed through as a single operation; as late as 1587, Messrs. B. Agosta, N. de Ruggeri and G.P. Fruggia started to demolish their houses, to be rebuilt to designs approved by Vespasiano[142], suggesting that, even at this date, there remained a few structures from an earlier fabric.

None of this is intended to detract from the historical significance of Sabbioneta's urban form; it might, indeed, throw into greater prominence the single-mindedness as well as the originality of Vespasiano's method and achievement. It is to suggest, rather, that the ideas and solutions which he deployed were not simply taken 'off the peg' but developed out of a continuous and thoughtfully empirical interaction between his long-term intentions and the immediate circumstances in which they were applied. Like the social and institutional programme which we encountered in the first chapter, we might here understand Vespasiano's architectural strategies at Sabbioneta as an 'art of the possible' and his reading of architectural theory less a search for prescription than a source for worthwhile experiment.

139. Quoted in A. Puerari, Op. Cit.,p.1. Nizolio's words are here paraphrased and considerably amplified by Racheli, Op. Cit.
140. E. Rossi and R. Marchini, Op. Cit., p.55.
141. See The Jewish Encyclopedia, London, 1900, p.586.
142. N. de Dondi, Op. Cit., p.331.

Vitruvius, as we have noted, took the (male) human body, held to be the most perfect manifestation of natural order, as the paradigm of the symmetry which buildings ought to exhibit:

> *Thus in the human body there is a kind of symmetrical harmony between forearm, foot, palm, finger and other small parts; and so it is with perfect buildings[143].*

The idea that God's creation, examined in the light of human reason, would reveal an ideal mathematical order was not, in any case, unfamiliar even during the Middle Ages; Villard de Honnecourt, in his *Notebook* made between 1225 and 1250, shows faces and figures constructed around triangles, pentagrams and grids[144]. Apart from the authority of Antiquity, however, what seems to have attracted renaissance writers in the vitruvian interpretation was its derivation of a series of simple, whole-number ratios which could be applied directly in the dimensions of buildings. According to medieval building practices, where the designer was directly involved in setting out dimensions on site, irrational ratios were as easy to achieve as whole numbers, provided they could be set out with a line. Ratios of 1 : √2 or of the side of a square to its diagonal, are common in Gothic architecture as are dimensions in the ratio 2: 1+√5, the 'golden section' constructed by adding to the short side of a double square the length of its diagonal[145]. Luca Pacioli, in his treatise *De Divina Proportione* (first published in Venice, 1509[146]), closely following the theoretical work of Piero della Francesca, still proposes the Golden Section as an ideal ratio applicable in painting but, when he confronts architectural issues directly, he falls back upon whole number measurement derived (without acknowledgement) from Francesco di Giorgio[147]. Increasingly, during the Renaissance, the designs of buildings were transmitted by means of drawings and figured dimensions so that irrational ratios had to be avoided as far as possible. Here, the vitruvian formula was irresistible as stated by Vitruvius with disarming simplicity:

> *For the human body is so designed by nature that the face, from the chin to the top of the forehead and the lowest roots of the hair, is a tenth part of the whole height; the open hand from the wrist to the tip of the middle finger is just the same; the chin to the crown is an eighth, and with the neck and shoulder from the top of the breast to the lowest roots of the hair is a sixth[148]. And so on.*

For Francesco di Giorgio, this was good enough:

> *Therefore it is not by accident that the numbers found in the divisions of the human body should constitute its beauty by reason of proportion and measure. It remains for us to take the same [measures] in the composition of all buildings[149].*

Like his text, Francesco's drawings are littered with images of the human body superimposed, often in a somewhat opportunistic manner, upon plans, facades or the profile of columns or mouldings, their presence, in either case, effectively creating a mood without the need for rigorous explanation. In Cataneo's treatise, the image of the body is Christianized as the perfect body of Christ, but similar proportions are derived from it[150].

143. Vitruvius, Op. Cit., p.14.
144. See Carnet de Villard de Honnecourt Paris, 1986, plates 36-38.
145. See Otto von Simson, Cit., pp.14-20 and 208-211.
146. This reference is to the edition, with summary of Pacioli's life and work by Giuseppina Masotti Biggiogero, Milan, 1956.
147. H.W.Kruft, History of Architectural Theory, London and New York, p.63.
148. Vitruvius, Op. Cit., p.72.
149. Francesco di Giorgio, Op. Cit., p.69.
150. Pietro Cataneo, Op. Cit., p.36.

In their haste to arrive at a set of whole numbers for immediate application in the setting out of buildings, Francesco di Giorgio and Cataneo undoubtedly missed some of the refinement with which more subtle philosophers wished to invest the idea of the body's perfection. Marsilio Ficino is not inclined to state the case in such literal terms:

> *The beauty of the body lies not in the shadow of matter, but in the light and grace of form; not in dark mass, but in clear proportion; not in sluggish and senseless weight, but in harmonious number and measure. But we come to that light, that grace, proportion, number, and measure only through thinking, seeing, and hearing[151].*

The notion that the ideal beauty of the human body could be apprehended, not only by thinking and seeing, but also by hearing, was not lost on Alberti. The theoretical identity of visual and musical harmony, though ignored by Vitruvius, was an idea as old as the thought of Pythagoras. Abelard, in the twelfth century, had connected this idea with the biblical dimensions of the temple of Solomon[152]. In Alberti's view, the variety of proportions to be found in individual human bodies, and the fact that one person might prefer one but another, another, rendered human measurements an insecure basis for a universal system of harmony; he is happy that the orders should reflect human proportions for the very reason that their different 'character' Doric sturdy, Corinthian slender and Ionic (in between, as though composed of both) allowed the introduction of individual preference into the ornament of buildings[153]. But when it came to the major setting-out dimensions to be employed in architecture Alberti derives his preferred ratios from the numerical structure of the tetrachord.

> *I affirm again with Pythagoras: it is absolutely certain that Nature is wholly consistent. That is how things stand.*
>
> *The very same numbers that cause sounds to have that concinnitas, pleasing to the ears, can also fill the eyes and mind with wondrous delight[154].*

From the model of diatonic musical harmony, Alberti derived a set of ideal ratios expressed in whole numbers:

short areas	1 : 1, 2 : 3, 3 : 4.
intermediate areas	1 : 2, 4 : 9, 9 : 16.
long areas	1 : 3, 1 : 4, 3 : 8.

In Vespasiano's ducal palace at Sabbioneta, the plan dimensions in nineteen out of the twenty-three major spaces on the ground floor and first floor produce ratios within 3% of the albertian prescription. Given the practical difficulties involved in superimposing two different plan arrangements within a system of load-bearing walls running through the two floors, the limited range of wall thicknesses which could be obtained using standard bricks and the inevitable 'left over' dimensions which had to be taken up somewhere in the plan, one could say that if Vespasiano was intentionally using albertian ratios, he did rather well at making them fit together[155].

151. Marsilio Ficino, Op. Cit., p173.
152. Von Simson, Op. Cit., p.38.
153. Alberti, Op. Cit. , p.303.
154. Ibid. p.305. Alberti's musical numerology is elucidated in R. Wittkower, Architectural Principles in the Age of Humanism, London, 1949, Part IV.
155. The author is fully aware of the pitfalls awaiting anyone who attempts to analyze the proportions of buildings; without precise knowledge of the unit of measurement in use, without knowing how the work was set out - on the centre-lines of structure, the centre-lines of openings and voids or to the boundaries of spatial zones, one can never be sure that one is correctly reading the designer's intention. This is especially so in the case of complex columnar architecture, such as Gothic, less so in a case such as Vespasiano's ducal palace where one is, at least, dealing with simple, unarticulated rectangles. Wittkower is, of course, predisposed to corroborate his own interpretation: (Op. Cit. . p.99) "Whenever one meets ratios of the series 6, 8, 12, 16, 18, 24, 27, 32, 36, 48, etc., it is safe to presume that this is not casual but the result of reflections which depend directly or indirectly on the Pythagorean-Platonic division of the musical scale." It is not improbable (nor even, in fact, particularly surprising) that the practice of architecture should reflect, in this way, the overwhelming consensus of the contemporary discourse.

Similar ratios are to be found in the Palazzo Giardino. This plan, whose Pt 1 ~2 apparently episodic sequence of variously dimensioned spaces prompted a Frenchman to comment, in 1898: "by their dimensions, their ornament and the small scope which they offer for practical life, [these] must clearly have been intended for princesses"[156], nevertheless achieves albertian proportions for most of the rooms. The Sala degli Specchi falls within 1% of the comparatively uncommon 'long area' ratio of 3 : 8.

More surprising, perhaps, is the apparent consonance between the 056 so-called Galleria degli Antenati and the space outside it. This comparatively small room, which was Vespasiano's studiolo, occupies the centre of the first floor of the ducal palace (a position in which one might have expected to find a large room, the principal salon) and the ratio of its short side, the window wall, to its extension back into the building is 4 : 9. The wall at the back which separates it from a small lobby is non-structural, making it more unlikely that its position was dictated by other than aesthetic motives. The window of this room also occupies the centre of a short end of the piazza outside and this, also, has a proportion of $4 : 9 \pm 3\%$. If this was, as one might like to believe, a relationship set up self-consciously between the major symbolic space of the city and the room in which Vespasiano worked and kept his private library, then it is a development of the albertian notion of concinnitas far beyond what was generally attempted, rendering in concrete terms the harmony of a ruler and his subjects.

> *For, as we experience every day, when two strings or lyres are tuned to the same pitch, whenever one is plucked the other vibrates[157]. (Fig. 2.4)*

156. C. Yriarte, "Sabbioneta, la Petite Athènes", in Gazette des Beaux Arts, XL T.19, p.123.
157. Marsilio Ficino, Op. Cit., p.174.

The architectural or pictorial effect

The architecture of Sabbioneta is almost entirely a-stylar, depending hardly at all, other than in small-scale decoration, upon the use of the orders. Two principal reasons for this seem to suggest themselves:

057

1) Vespasiano, though not impoverished, was not in a position to spend at anything like the level available, for instance, to his cousin Guglielmo, who could not only maintain an entourage at Mantua of a thousand dependants, twenty country and suburban residences as well as palaces in Rome, Venice and Milan, but had available in his private coffers a cash sum of two million gold scudi.[158]. Sabbioneta had, in relative terms, to be constructed on a shoe-string. Sabbioneta was, moreover, remote from any source of building stone, an expensive commodity to transport, and consequently lack local expertise in refined stone carving. In the few cases where detached columns of stone do appear at Sabbioneta, they are evidently reused components of earlier buildings (for instance, the very crude and apparently medieval columns on the ground floor of the Palazzo della Ragione) or, like the genuinely antique column of Minerva, said to have marked the symbolic crossing of cardus and decumanus , brought as a trophy, by Vespasiano's father, from the sack of Rome. Internally, the orders could be rendered as pilasters in stucco and, as such, they appear (Corinthian) in the Sala degli Specchi of the Palazzo del Giardino and (Ionic) in the church of the Incoronata. Scamozzi's Doric half-columns on the upper floor of the theatre are, similarly, worked in plaster but this procedure, probably introduced by Giulio Romano in the Palazzo Té in Mantua and widely followed by Palladio, was not generally adopted at Sabbioneta.

2) We have seen that Vespasiano was capable of producing drawings for military installations and have evidence, noted earlier, that he sent drawings for the Corridor Grande from Spain. It does not follow from this, however, that he had the technical skill to make drawings of the orders or of other sculptural ornament. Most of the architects who did make designs for ornamental sculpture were, themselves, painters and there is no evidence that Vespasiano (or, indeed, Bottacci, his site superintendent) had such accomplishments. When this sort of work was essential, as in the case of Vespasiano's funeral monument, for which the marble was imported from Rome, the design was commissioned from an expert, Giovanni Battista della Porta from Porlezza[159].

For whatever reason, the architectural effect at Sabbioneta is achieved with only a very limited use of the decorative repertoire of High Renaissance architecture. (Fig. 2.5) A considerable part of the treatises lay, therefore, beyond the scope of Vespasiano's project and it is hardly surprising, by the same token, that the architecture of Sabbioneta has played little part in perceptions or accounts of the development of architectural style. The only decorative innovation that seems to have attracted comment at the time is the series of richly carved ceilings and panelling in a variety of rare species of wood which are still preserved in the ducal palace; the source for this, if it is to be found in any ancient precedent, is not vitruvian but apparently Judaic. Vespasiano's friend Bernardino Baldi commented:

158. A. Paolucci, I Gonzaga e
l'Antico: Percorso di Palazzo
Ducale a Mantova, Rome, 1988,
p.47.
159. A. Puerari, Op. Cit., pl. 26.

In the time of Solomon, and particularly, perhaps, in Phoenicia and Judea, great use was made, in the ornament of regal buildings, of precious wood such as Cedar, Acacia and also Olive: so it is written that the forty-five columns of his house of Lebanon were made of Cedar wood. This practice of lining walls with precious wood I have seen revived with great skill by the most excellent Vespasiano Duke of Sabbioneta who, in the magnificence of his buildings and in the nobility of his mind is quite exceptional, deserving comparison with the most famous of the ancients.[160]

It could well have been Baldi who had provided this obscure reference in the first place, but we have already noted in Vespasiano an inclination towards experiment and the appetite of a collector.

When, in 1962, the *Architectural Review* dedicated a large part of its special Townscape issue to a visual analysis of Sabbioneta[161], Ivor de Wolfe, the author, had hardly anything to say about the architecture of individual buildings but a great deal about the composition of the city as a sequence of contrasted spatial events. The interest of this text for our current enquiry lies in the fact that it represents an architect's way of looking at a city, concerned with what is visibly there rather than what, according to a predetermined model of 'the renaissance city', should be there. Ivor de Wolfe's analysis of Sabbioneta is designed to bring out two main points:

1)   *The arrangement of Sabbioneta's streets, far from promoting an atmosphere of rational calm and clarity, deliberately closes views and withholds any simultaneous experience of the city's various components. In any other case than a custom-built town made to the order of one customer, the tailor himself, one could hardly speak with such certainty, but here behind every ploy we have a right to assume deliberate intention. Thus only once in the whole canyon's journey [the 'canyon' is the long narrow street which crosses the northern edge of the main piazza, linking the church of the Incoronata with the north-eastern extremity of the city] are we allowed even a glimpse of the rest of Sabbioneta. All other openings are T-trapped until, as per Alberti's instructions, the Via Prato Raineri runs up under the town wall (so adding several cubits to its stature) before itself being trapped and made to take the last long leg back to the Gate the other end, the Porta Imperiale.*

By 'trapping' de Wolfe means the recurrent device of blocking a straight view from one end of a street to the other. The albertian reference is to Book Four of *On The Art of Building*, in which Alberti sets out principles for the design of various sorts of road; distinguishing between large and powerful cities, whose main streets should be straight and very wide, while those in 'a settlement or a fortified town' would be better not straight, making the town appear larger than it was. He goes on to comment upon secondary roads:

Nonmilitary roads will be similar, except perhaps in this respect: if built in straight lines, they will make a better match with the corners of the walls and the parts of the buildings. But I notice that the ancients preferred to give some of their roads within the city awkward exits, and others blind alleys, so that any aggressor or criminal who entered would either hesitate, being in two minds and unsure of himself, or, summoning up the courage to continue, would soon find himself in danger[162].

160. Bernardino Baldi, Descrizione del Palazzo Ducale d'Urbino, included in Memorie concernente la città di Urbino, Rome, 1724, p.514.
161. Ivor de Wolfe, "The Street" and "Sabbioneta" in Architectural Review, Vol.131, No.784, London, 1962.
162. Alberti, Op. Cit., p.107.

Noting here with approval the same apparent characteristic of ancient Rome which so deeply offended Cataneo, Alberti makes a tactical military argument which, as it happens, Cataneo flatly rejects:

I have to laugh at those who claim streets should be narrow so as to be easier to defend; that when the enemy has penetrated the walls one can more safely defend the rest and drive him out again. This is not to deny that narrow streets are better to fight in than wide ones: but I still say that a city or castle is in trouble which, having failed to keep the enemy outside the walls, expects then to defend the remainder by fighting in the streets[163].

This is not the place to discuss the significance of de Wolfe's attempt to recruit Alberti and Vespasiano Gonzaga to the cause of Townscape and the picturesque tradition; we cannot, in any case, be sure that Vespasiano was responding, at Sabbioneta, to Alberti's advice but it does appear probable that his motive, in so regularly breaking the open street grid, was aesthetic rather than military: an experiment which he found interesting (or perhaps, as we shall suggest in the final chapter, his response to a more private impulse). De Wolfe gives us, if nothing else, a way of looking at Sabbioneta which allows it to escape from the accepted model of the 'ideal' renaissance urban form.

On the surface the plan is as the guide books and scholars describe it, star-shaped, formal, grid-ish, fortified, yet not one of these aspects has any real bearing on the end product which is of an extremely subtle, romantic, synoptic sort, deeply opposed to what is widely regarded as the Cinquecento ideal - through-way bypassing the town square - T-junctions to all exits - lead-ins - street lengths reduced to a minimum - entrance gates masked - all exits to town masked - all views of the world excluded - no rational plan - no quick picture - no geometry - no grasp permitted of the master-plan or underlying rationale - on the contrary, surprise, anticipation, mystery, frustration.... etc., etc.

2) The monumental structures of Sabbioneta are deployed in such a way as to leave the possibility of alternative readings: they can be understood both as elements delimiting the space onto which they front and, at the same time, as freestanding objects within an implied larger urban space. (Fig.2.6) De Wolfe develops this point in relation to the main piazza and the impossible predicament forced on the planner when two street apertures are required at one corner.

Vespasian had four at two and took steps to cure the lateral leak by projecting the palace stair across the aperture, adding two man-size bollards for good measure. [....] he caused the Palace to tower above its neighbours in such a way as to suggest that it, the Palace, like the Duomo at Florence, is just another of those quart-size dirigibles, parked in a pint-sized open space (a ploy which causes the streets to vanish and reappear as part of the pint-sized effect). For photography the point is better made at the other end of the Piazza for there Vespasian repeated the gimmick in reverse, by reducing instead of increasing the height of the frontage. Upon this frontage he then clapped a single flattened roof and, behold, no frontage - instead a charming little pavilion. A pint-sized pavilion planted in a quart-sized piazza whose quart-sized boundaries appear (by means of uniform roof lines and T-traps) to be extended round the pint-sized pavilion.

163. Pietro Cataneo, Op. Cit., p.8R.

Whether the 'man-size bollards' were indeed placed there as part of Vespasiano's original design is open to question (bollards were a vital ingredient in the apparatus of Townscape) but Vespasiano did put his statue in that space[164]. De Wolfe may have missed the obvious political symbolism in the disjuncture of scale between the ducal palace and the Palazzo della Ragione but his observation is nevertheless valuable. A similar strategy is to be seen in the way that the Corridor Grande can be read both as lining to the fabric of the blocks behind it and, alternatively, as a freestanding structure. One does not have to impute similar motives, but it might still be legitimate to suggest that Vespasiano deployed, at Sabbioneta, strategies of urban composition which seem to have foreshadowed some of the preoccupations generally associated with Camillo Sitte and the late nineteenth century[165].

Of the four architectural treatise writers whom we have considered, although all but Alberti combined illustration with text, it was only Francesco di Giorgio who had the graphical skills to indicate pictorially the effect which a city (Filarete illustrates only individual buildings) designed all'Antica should aim to create. Three such drawings (folio 86V and 87) show maritime cities viewed through the harbour entrance, enabling a major urban space to be seen axially while a variety of structures appear rising above the general skyline and behind the city walls at either side. (Fig. 4.1) The suggestion of a freestanding octagonal structure placed on the main axis of a square in two of these views links these drawings with 'ideal' urban settings depicted in painting and, in particular, in one attributed to the school of Piero della Francesca which hangs in the ducal palace at Urbino. Together with the inlaid panels of two doors of the same palace, on which, even if he was not the principal architect, Francesco di Giorgio is known to have worked, this image constitutes, more than any other, our received notion of what 'the renaissance city' was supposed to be like. In this respect, Sabbioneta does not reflect the painters' ideal conception of city space at all: the insistent grid which, in all these representations, is marked out on the ground surface (as it is in Pius II's piazza at Pienza) is absent at Sabbioneta while the octagonal church of the Incoronata is neither freestanding nor axial. We have already seen that the relationship of monumental structures to urban space at Sabbioneta is, contrary to the suggestion of these pictorial cities, consistently ambiguous.

The image of a cluster of towers and domes rising above a city's walls was not new in the Renaissance: cities are represented like this in countless medieval examples; but it is in this respect that Sabbioneta does appear to resemble the drawings of Francesco di Giorgio. It can hardly have been by accident that Vespasiano grouped all the tall structures of Sabbioneta (in addition to those visible today, there was also a tower at the rear of the ducal palace) in the north-west corner of the city where they fill the skyline as one approaches the Porta Vittoria. For a long time the only gateway, this approach to Sabbioneta seems to have been the preferred one and it was in the space outside this gate that events such as military parades (and executions) took place. Again, then, we can see Vespasiano cultivating a view of his city in which the precise location of its parts is obscured. In the south-eastern half of the city, by contrast, the pattern of the streets is comparatively spacious and relaxed, having more the atmosphere, on a smaller scale, of Ercole d'Este's new district at Ferrara.

164. De Dondi, Op. Cit., p.338 (entry for 31st May, 1588).
165. De Wolfe refers frequently to Sitte, whose Städte-bau nach seinen künstlerischen Grundsätzen was first published in Vienna in 1889.

Cities were also represented, of course, in stage scenery:

Three types of drama are performed in a theatre: tragedy, recounting the misfortunes of tyrants; comedy, unfolding the cares and anxieties of the head of a family; and satire, singing of countryside delights and pastoral romance[166].

For these three types of presentation, appropriate settings were constructed and, as technical skill in the depiction of realistic perspective space developed in the early sixteenth century, so did the public's appetite for illusionistic space represented upon the stage and the construction of three-dimensional settings in which, by the exaggeration of diminishing sight-lines, the actors were made to appear as though standing in the foreground of deeply extended urban vistas. For tragedies, the scene was supposed to portray fine palaces while comedies could be set amongst more everyday and less dignified structures, so that gothic or grotesque elements are more commonly found in comic scenes; in practice, however, it was the variety, even the irregularity of the architecture which most often dominates the effect. These are not unified or serene compositions; cornice lines are not uniform as they are in the painters' evocations of ideal city space (and as recommended by Alberti[167]) and their intention seems as much to divert ("perhaps also women or others danced up there to make merry while the plays were going on") as to instruct. In Baldassare Peruzzi's drawing for a tragic scene, the Colosseum and Hadrian's mausoleum loom above renaissance and gothic palaces and porticos to produce an impression more fantastic than dignified. (Fig. 5.7) Even in Sebastiano Serlio's somewhat bowdlerized versions of Peruzzi, attached to the second book of his treatise[168] which deals with perspective, it is the variety of architectural forms and types which clamour for attention, rather than their conspicuous order. Much has been made of the 'theatrical' quality of Sabbioneta's urban scene and of its reciprocal reconstruction in Scamozzi's fixed set in the Teatro Olimpico [169]. It is certainly true that devices akin to the heightened perspective of the fixed scene are visible in the space of the city: the height of buildings tends to reduce as the streets run away from the main piazza; many of the buildings are revealed only as corners pushed into the street vista; individual structures are, in many cases, particularized by changes of material, scale or articulation. It seems very likely, in fact, that Vespasiano had in mind images such as Peruzzi's tragic scene and wanted Sabbioneta to suggest something of the same diversity.

166. Alberti, Op. Cit., p.273.
167. Ibid., p.262.
168. Sebastiano Serlio, Il Secondo libro d'Architettura (Prospettiva) first published in Paris, 1540. Serlio's writings have been omitted from the general review of treatises in this chapter since Book VIII, in which, if anywhere, a theory of urban planning and design may be set out, has not yet, even today, been fully published. (See Hanno-Walter Kruft, Op. Cit., p.74).
169. The important text, from which most others are derived, is Kurt Forster, "Stagecraft and Statecraft: the Architectural Integration of Public Life and Theatrical Spectacle in Scamozzi's Theatre at Sabbioneta" in Oppositions IX, (1977).

We have seen that, to the trattatisti, the idea of a theatre was a strange one and that these writers had some difficulty imagining what sort of thing would go on in such a structure. Even, perhaps, on account of its very strangeness, as well as through the splendid devices of colour and lighting, the theatrical spectacle of sixteenth-century Italy conjured up an air of enchantment (Ariosto's evocation is quoted in Chapter 1) which must have gone far to compensate for the remoteness of the dramas which were presented. Such an air of enchantment seems to have been in Vespasiano's mind when he designed and embellished his city, and an important ingredient towards this was the late medieval Castello which filled one side of the Piazza d'Armi. In de Dondi's account there are constant references to works, of a generally decorative nature, applied to parts of this venerable structure. Variously describing as turrets, spires, lanterns or domes, erected upon the torrioni, de Dondi was evidently at a loss to name correctly the trappings of a chivalric architecture which seems to have referred as much to northern european as to local precedents. A pointed roof on one of the towers was taken down and rebuilt to a reduced pitch; heraldic devices were added in many places and a gilded angel crowned one of the pinnacles[170]. As it would have appeared from outside the city, set back behind a wide expanse of the moat, Vespasiano's Castello seems to have embodied the enchanted world of the romances which, in the works of Ariosto and Vespasiano's friend Torquato Tasso, still provided sixteenth century Italians with some of their favourite reading. Tasso describes a castle in which a number of christian knights were ensnared by the enchantments of Armida:

> *so many lamps made their appearance round about that the air was clear and bright with them. The castle glows as does the lofty stage in a decorated theatre amid festivities at night[171]*

We have seen, then, that the architecture of Sabbioneta, though clearly belonging to the same broad culture as that in which the architectural treatises of the Renaissance were produced, cannot, without distortion, be reduced to the physical manifestation of contemporary written theory. There is no sanction in the treatises for the elision at Sabbioneta of ducal, representational structures with the domestic fabric of the city, the witholding of an explicit spatial hierarchy for the deployment not of one ideal bastion type but of the whole available range of bastion shapes, for the pragmatism with which topographical accidents are absorbed into a flexible but highly controlled order. Nor, in the treatises, is there to be found any precedent for the 'harmonisation' of a room with the public external space upon which it opens and certainly none for the violent and sometimes disturbing disjunctures of scale, the cultivated ambiguity of free-standing and embedded form, the restless variation of texture and material which characterise Vespasiano's city. From the built evidence at Sabbioneta, one might infer that its creator was an enthusiastic, though critical reader of the treatises but also an individual for whom architecture was a means to externalize a complex, often contradictory and passionate nature.

170. N. de Dondi, Op. Cit., p334.
171. Tasso, Op. Cit., Canto 7, 36.

Lacking the means (perhaps, even, the desire) to emulate the sculptured magnificence of the architecture of contemporary Rome, Venice, Florence or Genoa, Vespasiano had no choice but to resort to architectural devices which, from the historical perspective of four centuries, may now be seen to carry the marks of a highly original creative intelligence. To the extent that Vespasiano's architectural activity took place close to, or even beyond, the limits of the architectural discourse of his time, however, the originality of his work at Sabbioneta was largely invisible in his own day and has remained so almost until the present. The 'reinvention' of Sabbioneta as an exemplary object of study by architects in comparatively recent times, when the architectural discourse of the Renaissance had finally run its course, may testify to the extent to which the consolidation of a profession and a theory of architecture might also have served to suppress the recognition of that which it was unable to encompass.

Pt 2

~3)

Politics.
Expectations of
Nobility and the
de-personalization
of power.

068

069

What man that sees the ever-whirling wheele
Of Change, the which all mortall things doth sway,
But that thereby doth find, and plainly feel,
How Mutability in them doth play
Her cruell sports to many mens decay?
Which that to all may better yet appeare,
I will rehearse, that whylome I heard say,
How she at first herselfe began to reare
Gainst all the gods, and th'empire sought from them to beare.

[....]

For she the face of earthly things so changed,
That all which Nature had establisht first,
In good estate, and in meet order ranged,
She did pervert, and all their statutes burst:
And all the worlds faire frame (which none yet durst
Of gods or men to alter or misguide)
She alter'd quite; and made them all accurst
That God had blest, and did at first provide
In that first happy state for ever to abide.

Ne shee the lawes of Nature onley brake,
But eke of iustice, and of policie;
And wrong of right, and bad of good did make,
And death for life exchanged foolishlie:
Since which, all living wights have learned to die,
And all this world is woxen daily worse.
O pittious worke of Mutabilitie,
By which we all are subject to that curst
And death, instead of life, have sucked from our nurse![172]

172. Edmund Spenser, The Faerie Queene, Cantos on Mutability, (first published 1609) in The Works of Edmund Spenser, London, 1850, Stanzas 1, 5 &6, p.342.

To describe as 'uneventful' the times in which Vespasiano Gonzaga lived Pt 2 ~3
requires a retrospective view that was unavailable to him or to his contemporaries.
To observe that none of the major political, religious or cultural crises perceptible in
Europe at the end of the fifteenth century had been decisively resolved at the end of
the sixteenth: that the military advances and reversals, critical though they may have
seemed at the time, amounted to little more than a rehearsal of the major struggles
for national dominance of Europe and the New World which were to shatter the life 070
of the succeeding century: that a stalemate persisted throughout the century in the
confrontation of Christian and Islamic powers or that the disintegration of a Catholic
hegemony in Europe could still be seen, when the sixteenth century ended, as a
problem to be contained rather than the irreversible split which was clearly evident
a few decades later: to see the sixteenth century as a period of comparative stand-
still in the crucial developments of western history is to take a long-term perspective
sharply at odds with the lived experience of millions of individuals. While there may
be grounds for maintaining that the sixteenth-century was, if anything, a period of
consolidation - consolidation of national power-bases, of the church, of hereditary
privilege, consolidation of colonial enterprises or, indeed, of the cultural upheavals
which characterised the previous century - it would be necessary to add, nevertheless,
that the direction in which Europe was pointing at the end of the century was very
different from anything which could have been anticipated at the end of the fifteenth.
One might say, with greater justice, that the critical developments of the sixteenth
century were evolutionary rather than climactic. While it may be fair to suggest that the
world into which Vespasiano was born was still, in many important respects, the same
world in which, sixty years later, he died, the intervening years had seen a decisive
shift in probabilities, political, military, cultural, to the extent that the upbringing
and the education which he received in the first fifteen years of his life could not, in
themselves, fully equip him for the conditions under which much of his future life was
to unfold. The expectations which he brought with him from childhood could not,
without redefinition, be measured against the achievements and the disappointments
of his subsequent career.

Vespasiano's working life was spent, as it turned out, close to the
epicentres of decisive change in the inter-related but nevertheless distinct arenas
of politics and warfare, and it is with these that the two following chapters will be
concerned.

*And when the time comes let us make the rounds; for I intend to cleanse this
isle of every sort of impurity, and of your vagabond, idle and ill-conditioned
persons. For I should like you to know, friends, that your vagrant and lazy
sort are the same thing in a state as drones are in the hive, eating up the honey
the workers make. I intend to favour labouring men, preserve gentlemen's
privileges, reward the virtuous, and above all respect religion and honour the
clergy. What do you think of that? Am I saying something or cracking my
brains for nothing?[173]*

*173. Miguel de Cervantes
Saavedra, Don Quixote, trans.
J.M.Cohen, London, 1950,
p.781.*

To a reader in the late sixteenth century it was, in itself, comical to imagine that a man of the people might undertake the duties of a governor just as the nostalgia of his aristocratic master for the world of chivalric romance was seen, comically, as evidence of a deranged mind. A present-day reader would hardly find these circumstances intrinsically amusing, needing the added ironic twist of Sancho's evident ability in his improbable role and the progressive revelation that Don Quixote was, in many respects, less mad than those around him. The tangle of beliefs, prejudices, aspirations and self-deceptions out of which, during Vespasiano's lifetime, the idea of nobility was concocted is entirely alien to our modern, bourgeois understanding of human relationships and power, in which we expect to see reflected conditions, either personal, economic or ideological, which we can recognise as realities. That Vespasiano belonged to the nobility is a fact, however, of such fundamental importance in shaping the opportunities, the expectations and the outcomes of his political career that it is worth devoting a few lines to investigating some of the meanings which the concept of nobility might, in his day, have carried.

At its crudest definition, nobility entailed the right to bear arms, the expectation of a life free from menial labour and a broad exemption from most forms of taxation. It implied membership of the constituency from which, other things being equal, the leaders of civil, religious and military affairs would be drawn though not an automatic right to such a position of leadership. A nobleman, however insignificant, was expected to dress appropriately and to wear a sword, to be treated with deference by his inferiors and to defend his honour as a point of principle. Like the clergy, the nobility was seen as an institution ordained by God: the respect due to its members related to the institution and not to the personal attributes of individuals, however much, in theory, noble status entailed moral and personal expectations not applicable to commoners. As the church stood in relation to Christian belief, so the nobility stood in relation to the tradition of chivalry[174] and a nobleman was seen to be the carrier of this valiant and high-minded ethos whether his personal behaviour exemplified it or not, just as it was regarded as natural that few members of the clergy would, in their personal lives, demonstrate the values of Christianity. Parallel, as it was in many other respects, to the church, the order of nobility was entirely non-productive, a burden to be carried by the rest of society with no reciprocal benefit of a tangible nature.

Noble status could be inherited, it could be bought or it could be won *de facto*. In the words of Stefano Guazzo, an acquaintance of Vespasiano whom we shall meet later in a different connection:

> ....*some falling to define gentry, have sayde it be the dignitie of the fathers and ancestours, others the ancient patrimonie, others riches joined with vertue, others vertue onely.*[175]

Like membership of the clergy, the advantages enjoyed by the nobility were such that those who possessed them were unlikely to give them up while, to those in a position to confer noble status, the Emperor, kings or princes, the sale of titles - essentially a down-payment on tax exemption - represented a valuable source of ready cash. By the second half of the sixteenth century, the coinage of nobility (to use Guazzo's metaphor) was considerably debased: not only Spain harboured the impoverished remnants of rural feudalism; the hidalgos of Spain had their counterparts in Italy:

> *And if you doe but looke about these mountains without going any farther, you shall see some houses so ful of Gentlemen, al companions and equalles in this seigneorry, that every one of them hath scarce a little hole to shrowd himself in: and they come at diverse doores so thick as it were conies out of a Berrie. [rabbits out of a burrow]*[176]

174. For a brilliant analysis of the role of chivalric ideology as it survived into the late Middle Ages and Renaissance, see J.Huizinga, The Waning of the Middle Ages, trans. F.Hopman, Harmondsworth, 1965, p. 54 ff.
175. Stefano Guazzo, The Civile Conversation, trans. George Pettie (London, 1581) Ed. E.Sullivan, London and New York, 1925, Book 1, p.175.
176. Ibid., p.189.

The cities, too, were crowded with 'cavaliers' of various descriptions, those who had bettered themselves through trade and had now assumed respectability[177], those struggling to keep up appearances (like Amilcare Anguissola of Cremona, father of Sofonisba, the celebrated painter at the court of King Philip, the failure of whose investments in property and in the perfume trade brought him to a state of near destitution from which he was partially rescued by his enlightened investment in his daughters' education[178]) or, for that matter, the knighted urban low-life so well known to the English in Shakespeare's portrayal of Sir John Falstaff and his circle.

Nobility could be the expression of upward social mobility but it could also be the cover beneath which downward mobility might, however thinly, be disguised.

At the more rarified end of the aristocratic spectrum, the nuances of nobility were equally complex; those who could demonstrate an ancient line of descent - the Estense dukes of Ferrara, the Orsini and the Colonna of Rome (Vespasiano was particularly proud of his maternal Colonna heredity, adding the name to his own family name) or the descendants of imperial Roman families such as the Paleologhi and the Caetani occupied a position of special prestige but yielded, nevertheless, in effective status to the offspring of emperors, kings or, on occasion, popes. Don Juan of Austria, illegitimate son of Charles V, could assume, as of right, the glamorous military undertakings for which Vespasiano (probably as well qualified) would have given anything, and it was on account of being the same emperor's grandson (again through an illegitimate line), rather than as a proven leader, that Alessandro Farnese was allowed to take over the Flemish campaign. Those families, like the de' Medici or the Gonzaga whose nobility, though of comparatively recent origin, was founded in the possession of real political power, could compete for the top honours only to the extent that the reality of their power-base continued to be demonstrated while those, like Agostino Chigi, whose entrée to aristocratic circles derived almost entirely from his specatcular wealth, remained vulnerable to little snubs in matters of real social prestige.

The distinction between material and symbolic matters in the perception of noble status was not precisely drawn: the elaborate forms and rituals associated with hunting were, for instance, a clearly understood component in the representation of high nobility, so that Luigi Gonzaga, founder of his dynasty, could be so humiliated by the superior array of falcons and dogs at the disposal of Bernabò Visconti of Milan as to feel obliged to concede to him all his possessions. The same protocol demanded, of course, that Visconti, in return, must demonstrate his magnanimity by letting Luigi have back his possessions subject to an annual tribute - as a reminder - of two hounds and two sparrow-hawks[179]. The accoutrements of hunting (as opposed to its practice, as an economic activity by the lower orders, still tolerated within limits during the sixteenth century) were understood as expressive of the atavistic foundations of aristocratic culture, and the vulnerability of their prestige in this respect was a matter which the Gonzaga were quick to redress: already, at the beginning of the sixteenth century the gift of dogs, horses or birds of prey from the Gonzaga was an honour which kings and popes took seriously.

177. Giovanni Muto, "Centro e periferia: le relazioni tra la corte di Madrid e il ducato di Milano e tra XVI e XVII secolo" in Various authors, Sofonisba Anguissola e le sue Sorelle, Cremona, 1994, pp. 177 & 178. The aristocracy of Milan was of predominantly urban, non-feudal origin and was, in a large number of cases, involved in mercantile activity.
178. Rosanna Sacchi, "Intorno agli Anguissola" ibid.,p. 346.
179. See Giancarlo Malacarne, Le Cacce del Principe, Modena,1998, p.58 and generally. On the subject of hunting by commoners, the same work (p.48) quotes a revealing account, written by his game-keeper to Federico Gonzaga II, describing the trouble he had with some soldiers who were passing through Pergognaga and who, despite being told that hunting belonged there to the Marquis, paid no attention, saying that they wanted to kill hares and pheasants.

In practice, of course, the possession of great power or wealth could be converted, over a few generations, into the status of hereditary nobility through inter-marriage amongst the leading dynasties, so that discrepancies would become, with time, less visible. It was also in the social arrangements associated with marriage that the perceptions of comparative noble status came, most directly, to be expressed in cash terms. In marriages between families of equivalent status, the size of the dowry would be a simple reflection of the wealth and dignity assumed by both but dowries could be adjusted upwards or downwards in order to reflect the extent to which one family was doing the other a social favour in agreeing to the marriage. Vespasiano's maternal grandfather provided in his will that should his daughter Isabella be married to Ippolito de' Medici, her dowry should be 30,000 ducats but that in the case of her marriage to Luigi Gonzaga, Vespasiano's father (which took place soon afterwards), it would be only 10,000. Vespasiano's second marriage, to Anna d'Aragona, who was related by quarter consanguinity to King Philip, was accepted only reluctantly, and on the king's insistence, by her family, presumably because they had been expecting a more advantageous outcome in respect of her elevated rank. Negotiations over the payment of her dowry remained inconclusive long after her death.

If the ideological foundation which, inherited from the Middle Ages, still sustained an uncritical belief in the superiority of the nobility during the sixteenth century had its roots in the traditions of chivalry and if, at least in theory, to have embraced the order of knighthood was originally conceived as a personal, rather than an hereditary-commitment, the prestige of ancestry during the Renaissance drew also upon new models and arguments. Not only was there a change in style and emphasis, as noted by Huizinga:

> *The thirst for honour and glory proper to the men of the Renaissance is essentially the same as the chivalrous ambition of earlier times, and of French origin. Only it has shaken off the feudal form and assumed an antique garb.* [180]

Nobility of ancestry had come, in any case, to represent a value in itself. In *The Book of the Courtier*, Castiglione sets out an argument which was frequently echoed:

> *So, for myself, I would have our courtier of noble birth and good family, since it matters far less to a common man if he fails to perform virtuously and well than to a nobleman. For if a gentleman strays from the path of his forbears, he dishonours his family name and not only fails to achieve anything but loses what has already been achieved. Noble birth is like a bright lamp that makes clear and visible both good deeds and bad, and inspires and incites to high performance as much as fear of dishonour or hope of praise; and since their deeds do not possess such noble brilliance, ordinary people lack both this stimulus and the fear of dishonour; nor do they believe that they are bound to surpass what was achieved by their forbears. Whereas to people of noble birth it seems reprehensible not to attain at least the standard set them by their ancestors. Thus as a general rule, both in arms and in other worthy activities, those who are most distinguished are of noble birth, because Nature has implanted in everything a hidden seed which has a certain way of influencing and passing on its own essential characteristics to all that grows from it, making it similar to itself. We see this not only in breeds of horses and other animals but also in trees, whose offshoots nearly always resemble the trunk; and if they sometimes degenerate, the fault lies with the man who tends them.* [181]

180. J. Huizinga, Op. Cit., p. 68.
181. Baldessare Castiglione, The Book of the Courtier, trans. George Bull, London and New York, 1976, p. 54.

There are, of course, two parts to this argument which do not properly belong together - unless we are to suppose that horses or trees are incited to virtuous deeds by the fear of dishonour. Nevertheless, the main point, that noble ancestry gave those who had it something to live up to (anticipating, in a sense, the Freudian concept of the Super-Ego), is one that was certainly not lost on Vespasiano Gonzaga. Indeed, there is plenty of evidence to suggest that Vespasiano was inclined to take the ethical implications of his noble birth quite literally, that he was almost morbidly obsessed with the tutelary presence of his ancestors, and that the internal tensions engendered by his understanding of his inherited obligations were seldom far from the surface:

> *It is only a game for me to promote the welfare of these my subjects who throng round me whenever I go out in public, only a game to raise new walls, to give life to material things while I am so much diminished in spirit.* [182]

On the other hand, while earlier notions of chivalry might have pointed to a life of personal privation, an almost monastic ideal of other-worldliness, the magnificence and the munificence, the desire to mark the world permanently with the record of their greatness required of the ambitious nobleman of the Renaissance - amongst whom we must certainly include Vespasiano - a corresponding access to the finance required to achieve these things. In the words of Stefano Guazzo:

> *Though riches can adde no degree to gentrie, yet they are a readie instrument to put in practise certain vertues belonging to gentrie.* [183]

And those who combine nobility of birth with substantial wealth are termed (in Pettie's Elizabethan translation) 'absolute gentry'. If, then, the 'natural' activity of a nobleman was the service of a prince and if Guazzo, like Castiglione, is at pains to stress that 'service' of this kind was a voluntary state not to be confused with that of a menial servant constrained, against his will, to work for wages, it is also clear that Vespasiano, whose ambitions were certainly those of an 'absolute gentleman', had little choice but to earn the cash needed for his projects in the service of King Philip II in Spain. Only during the last years of his life, subsequent to the death of his mother and his inheritance of extensive properties between Rome and Naples, did Vespasiano begin to dispose of an independent income commensurate with the magnificence of his ambition.

182. *Letter to Guglielmo, duke of Mantua, quoted in Marzio dall'Acqua, "Il Principe e la sua Primogenita" in Atti del Convegno, cit. p. 39.*
183. *Guazzo, Op. Cit., p. 186.*

Whether it would be more correct to see it as evidence of deep structural change or as the historical impact of two very different personalities, there can be little doubt that the transformation in the aims, method and style of government, affecting a large part of western Europe, which took place with the succession of Philip II to his father Charles V was a circumstance of considerable historical significance. While Charles had united, in his own person, the dominion of a substantial part of western Europe and of the New World with the symbolic legitimising role of the secular head of Christendom, in the succession the latter role devolved upon Charles' brother Ferdinand while it was Philip who inherited the effective power of kingship. The image of Philip as a miserable, mean-minded, devious and bigoted bureacrat popularly held amongst protestants ever since his time[184] is one whose correction by writers such as Henry Kamen[185] has been long overdue. Equally, the perception of Charles V as heroic defender of Christendom, ebullient hero of the battlefield, magnanimous and cultured, though it has generally earned him the affection of subsequent generations, cannot, upon closer scrutiny, be accepted without reservation. Charles' abdication in 1556 is to be understood, not so much as the theatrical termination (prompted by ill-health) of a brilliant reign, as the reflection of a changed mood and his own sober realization that his combined management of the Empire and exercise of regal authority was not - in today's language - sustainable. He had bankrupted his dominions with little, either political or military, to show for it; his resistance to Turkish expansion had been of no more than token significance; his belief that the divisions of the church could be resolved purely by the force of his own prestige and charisma had proved unfounded and he had barely even attempted to set in place the instruments which would have made effective government over his vast territories into a practical possibility. Though constantly on the move, constantly in person at the scene of some new crisis, Charles may have lived up to his contemporaries' idea of what an Emperor should be like but had failed to give political substance to the idea of Empire.

It is true, no doubt, that Philip was disinclined, by nature, to confront political crises face to face; that he would instinctively avoid the placing of unqualified confidence in any of his subordinates and that he would only pass on to them as much information as would point them in a direction of his own choosing, while the complete picture, constructed through hours of careful investigation, he would keep to himself. It is true that he would manipulate and exploit the temperamental attributes of his associates - the stubborn bellicosity of the Duke of Alva or the smooth pragmatism of Cardinal Granvelle or the impetuous gallantry of his half-brother, John of Austria - as and when it suited his own purposes, abandoning them without compunction if they should become inconvenient. It is clear that Philip would play for time in those circumstances where his father would have seized the initiative and that his legendary prudence frequently masked the absence of any idea what action he should take. It is equally clear, however, that Philip's tactics were, in general, effective against those who played according to the old rules - the French, the Italians and Portuguese and his own Castilian nobility - but less so when confronted by opponents for whom those rules did not apply - the Dutch Calvinists, the English corsairs or, for that matter, the international banking community. His method of government can be seen, then, as an attempt, possibly an insufficient attempt, to retain control over events which were unfolding in increasingly unfamiliar ways. In the words of Friedrich Heer:

> Philip saw himself as responsible for the spiritual and physical well-being of twenty nations. It was this sense of responsibility that chained him to the desk at which he spent eight hours a day and turned him into a re burocrata, the first man, as one writer put it, 'to attempt to guide the course of the world from a writing-desk' (Alexander von Randa). He would fall asleep at his work and be found slumped over it in the morning.[186]

184. William H. Prescott, History of the Reign of Philip II, London, 1855 is an outstanding example.
185. E.g. Henry Kamen, Philip of Spain, Newhaven and London, 1997.
186. Friedrich Heer, The Holy Roman Empire, London, 1996, p.187.

If it has been unusual, in the case of monarchs subsequent to the reign of Philip II, to conduct the bureaucracy of government in person and more common for ministers of the crown, rather than the crown itself, to be behind the writing-desk, it must be admitted, also, that the image of Charles V, the last (it might be said) to attempt to guide the course of the world from the back of a horse, can only appear, by comparison, as distinctly archaic.

When, in 1572, Vespasiano Gonzaga was appointed King Philip's viceroy in Navarre and governor of Guipuzcoa, his experience in civil administration could hardly be described as extensive; unlike the Spanish nobility from which the holders of such offices were normally recruited, Vespasiano had not enjoyed the exercise of semi-autonomous feudal dominion over a large territory and the government of his diminutive states in Lombardy had, during much of the time that he was responsible for it, necessarily been delegated in his absence. Such a mark of confidence on the king's part could be based more upon the king's knowledge of Vespasiano's character than upon any clearly demonstrated track record. It seems, however, that Vespasiano had already attracted a modest reputation for his grasp of legal issues: as early as 1559, we find him, in the distinguished company of Ercole II, duke of Ferrara and Marc'Antonio Colonna, duke of Tagliacozzo, called upon to adjudicate in a bitter and protracted verbal duel fought out between two noblemen of Pistoia according to the elaborate protocol of personal honour.[187] Touchstone's account, in *As You Like It*, was not unduly remote from the reality:

> *O sir, we quarrel in print, by the book; as you have books for good manners: I will name you the degrees. The first, the Retort Courteous; the second, the Quip Modest; the third, the Reply Churlish; the fourth, the Reproof Valiant; the fifth, the Countercheck Quarrelsome; the sixth, the Lie with Circumstance; the seventh, the Lie Direct. All these you may avoid, but the Lie Direct; and you may avoid that too with an 'if.' I knew when seven justices could not take up a quarrel; but when the parties were met themselves, one of them thought but of an 'if,' as, 'If you said so, then I said so'; and they shook hands, and swore brothers. Your 'if' is the only peace-maker; much virtue in 'if.'[188]*

More seriously, Vespasiano had extracted the emperor Maximilian, King Philip of Spain and his cousin Guglielmo, duke of Mantua from an embarrassing situation, acting variously on their behalf in the 'affair' of Casale in 1567[189]. This episode is worth a moment's attention, not only because it illustrates, in microcosm, the process of political transformation which was taking place more generally in Italy during the sixteenth century but also, more particularly, because it brought to King Philip's attention those abilities for which Vespasiano was to become a valuable instrument in the implementation of his governmental strategy.

187. Dean and Lowe, Op. Cit., p.208.
188. William Shakespeare, As You Like It, Act V, Scene IV.
189. The account which follows is largely based upon that of A. Carli, Op.Cit., pp.115 ff. Carli, writing at the time of Italy's rediscovery of national identity, is at pains to rebut the suggestion that the people of Casale were in a state of illegal revolt, wanting, on the contrary, to characterize their struggle as a last flicker of resistance to the imposition of foreign rule.

Casale, situated within, but not subject to the state of Monferrato, had survived as an autonomous 'republic' under the protection of the Holy Roman Emperor and administered by an independent proconsulate nominated by the city 'elders'. With the marriage of Margherita Paleologa to Federico, first duke of Mantua, Monferrato passed into the hands of the Gonzaga, though its government was fronted by Margherita, who was known locally, so as not to cause unnecessary provocation. Situated on the river Po at a natural point of entry to northern Italy from the alpine passes of Savoy, Casale was seen as vital in the imperial and Spanish system for the encirclement of France and in the course of the skirmishes preceding the treaty of Cateau-Cambrésis of 1559 it was occupied successively by Spanish, German and French forces. In the peace settlement, Casale was definitively ascribed to the duchess of Mantua through whom it was now ruled by her son, Duke Guglielmo. In 1562 the people of Casale were informed that their liberty was revoked: needless to say, their protests were ignored, their attempts to retain eminent lawyers blocked by the duke, whose enormous wealth had enabled him to buy off all the experts, and the 'orator' who was despatched to Vienna to plead directly with the emperor could achieve no more than a bland expression of the imperial desire to see the matter settled peacefully. The matter was not settled peacefully: in response to the deployment of imperial forces, the people of Casale hurriedly constructed a fortress which, hastily put up and inadequately armed, was less a threat than a provocation to the duke but sufficient, nevertheless, to bring in Spain to his support and to get the city surrounded by Spanish, Mantuan and Monferrato troops. Further provocations on both sides, together with the death, in 1566, of Margherita Paleologa, brought matters to a head. Lacking the confidence to act on his own in these circumstances, the duke summoned the assistance of his cousin, Vespasiano Gonzaga.

Vespasiano took care to clear this commission with the Emperor and King Philip before joining Guglielmo at Casale. By this time, the duke's leading opponents, Corrado Mola and Oliviero Capello, had absented themselves from Casale and, with the protection of the duke of Savoy, were evidently assembling a party with the intention of breaking into the Castello (whither Guglielmo had now retired) killing the Mantuan garrison and taking the duke and duchess hostage. Acting on a tip-off, Vespasiano gave the pre-arranged signal of a cannon shot to call in fresh forces from outside the city, changed the guard at all the gates, constrained the people to stay indoors while, during the whole night, he moved with his troops from one part of the city to another so as to confuse and to frustrate the intended strike of the insurgents. Shortly afterwards, a second plot was uncovered by which the duke and duchess were to be assassinated in the church during the mass for the ordination of a new bishop; warned again, at short notice, Vespasiano was quickly in command of the situation, activating the troops who were ready in the piazza, ringing all the church bells and placing the city under strict curfew. The duke (who was nothing if not punctilious in matters of religious observance) was able to hear out the remainder of the mass without disturbance. Rather than risk a further attempt, the duke made a hurried departure for Mantua, giving orders for the assassination of Oliviero Capello and the arrest of many leading citizens, while Vespasiano was left to reimpose order.

Invested as vice-duke and governor of all Monferrato, representative (contrary to the preference of Guglielmo, who mistrusted his independence) of the reality of Spanish power, though technically without the authority of the Emperor, Vespasiano acted with speed, resolution and sufficient severity:

> *He remained there with his troops and a company of the Duke's mounted Archibugiers, together with other companies of lombard italian troops, and began, without making any concessions, to treat these citizens considerately, avoiding any bloodshed while setting up numerous trials from which those found guilty were referred for the final decision of the Duke. [Of one hundred and twenty leaders of the revolt who were arrested and (according to the custom of the day) tortured, five were executed and a large number imprisoned.] His sole objective was to place a yoke upon this city which, for the future, it must bear patiently without being able to shake it off and in this he succeeded; in this way, he left in place all the conditions which the Duke required but did so with such dexterity that he was held in affection by the city, being invited by the leading nobility to sumptuous feasts and splendid entertainments.[190]*

Of the 'splendid entertainments' we shall have more to say in a later chapter. When the imperial envoy finally arrived from Vienna bearing the Emperor's instruction that newly imposed taxes should be revoked and certain rights restored to the people of Casale, Guglielmo wanted to ignore it and insisted that new *capitoli* be publicly proclaimed in church. Vespasiano absented himself from the 'celebration' arranged to accompany the imposition of the duke's laws, going instead to Milan where he negotiated with the governor, King Philip's representative, the remission of new and retrospective taxes.

Seen from a modern perspective, the story of the suppression of traditional liberties in Casale is far from edifying and the role played in it by Vespasiano Gonzaga cannot be seen altogether without distaste; it is easy to see, on the other hand, how King Philip, reading his governor's reports of these events (and it must be said for Philip II that he made it his business to be very thoroughly informed in matters such as this) would recognise in Vespasiano the type of an administrator in whom he could place considerable trust. Vespasiano had used only the degree of force and repression that was necessary to achieve his objectives: he had never allowed a situation to develop in which his ability to control events could have been doubted: he had negotiated a minefield of conflicting interests, the technicality of law and the reality of effective power, in a way which only alienated those who were in direct opposition to these. This was the style of government to which, with varying degrees of success, Philip aspired: minimum confrontation, minimum cost, minimum compromise.

In 1568, the matter of Casale being settled, Vespasiano let it be known that he would be available in the service of King Philip and by December of that year he was in Madrid, writing to Guglielmo: "I am well and may delay my return for several days. His Majesty has indicated his intention to employ me, I know neither where nor how: time will show."[191] Several days turned out to be ten years during which, as we shall see, Vespasiano's hopes of military distinction were progressively extinguished. His elevation to the post of Viceroy of Navarra was, nevertheless, evidence of his quiet success in the intricate processes of court politics. In October, 1572, Vespasiano wrote to his friend Ottavio Farnese:

190. Campana, Vita di Filippo II, quoted in Affò, Vita di Vespasiano Gonzaga, p.40.
191. Quoted in R. Tamalio, "Vespasiano Gonzaga al servizio del Re di Spagna in Spagna" in Atti del Convegno , cit., p. 125.

This is the present state of my affairs: the King, to start at the top, not only from what people tell me but also from what he has confided in letters by his own hand, holds me in esteem and and remains satisfied with my services. In the Councils of State and of War I have no close friends nor anyone who would take up the cudgel for me, since this is not their way, but neither am I a target of their hostility because the King watches what they say and they all speak well of me; I speak when I need to and have no enemies amongst them, which is no small achievement. Cardinal Espinosa died recently, who favoured me, but a bit less than people might have imagined; quite simply, I owe a lot to his memory in spite of the fact that his reputation was believed, at the time, to have been dented so that those of us who were in the same boat might have been at risk; but I have always followed the advice of Scipio to Jugurtha, that he should respect the collectivity of Rome and not individuals, and I have avoided being tied to a single person but aimed to give a bit of myself to everyone, because to embrace a single cause and reject the others is to give a hostage to fortune. [192]

Cardinal Espinosa had enjoyed a short but brilliant period of influence with king Philip but lost the king's confidence through his high-handed treatment of grandees and his reluctance to conduct business in writing. When, during an altercation, Philip called him a liar, the shock seems, literally, to have killed him. Philip's characteristically careful double negative: "I am not among those who will not miss the Cardinal"[193] is echoed in Vespasiano's cautious definition of his own position; seeking, as far as possible, to remain on cordial terms with everyone while placing complete trust in no-one: circumspect, unobtrusive and reticent.

Viceregal power in Navarra was probably more symbolic and ceremonial than effective in reality: the indigenous nobility had control of their own militias and governed their territories with full feudal authority while King Philip made little attempt, as he did in Castile, to extend his direct control there since the potential return for this in terms of cash or manpower was too small to justify the effort.[194] The cost of military activities of the crown had to be met from local taxation which was, in fact, seldom opposed by the ruling nobility since they were largely exempt from it but the burden imposed as a result of costly defensive provisions against the French did, in 1573, provoke the despatch of a lawyer to Madrid with a list of complaints relating to Vespasiano's administration. Acting as the king's agent in the implementation of policies which the king was unable to finance adequately, inevitably the focus of local hostility, Vespasiano was evidently uncomfortable. In the same letter to Ottavio Farnese, he confided his misgivings:

....I am trying to get myself removed from here, not that the King did not intend to give me more than if he had entrusted me with Flanders. The truth is that this post, sufficient in itself to satisfy the ambition of many Nobles who have held it and which, with the addition [Governorship of Guipuzcoa] which His Majesty has made to it, may not be the first in Spain but is not second to many, is so inconvenient to my personal circumstances, so remote from my State, my children and my friends that I am requesting, which I fear he may consider hasty, that he employ me in another place more suited to my needs.

192. Ibid. Note 38.
193. H.Kamen, Op. Cit., p.148.
194. See John Lynch, Spain Under the Habsburgs, Oxford, 1965, p. 10 and elsewhere.

Without friends, remote even from the court at which he could enjoy the personal favour of his king, Vespasiano, like Sancho Panza when he was 'governor' of an imagined island, was beginning to miss the company of those whom he knew well and with whom he could feel relaxed. His unconvincing assertion that the vice-regency of Navarra was an honour equivalent to the governorship of the Netherlands (Vespasiano's predecessor at Navarra, Juan de la Cerda, duke of Medinaceli, was entrusted with the Netherlands in 1572[195]) gives a clear indication of the scope of Vespasiano's ambition as well as his growing awareness that he was unlikely to achieve it.

The 'other place more suited to my needs' appears to have been a governorship in Italy though, again, Vespasiano dissimulates his hopes. In 1575, now viceroy of Valencia, he wrote to his cousin Guglielmo:

> ....this city, even though it may delude itself, professes to compare in this respect [the number of lesser nobility] and in its amenity with Naples, although in my opinion it must settle for second place; [....] The house in which the viceroys live is quite impressive and is called Il Reale. The viceroy's salary is better than that of Sicily, he is provided with foot and mounted guards and other perks which, to avoid boring your Highness, I will pass over. In any case, what I wanted was not a governorship in Italy since, being excluded from states of real importance, I would not want to exchange this one, but to see again my own possessions and, not the least consideration, to kiss your Highness' hands which I have sorely missed. I have, in the end, settled for this post to serve a king to whose affection I am particularly obliged and on account of some assurances which he has privately given me but with which I will not burden your Highness; enough for you to know that I am content with this job more than I would be with any, at present, in Italy where, currently, ministers are exposed to the risk of disgrace, do not earn honour and are beset by the troubles of those who sail in this sea of vanity. [196]

There are many things, as we shall see, which Vespasiano was not telling his cousin (whom he had no reason to trust) but the note of disillusionment in this letter is nevertheless unmistakable and sincere. Four years later, finally back in Sabbioneta, his congratulation of the young Alessandro Farnese, on the occasion of his promotion in the Netherlands, is tempered with a frankly embittered epitaph upon his own career in the service of King Philip:

> The quest for honour and glory is a fine thing so long as one comes well out of the intrigues, as I trust your Excellency will, but it must have clear limits and aims; otherwise, it is like trying to grab hold of the moon by its horn so that the more one climbs to the top of mountains, the more it recedes; the victim of ambition, one can easily slip into vanity. Please forgive my talking like this which really is because of the love which I bear you and my wish to see the greatness of your house perpetuated in these undertakings beyond the scope of my class of lesser fibre. Do not think that I am speaking of myself, who want nothing now but to rest, as I have given [king Philip} to understand, but I am speaking in general of nobility in my position. [197]

195. Henry Kamen, Op. Cit., p.144.
196. Letter to Guglielmo Gonzaga, duke of Mantua, 1575, quoted in R. Tamalio, Op. Cit. in Atti del Convegno, note 59.
197. Ibid., p. 142.

Vespasiano Gonzaga's political career in the service of Philip II had been, on paper at least, an outstanding success; he had achieved a position which, in his own words, 'may not be the first in Spain but is not second to many' and he had, to a great extent, done so through personal merit rather than family connection. And yet, as the quotation above clearly reveals, it was a career which left him deeply dissatisfied: in terms of the quest for honour and glory, of deeds worthy of his ancestors, deeds which would be spoken of by future generations, there was nothing to show for it. One must, indeed, search hard in the indices of the histories of Philip's reign for any mention of the man who governed first Navarra and then Valencia as the king's direct representative[198]. It seems that the very quality which had made him so valuable an instrument of royal policy had been Vespasiano's ability to make himself invisible.

Vespasiano had, of course, a political existence in his own right, concerned with his personal interests and the relations between his own states and those with which they were in immediate contact; here, in a world largely untouched by historical change, we can see, unbridled, the expression of his libido and the transformation of its mood over a period beginning before his entry into the political service of King Philip and extending into the twelve years of his 'retirement'. If, in the service of the king, Vespasiano might have appeared calculating, a discreet and smooth dissimulator of his real thoughts and motives, the record of his early activities as a local land-owner suggests that, in dealing with neighbours and rivals, he was headstrong, self-centered and vain.

In 1563, the year following that in which he had obliged his subjects of Sabbioneta to live within its new walls, Vespasiano became embroiled in an unseemly squabble with his cousins, the Gonzaga of San Martino dall'Argine, four brothers, Pirro, Scipione, Ferrante and Giulio Cesare whom their father, Carlo, had entrusted to Vespasiano's care while his widow, Emilia, was in control of their possessions. Like Sabbioneta and Bozzolo (as Vespasiano was later to find to his disadvantage) San Martino was a 'feudo maschile' and succession was reciprocal amongst these three in cases where there was no male heir to any one of them. Strictly speaking, therefore, one of the boys should have received the inheritance and Emilia's position was irregular. Belonging to this family was some land at Commessaggio, immediately adjoining that of Vespasiano and to which, on this flimsy technicality, Vespasiano now laid claim. There is clearly more to the story of this dispute than appears in the record (which is, in any case, largely dependent upon the testimony of an interested party, Scipione, whose 'Commentar Rerum suarum', in manuscript, came into the hands of Irene Affò[199]) but it appears to have mushroomed out of control due to the intransigent postures adopted both by Vespasiano and by Emilia. Vespasiano was piqued because, when he was in Milan, Pirro, returning from Genoa, ought to have stopped off to pay his respects but, instead, travelled directly by boat from Alessandria to Casalmaggiore on the Po. Perhaps more revealingly, Vespasiano found it irritating that Emilia wanted to copy and rival him in all sorts of ways "parem sibi omnibus in rebus vellet".

One would like to know more about Emilia and in what respects she sought to compete with Vespasiano: it can hardly have been in terms of his military career and if it had been merely a matter of domestic etiquette it is hard to see why Vespasiano would have minded. If, on the other hand, she had been trying to rival his architectural undertakings, this could have touched on a more personal nerve. If she did so, nothing is known about it but it is well known that her son, Giulio Cesare (who, like Vespasiano, spent much of his life at the Spanish court), was responsible for major architectural interventions at Pomponesco and Isola Dovarese while Pirro commissioned extensive work at San Martino dall'Argine[200]. Perhaps, at least, we can tell from where such a spirit of emulation might have originated.

198. Given the historical standpoint from which it is written, Vespasiano's four citations in Fernand Braudel, The Mediterranean and the Mediterranean World in the Age of Philip II, trans. Siân Reynolds, Los Angeles, 1995, would tend to confirm, rather than to refute this assertion.
199. I. Affò, Vita di Vespasiano Gonzaga, cit. pp. 32-3, 37, 41-2, from which this account has largely been extracted.
200. See M. Galerati, Architettura Scala Urbana, Florence, 1979, pp. 137-144.

In the first round of litigation, Emilia played the advantage that her son Scipione was well-placed in ecclesiastical circles[201] and could influence his senior colleague, Cardinal Ercole Gonzaga, brother of the first duke of Mantua, to intervene on their behalf; unfortunately, Cardinal Ercole died before anything had been achieved. Vespasiano retaliated by raising the stakes, demanding now not only a part of Commessaggio but the entire property of Emilia's family; this drew the boys' uncle Federigo, signor of Gazzolo, into the dispute and he, together with the young Scipione, set off to the imperial court at Vienna to lodge their complaint. Vespasiano countered this move by arguing, through his lawyer, that the matter should be referred to the Senate at Milan (where, presumably, he could count on support) and when the emperor decided, instead, to refer the affair to the impartial judgement of Ottavio Farnese, duke of Parma (later to become a close personal friend of Vespasiano), the eminent parmesan lawyer retained by Vespasiano discreetly advised him that his case would not stand.

Rather than give up at this stage, Vespasiano attempted to undermine the credit of Federigo and the brothers at the imperial court, accusing them of misrule in their fiefdoms and arguing that their privileges should be revoked. Emilia deftly rebutted these insinuations and the emperor's response was non-commital. One can imagine that, by now, to all but the main protagonists, this dispute had come to be nothing but a troublesome waste of time; the duke of Parma wanted to find a sensible compromise and suggested to Pirro and Scipione that they might give up half of Commessaggio. They, however, believed that this would be insufficient to pacify Vespasiano and (without telling their 'proud and tenacious' mother) proposed, instead, that he could have the whole of Commessaggio if he would drop his claim on their other possessions. And so, four years after it had started, this un-edifying wrangle was ended.

Once a solution had been found in which personal pride could be saved on both sides, it seems that Vespasiano and the Gonzaga of San Martino became good friends (as members of a family should be, Affò reminds us) and in the continuing saga of the brothers' efforts to retain their possessions, the role played by Vespasiano was evidently benign. Shortly after his arrival in Spain, Vespasiano received news from Scipione that he and his brothers were in trouble again, this time largely of their own making: they had turned their uncle Federigo out of Gazzolo 'because he had usurped it' and Federigo, now in Mantua, elderly and without an heir, had made up his mind to assign his rights (or claimed rights) to the duke Guglielmo. Without a moment's delay, Guglielmo had sent a party of heavies to Gazzolo, where Giulio Cesare was in no position to resist and, with appropriate protests, had no choice but to withdraw. Vespasiano wrote at once to the duke, making three points:

1.   Like himself, the duke had been appointed a guardian of the four brothers and it was unworthy to treat them in this way.
2.   In the contract of 1478 between Federigo, Marquis of Mantua and his brothers, the former had renounced 'for himself and for his successors' any claim on San Martino, Gazzolo, Commessaggio, Rodigo and the other territories; titles in these fiefdoms would, if there were no immediate heir, revert to the nearest descendant of Gianfrancesco Gonzaga, one of the brothers party to this contract.
3.   The brothers would be forced to seek the protection of a more powerful ruler, "it being human nature rather to throw oneself into the hands of a hostile stranger than into those of a relative, on whose support one should be able to rely but from whom one has received injury".

201. According to Affò, Scipione was already a cardinal, but this seems unlikely and is contradicted by the entry in de Dondi's diary according to which "Scipione Gonzaga, brother of Pietro and Giulio Cesare was made a cardinal by Sixtus V'" in 1587.

In order to give credibility to his last point, Vespasiano sent word to his auditor, Riniero Raineri, that he should put it around that the brothers were planning to declare themselves dependants of the duchy of Milan, this being a quite reasonable thing to do since much of their territory was in the Cremonese and the reasons for its attachment to Mantua no longer held good. He also advised the brothers to retain the services of a lawyer named Cravetta, in Turin, whose reputation extended more widely than that of the duke's lawyers, and who would charge 200 scudi or a little more.

It is unlikely that Vespasiano took all this trouble entirely out of love for his previous opponents. He knew Guglielmo too well to believe anything but the worst of his motives. Defending, in principle, the San Martino brothers' rights, he was giving notice of his determination to look after his own interests in spite of his detention in Spain. In this, he was undoubtedly well advised.

In the event, things followed a familiar course: both parties put their case before the emperor (Scipione, with greater success); the emperor, very reasonably, proposed that Gazzolo should be put back in the hands of Federigo as an interim measure while the duke of Ferrara worked out an amicable settlement; the emperor's plan could not be implemented because Federigo died, leaving all he had to Guglielmo, who sent troops to take Dosolo while Pirro and his brothers were able to retake Gazzolo. Twenty-one years later, when Vespasiano died, things had not really settled down: Bozzolo was now also up for grabs because its ruler, Federico, had sided with the French and the emperor had divested him of his rights; the San Martino brothers had a strong case to inherit Sabbioneta (and Commessaggio) because of the reciprocal male inheritance statute; the young duke Vincenzo of Mantua (or his advisors) proposed a deal whereby the San Martino brothers could have all the rest if he could have Sabbioneta. Finally, as we have seen, Vespasiano's son-in-law had to pay out a large sum of money (which he could afford) for the title of the duchy of Sabbioneta (which he didn't particularly want).

The numerous expeditions across the Alps occasioned by this string of events which, one has to imagine, had its counterpart in countless other disputes in other parts of the Italian peninsula, may have been good news for the inn-keepers along the way but can only be seen as a spectacular waste of human endeavour; in every case (as also in the affair of Casale) the Emperor's reply was non-commital, his desire unenforcible. It is as though the length and difficulty of the journey was a necessary, though little more than symbolic, demonstration of each side's determination.

In all this, (the most protracted but by no means the only site of Vespasiano's entry into the scramble for material or political gain), we can see that the fiction of imperial rule, the aspirations of chivalry and noble magnanimity, the sustaining myths of a traditional aristocratic society, could be little more than a thin veneer masking a political culture in which legality was, as a matter of course, perverted and undermined in the name of rapacious and ruthless self-interest. We can see that Vespasiano was able to inhabit this world as readily as he could that of King Philip's meticulous and, by comparison, modern legal bureaucracy. It must be admitted that the moralizing tone of many of his statements (his admonition to Guglielmo, for instance, that justice is a sea in which small ships sail as well as big ones, and there should be no distinction of subjects or greater or lesser princes[202]) would have carried greater force if his own conduct in this respect had been without blemish.

202. Letter of 2nd Feb. 1570 to the duke of Mantua, quoted in Daniela Ferrari, "Vespasiano e I Gonzaga di Mantova" in Atti del Convegno, p.226.

Whatever we might think today, Vespasiano was a man upon whom it was considered appropriate to bestow the highest honours. The order of the Golden Fleece, awarded him by King Philip in 1585 may, as has been suggested, have been also a golden handshake[203] but it placed him, nevertheless, among the élite in Europe of his day and his election to the nobility of the Venetian republic in 1586 appears to have been unsolicited and without ulterior motive. In 1564, Sabbioneta was elevated by the emperor Ferdinand I to the status of a Marquesate, in 1576, by Maximilian II, to Principality and the following year, by Rudolf II, to an independent dukedom (independent, that is, of any intermediate power below the emperor and critically, so far as Vespasiano was concerned, independent of the duke of Mantua). To have retained the favour of three successive emperors while committed to the service of the king of Spain was, in itself, a balancing act of some dexterity, (given that relations between these arms of the Habsburg dynasty were seldom without tension), though it was reported (by informants of the duke of Mantua), probably correctly, that the dukedom was purchased for the sum of 4,000 ducats[204].

The negotiations leading to Sabbioneta's elevation had to be conducted with the greatest secrecy, for it was certain that Guglielmo would have tried to prevent it (Guglielmo never offered a word of congratulation) and in this, as in many other important commissions, Vespasiano was ably and loyally represented by his kinsman Ercole Visconti. The long periods of his absence from Italy meant that Vespasiano had to place considerable trust in his deputies: for the day-to-day government of Sabbioneta and, later, of his dominions in the south; for the oversight of his building projects and for the command of his small army; and in this respect he appears to have chosen well. He seems, in fact, with a few minor exceptions (the Raineri family was an occasional source of trouble), to have commanded the same unquestioning loyalty from those to whom he entrusted his affairs as that with which he served the king of Spain. If Sabbioneta, on Vespasiano's final return in 1578, had grown and prospered during his absence, this is an indication that the Visconti, the Zanichelli, the Mesirotti and others were fully committed to Vespasiano's project.

In his government of Sabbioneta, where he had neither opponents nor any master whom he must serve, Vespasiano could put into practice the political beliefs which he held by conviction. We have already noted that his city was intended to demonstrate, if only on a minute scale, principles which were, in his view, applicable elsewhere in Italy; we have noted his insistence that Sabbioneta should not depend, for its defence, upon mercenary troops, and he had already, during the '50s and '60s, legislated to oblige citizens to defend the state[205]. He issued statutes in 1563 to prevent lawyers charging excessive fees to poor people and in 1574 to prevent usury. In 1580, he reformed the 'Collegio' to control entry to legal practice. In matters of detail (his interventions and subsidies to stabilize the grain market and minimise the effects of poor harvests, for instance), Vespasiano showed a genuine concern for the well-being of the population[206]. But he did little to revise the Statutes of Sabbioneta which had been established in 1483[207] and there is no evidence to suggest that Vespasiano entertained any grand utopian fantasies concerning his government or that he wanted to interfere in the private lives of his subjects; his political programme was entirely pragmatic, like that of Sancho Panza: I intend to favour labouring men, preserve gentlemen's privileges, reward the virtuous, and above all respect religion and honour the clergy. Given its minuscule size, Vespasiano was not obliged to choose either to govern Sabbioneta from behind a writing desk or from the back of a horse but in both he showed himself a perfectionist. As Marzio dall'Acqua has noted:

> One has only to read at random any of his decrees to recognise the profound difference of tone which distinguishes them from those of other seigneurs of the time.[208]

203. Giancarlo Malacarne, "Gli Stemmi di Vespasiano Gonzaga del Ramo Cadetto di Sabbioneta" in Atti del Convegno, p.101.
204. Ibid. p. 97.
205. Alberto Liva, "Gli Statuti della Communità di Sabbioneta e la successiva legislazione di Vespasiano Gonzaga" in Atti del Convegno, p.281.
206. See Dondi, Op. Cit., pp 366, 376, etc.
207. Ibid. p. 279.
208. Marzio dall'Acqua, "Il Principe e la sua Primogenita" in Atti del Convegno, p. 41.

085

~4)

Warfare.
Heroic dreams and
technical realities.

For the Spanish cannot withstand cavalry and the Swiss have a fear of foot soldiers they meet in combat who are as brave as they are. Therefore, it has been witnessed and experience will demonstrate that the Spanish cannot withstand French cavalry and the Swiss are ruined by Spanish infantrymen. And although this last point has not been completely confirmed by experience, there was nevertheless a hint of it at the battle of Ravenna, when the Spanish infantry met the German battalions, who follow the same order as the Swiss; and the Spanish, with their agile bodies, aided by their spiked shields, entered between and underneath the Germans' long pikes and were safe, without the Germans having any recourse against them; and had it not been for the cavalry charge that broke them, the Spaniards would have slaughtered them all. [209]

Stone blunts scissors, scissors cut paper, paper wraps stone; if the Italians are absent from this description of a military stale-mate which was, nevertheless, more regularly demonstrated on their own territory than anywhere else, it was a state of affairs which many Italians might have been happy to perpetuate. In a country whose power struggles had traditionally been individualistic, shifting and indecisive, military force was accepted more as a necessary means for lending credibility to diplomacy than as an instrument of long-term strategic policy in its own right. Professional mercenary soldiers, recruited only for the short duration of a single campaign, loyal, if to anyone, only to the group of a hundred or less men to which they belonged, could not be sure that the 'enemy' might not be fighting alongside them in a few months' time while the commanders themselves faced opponents who might, in the next round of diplomatic re-alignment, become their allies. In the first half of the sixteenth century, only the Republic of Venice, to a less extent Milan and, for a short period during the papacy of Julius II, the Holy See supported standing armies of any consequence, able to achieve more than local or temporary objectives. It was in the interest of no-one to inflict more than token damage upon opposing forces and the incessant skirmishes which were the visible manifestation of political life in the peninsular were, in general, conducted upon this understanding [210].

Warfare, conceived as spectacular (if, incidentally, bloody and destructive) ritual, carried strong aesthetic resonances and the Italian predilection for cavalry was, at least in part, a reflection of this. The shock, therefore, which Italians experienced in the face of invading national armies from France, Spain and Germany between 1494 (when the French invaded Naples) and 1559 (when the peace of Cateau-Cambrésis established Spanish power over most of Italy on a permanent basis), was a shock as much to the Italians' idea of civilized manners as to their hopes of a significant national military role in the future.

Heavy artillery, though it loomed large in sixteenth-century perceptions of the horror of modern warfare, was only at a primitive state of development so far as field warfare was concerned. The transport of just five large cannon with their ammunition and ancillary equipment could require ninety-five carriers and a hundred pair of oxen [211] so that any hope of tactical surprise must have been frustrated, if only by the enormous dust-cloud which would accompany any substantial movement of artillery (warfare being generally a summer-time activity). Incapable of rapid deployment, artillery was effectively restricted to long-term siege (or the threat of it), static defence and, most importantly, to naval warfare; in 1590, the Venetian republic considered transferring all guns of pay-load rated at over fifty pounds from land to naval use [212]. The outcome of land battles remained, as it had been in classical antiquity, a function of superiority in the various modes of hand-to-hand fighting, and field warfare remained, at least in the imagination of sixteenth century Italians, a theatre for the display of individual acts of heroism within a system of generally agreed rules. During the sixteenth century, however, the emphasis of tactics was to shift irreversibly towards the primacy of fire-power and the technique of its deployment.

209. *Macchiavelli, Op. Cit., p.87.*
210. *See Paul Larivaille, La vita quotidiana in Italia ai tempi di Machiavelli (Firenze e Roma), (originally La vie quotidienne au temps de Machiavel (Florence et Rome), Paris, 1979) Milan, 1995, Cap III.*
211. *Ibid., p.109. De Dondi records in his diary for January, 1589 (Op. Cit., p. 343) the comandeering of 1000 oxen in the province of Cremona for the transport of a part of Philip II's artillery.*
212. *J.R.Hale, Renaissance War Studies, London, 1983, p.315.*

To Vespasiano Gonzaga, it probably seemed natural that he should follow a military career. His father Luigi was nicknamed il Rodomonte after the ferocious anti-hero of Ariosto's *Orlando Furioso*. In the service of the emperor Charles V, Luigi's brief career (at the age of thirty-two, when Vespasiano was only a year old, he was killed by a stray shot from an arquebus during an attack on Vicovaro) earned him the reputation of an exemplary condottiero and Vespasiano had his example to live up to. No sooner released from service as a page to the future Philip II of Spain, at the age of twenty, Vespasiano placed himself at the disposal of his elder cousin, Don Ferrante Gonzaga, a highly regarded captain-general of Charles V. His first engagement was in the siege of Parma where, on a harrying exercise outside the St Barnabas gate, he and his party were surprised by a sortie and in the ensuing skirmish many were killed on both sides. Vespasiano was left for dead but subsequently found only to be lightly wounded[213].

Undeterred by this minor setback, Vespasiano was off again in 1553 to join the force which the emperor was assembling at Innsbruck to drive the French out of Piedmont. This time he was given command of four hundred light cavalry under the standard of his stepfather, the prince of Sulmona. Admitted, also, to councils of war, Vespasiano lost no opportunity to demonstrate his commitment to the profession of a soldier:

> *A wonderful proof of his daring was seen when, moving on the heels of the enemy with his few soldiers, he sustained the attack of two thousand hardened Swiss infantry who expected to take him prisoner without difficulty. He, not in the least intimidated by such numbers and to encourage his own men, charged his horse directly at the enemy's ranks, breaking through as far as the third line, to their great consternation. Whirling his sword around him, he struck such terror into these people that, if his men had followed with equal resolve, he would certainly have defeated this force so much greater than his own. Pressed in by the throng, however, his horse was killed beneath him and, at the same time, he received a blow on the head from a heavy halbard, stunning him so that the sword fell from his hand and he fainted in what could have been a very dangerous predicament, had not the bravest of his followers come to his aid. In spite of this misfortune, the Swiss came out of it worst, being forced to retreat but taking with them, as supposed trophy of victory, Vespasiano's sword to be presented to Signor de Brisac, French Captain general. [....] Shortly afterwards, during a truce, Signor de Brisac and Don Ferrante Gonzaga were negotiating on behalf of their respective Monarchs and, at the end of a splendid banquet when the conversation turned to military matters, Vespasiano, who was there, received great praise from de Brisac who freely admitted that, if the day had turned out as the young man had deserved, that Swiss rabble would have been defeated. Recognising, therefore, that the sword, which had been lost only by mischance and could not count as a trophy of victory, he had it brought to him and graciously placed it between [Vespasiano's] hands, exhorting him always to do as he did, magnanimously emulating the glory of his ancestors[214].*

213. *Affò, Op.Cit., p.14.*
214. *Ibid., p.16.*

This account, which Affò has constructed from more than one source, seems likely to be a somewhat glamourized version of an event which did, nevertheless, take place. Whether, as also seems probable, Vespasiano was afterwards taken aside by Don Ferrante and told never again to take so irresponsible a risk with his own life and the lives of his men, we can never know; this was, however, the last occasion upon which Vespasiano appears to have acted so recklessly in the quest for military glory. Don Ferrante was, in any case, himself summoned to the emperor 'to answer certain accusations' and replaced as commander-in-chief of the imperial forces in Italy by Don Ferdinand of Toledo, duke of Alva. This man, with whom Vespasiano's fortunes were, for many years, to be bound up, brought a strategic, rather than a local interest to the conduct of imperial military policy in Italy[215] and was disinclined to pursue the campaign in Piedmont with great vigour so that Vespasiano, now, at twenty-four years of age, captain-general of the Italian infantry, could claim only temporary and inconclusive successes. The following year (1556) saw the final phase of Vespasiano's career in active warfare. The duke of Alva had turned his attention to the anti-spanish activities of the newly elected Pope Paul IV (Caraffa); this outspoken xenophobe (the Spanish were "heretics, schismatics, accursed of God, the progeny of Jews and Moors, the filth of the world"[216]) had annexed a number of small states around Rome whose rulers had been pro-Spanish and was forming alliances not only with the French but with the Turks as well. Vespasiano, in command of eight thousand Italian infantry, accompanied Alva's powerful force of Spanish veterans to recapture Pontecorvo, Anagni, Vicovaro (where Vespasiano was able to make amends for the death of his father) and Palombara. These events have been variously recounted so that, from William Prescott[217], we learn that the town of Anagni was "stormed and delivered up to sack, - by which phrase is to be understood the perpetration of all those outrages which the ruthless code of war allowed, in that age, on the persons and property of the defenceless inhabitants, without regard to sex or age," while Affò, on the contrary, assures us that Anagni was taken 'without bloodshed' and that after the storming of Palombara, Vespasiano demonstrated his compassion by protecting the women, children and the aged who had taken refuge in the Rocca[218]. Since it appears that the defenders of Anagni capitulated and opened their gates as soon as the Spanish artillery had been set ready on nearby high ground, it is improbable that convention would have been ignored and the citizens punished as though they had put up resistance; the clemency of Vespasiano towards those who were non-combatant was evidently recorded as unusual for the same reason. What is clear, in all of these engagements, is that the decisive factor was the use (or threatened use) of heavy artillery by Spanish forces and that the antiquated defences of these towns were inadequate to resist this form of attack.

The siege of Ostia, whose fortress was of comparatively modern design, proved to be a much more difficult undertaking; while the town gate was broken down after a short salvo the garrison commander retreated into the Rocca where he was able to hold out against heavy bombardment for seven days, by which time the attackers were running short of ammunition. The Italians, led by Vespasiano, were sent in to storm the Rocca and in this desperate assault Vespasiano had a large part of his upper lip blown off by a shot from an arquebus. The attack had to be abandoned and the fortress was subsequently handed over in a negotiated settlement. This marked the end of Vespasiano's career on the field of battle; his lip was skilfully treated (the remaining scar was a source of considerable pride to Vespasiano) He was able to continue in service of the duke of Alva, this time occupied in the fortification of Nola in readiness for an expected attack by the duke of Guise, sent by the French king in an attempt to revive the fortunes of the pope and his allies. The defensive installation, built at considerable speed, was presumably no more than earthwork and wattle, but it proved so effective that the French kept well clear of it and shortly afterwards the pope conceded defeat.

215. See W.H.Prescott, History of the Reign of Philip II, London, 1855, Vol. I, p.134: "He showed little of that romantic and adventurous spirit of the Spanish cavalier, which seemed to court evil for its own sake, and would hazard all on a single cast. Caution was his prominent trait, in which he was a match for any graybeard in the army; - a caution carried to such lengths as sometimes to put a curb on the enterprising spirit of the emperor."
216. Quoted in Carli, Op. Cit., p.49.
217. W.H.Prescott, Op. Cit., p.139.
218. I.Affò, Op. Cit., p.18

In the space of five years, then, Vespasiano had matured from an impetuous youth ready to risk anything for the sake of glory to a hardened, prudent and efficient soldier. He had learned the realities of modern international warfare and mastered its technology. The first phase of the building of Sabbioneta dates also from this period of his life, initiated at a time that his ability as a soldier had been demonstrated in terms of his courage more than his common sense. Two years after the Roman campaign and the capitulation of Paul IV, the peace treaty of Cateau-Cambrésis, in 1559, brought to a halt the French bid for dominance in Italy and inaugurated an extended period of comparative peace in the peninsula. This peace was bought, however, at the price of any remaining prospect for Italian self-determination. For a professional soldier, the traditional opportunities provided in the perennial skirmishes of Italian power-play no longer existed. No longer the pastime of aristocrats, the business of warfare was entering a more strictly 'professional' phase:

> *Having, since boyhood, found warfare more interesting than anything else, leaving father and homeland [I] went to seek out engagements not only in Italy but also in France, England, Scotland, Flanders and other parts of Germany. And I wanted to make a minute study of defense & offense in those things which seemed to me to be of value, not seeking understanding from those who believed that they understood better than me but that intelligence which appeared from my own researches. I can truly tell you that there are few fortresses which cannot be taken and this, in most cases, is because princes have given the work to an Architect, who sets himself to do things which do not belong to his profession, in which he has no judgement, and who will not listen to the accurate advice of a hardened soldier who, through long experience, sweat and study, has learned the art of offense and defense.* [219]

Gerolamo Cataneo, whose treatise *Dell'Arte Militare Libri Tre*, published in 1571, was among the most significant (and frequently copied) writers on the technique of warfare during the sixteenth century. In his Preface, he wants the world to know that his work has received the approval of experts:

> *I have had the opportunity of showing these, my endeavours, to some of the great gentlemen and famous captains of our time [....] and they have been praised by the most illustrious Vespasiano Gonzaga, an exceptional person, excellent in every noble quality, of which he has many times given proof through his courage, which reflects the nobility of his birth, through his accomplishment in letters and in arms, and every admirable pursuit; whose probity, invention, spirit and wisdom are such that there is nothing so great that it cannot be expected of him* [220].

219. "Cose narrate da M. Gio. Tomasso da Venetia, ingeniero eccellentissimo, già di Carlo Imperatore, or dell'Illustrissimo Dominio...." in Girolamo Ruscelli, Precetti della Militia Moderna, Tanto per Mare, Quanto per Terra Venice, 1572, p.40 V.

220. Gerolamo Cataneo, Dell'Arte Militare Libri Tre, Venice, 1571, (not paginated) Preface. The last part of this eulogy appears to have been lifted directly from Castiglione (Baldesar Castiglione, The Book of the Courtier, trans. George Bull, London and New York, 1967, p.281.)

All this eulogy is not, as it would normally have been, directed to a potential patron (the book is not dedicated to Vespasiano) but seeks, rather, to establish the immaculate credentials of a person who had praised Cataneo's book. One can see that the book could, indeed, have appealed to Vespasiano. Many renaissance treatises on aspects of warfare, in common with much written on the subject of architecture, must earn the stricture of Paul O. Kristeller that "They often seem to lack not only originality, but also coherence, method, and substance, and if we try to sum up their arguments and conclusions, leaving aside citations, examples and commonplaces, literary ornaments, and digressions, we are frequently left with nearly empty hands."[221] In Cataneo's *Arte Militare*, there is barely a reference to antique authority, hardly a single concession to literary style; where appropriate, information is tabulated or diagrammatically expressed. It is a thorough, systematic and rigorously empirical review of current military technology. Book I deals in the first chapter with the basic construction of geometrical figures: Chapter 2 sets out the principles of the design of bastions, clearly explained in terms of firing lines, with general layout and details drawn to scale (in Pietro Cataneo's *Quattro Primi Libri di Architettura*, dimensions are given in the text, and are almost impossible to relate to his plans). Chapters 3 and 4 respectively deal with the duties of the person with overall responsibility for defence of a fortress, and of the person responsible for day-to-day operations. In Chapters 5 and 6 there are instructions for attacking forces applicable where a) a fortress cannot be stormed and must be besieged and b) where it can be stormed, (Fig. 4.1) while Chapter 7 contains reciprocal measures for withstanding an assault. These last three chapters are illustrated with graphic scenes in which the positions of infantry, cavalry and artillery are clearly represented; the town which can be taken by storm is shown as one with obsolete towers at the angles and high curtain walls, similar to the 'ideal' arrangements proposed by Francesco di Giorgio. Finally, in Chapter 8 are set out the procedures for marching and encampment (with normative dimensions for the sleeping areas needed for various categories of soldier and horses) and, in Chapter 9, rules for dislodging and driving away an encamped enemy force.

The last Book of Cataneo's treatise consists almost entirely of tables for instant reference, showing how any number of men from a hundred to twenty thousand should be lined up correctly in ranks, together with diagrams for the arrangement of pikemen, archibugiers and cavalry 'according to modern practice'. (Fig. 4.2)

The second Book is entirely devoted to the new art of artillery warfare and consists of a series of 'examinations' in the knowledge which a bombardier must possess; this includes knowledge of all types of armament, their size, the weight of shot which they deliver, maximum and point-blank range, consumption of powder (and grade of powder) and ammunition for a day, together with details of ancillary equipment and running repairs. Also 'examined' is the making of gun-powder for a variety of purposes (given like recipes for cookery) and instructions how to make fireworks (for display) smoke-bombs, fire-bombs, flares and other devices for night-time operation. At the end of this book, Cataneo locates his text firmly within a modern, empirical discourse, referring to a controlled test carried out at Brescia on the 29th August 1564, in which a 50lb cannon was fired one hundred and eight times in five hours. This second Book opens with a remarkable profile of the personal qualities necessary for a bombardier:

> *Since those who want to can make use of the book on Fortresses which I have composed and published, while the ordering of troops for Battle is in the third part of the present work, it is necessary also to understand about gun-powder, artillery, artificial fire & Bombardiers; these are things without which making war, in the present day, would be useless: I have put down briefly those points which from my own experience and the advice of expert friends seem to be necessary.*

221. Paul Oskar Kristeller, Renaissance Thought and its Sources, New York, 1979, p.28.

And first I want to stress that the Bombardier must make every possible effort to win the friendship of everyone, & be agreeable to all. But because it is very dangerous, in this profession, to be on close terms with any sort of person, he must not put his trust in anyone, since this could lead to his death and the ruin of the whole enterprise.

Every Bombardier must know how to read and write, & be good with numbers; so that he can measure heights, depths and distances; and he must understand how to make powder, artificial fire, do repairs & deal with the other things that often crop up in warfare. And he should have great courage, so that he can inspire it in others; but he must never trust anyone to come near his Artillery, since they might spike it or do other damage.

These same must not be dissolute or sleepy, but must conduct themselves with prudence and sobriety; so that their intellect should not be impaired, leading to the loss of their own honour and the general victory ; this very often depends upon Bombardiers, & Artillery.

And because the smoke from nitrate salt & sulphur causes headaches, in this profession one must go on duty neither starved nor too full.

He must know also that, when he goes on duty, he must look out for himself and keep his powder away from fire....

The character whom we meet in this portrait - sober, cool-headed, solitary and mistrustful of others is a far cry from the dare-devil, swashbuckling image of military folklore. He has more the calculating reserve of a modern technician, the calm specialist who gets on with his job without seeking the limelight, bound by a code of correct procedure, suppressing personal emotion. He belongs to a world in which those who go to war do so with the single intention of winning, for whom it is not enough merely to demonstrate individual valour or to lend conviction to a diplomatic posture. (Bombardiers were not, as we have noted elsewhere, put on parade as objects for aesthetic enjoyment.) In the second phase of his career as a soldier, Vespasiano was to inhabit such a world and his role in it, like that of Cataneo's Bombardier, was, whether he liked it or not, primarily a technical one.

By 1568, when Vespasiano began his second period of direct service to Philip II in Spain, the peace of Cateau-Cambrésis had ended hostilities with France in the Italian peninsula while the defeat of the French at Valenciennes in 1567 was a decisive step towards the suspension of direct military confrontation between western Europe's two dominant military powers. Both sides had been stretched almost to breaking point by the economic burden of the conflict and both were subject to disruptive forces within their own territories sufficient to absorb their immediate attention. While the political fabric of France was under threat from the growing strength of the Huguenots, the security of the Spanish kingdom was undermined by insurgency in the Netherlands and the threat of local insurgency in Spain itself; French and English pirates were harrying Spain's Atlantic shipping, taking a toll on essential supplies of gold from America (the latter encouraged, as a matter of policy, by Queen Elizabeth I); and Turkish marauders in the Mediterranean were a menace to Spanish coastal settlements who might also, at any moment, join forces with the residual Moorish population in the south.

Against these elusive adversaries, real or imagined, neither crude military superiority nor the tactical prudence of commanders such as the duke of Alva, with whom Spain had imposed its political will upon much of western Europe, could provide a reliable (or financially sustainable) answer. Unlike his father, Charles V, who frequently rode with his troops into battle and matched the open aggression of his French opponents, Philip was disinclined by nature to confront a problem directly, preferring to manoeuvre and leave his options open. It was as the agent of Philip's vigilant policies that Vespasiano, now thirty-seven years old, was to occupy the following decade of his life and the military skills which he was able to demonstrate were more often preventive than aggressively proactive. It was more than a year, in fact, before he was given anything at all to do, being finally sent off, in 1570, to Cartagena 'to fortify it as an architect and to defend it as a general'[222]. Founded by Hannibal as the 'New Carthage' from which he mounted his invasion of Italy, this had been an important Spanish base after the Roman re-conquest and had, prior to Vespasiano's commission, relied for defence upon what remained of its Roman walls. During the excavations for the foundations of its new defences, a Roman amphitheatre was discovered, along with a quantity of sculpture and coins, much of which Vespasiano had sent back to Sabbioneta.

Sent to work with Vespasiano at Cartagena was Giovanni Battista Antonelli, a military engineer whom Vespasiano neither liked nor trusted; the Prudent King was presumably anxious to retain control of the operation by splitting the responsibility. Vespasiano did not, evidently take the 'threat' from the moriscos all that seriously:

> The Moors around here have been reduced to obedience but not all, because those who have tasted the pleasures of armed robbery on the road, more criminals than soldiers, take advantage of the terrain, coming out of caves to inflict damage; but it can't really be said that the war is not finished since the greater and better part of them have been brought under control, the others being a residue of the war like the quaternary, erratically feverish phase of a dangerous illness; I am writing this because I know that others claim differently [....] Those in the kingdom of Valencia, on my left, have never attempted an uprising and say that they would not do so unless the Turks had both salt and olives, by which they mean Ibiza and Majorca, and they mock the Grenadan Moors for their excessive haste. [...] I beg your Excellency pardon for my secretary's handwriting, as I hurt my right hand yesterday helping to mount a cannon.[223]

Evidently, Vespasiano's involvement with his artillery was 'hands-on'. Tactically, the importance of Cartagena was as a sea-port from which to police the coastal waters and as a point of delivery for supplies in case of emergency, but it was also significant as a garrison and a symbol of military presence during the systematic dispersal of the Moors into a barren hinterland from which, if they survived at all, they would be unable to make contact with Turkish expeditions that might arrive by sea. As a further precaution, Vespasiano and Antonelli constructed a string of hexagonal watch-towers, a means to deter pirate landings as well as a position from which to keep the land under observation. Despite the haste with which these works had to be carried out (Philip delaying his decision to act until it had become urgent) and the shortage of cash and labour which forced Vespasiano to impose two days a week compulsory labour on all adult males[224], Vespasiano had proved his worth in the implementation of Philip's vigilant tactics.

222. Luca Sarzi Amadè, Il Duca di Sabbioneta - Guerre e Amori di un Europeo del XVI Secolo, Milan, 1990, p.178.
223. Letter to Ottavio Farnese, 27th June, 1570, quoted in R. Tamalio, Op. Cit., Note 28.
224. Ibid. p. 179.

His reward was a posting, the following year, to Navarra, with the task of securing frontier defences aginst the Navarese province on the French side of the border where protestantism was believed to be gaining ground. Like other provinces only comparatively recently absorbed under Spanish dominance, Navarra retained its own laws and traditions and was unwilling to recognise Spanish sovereignty. As Philip had to be reminded by his deputy in Catalonia five years previously, "Here, your Majesty is seen as an individual in a contract."[225] While the city of Pamplona was hastily fortified with earthworks and brushwood, its fortress was of masonry (which still survives today), as threatening to the city itself as it was to any outside assailant; this was an act of provocation which the king was probably quite happy to delegate to a commander who was not even Spanish. Vespasiano evidently felt uncomfortable in this position and hoped, in any case, that upon completion of his immediate task, he would be allowed to take leave and get back for a while to Sabbioneta. Rather than release him, as he requested, the king appointed Vespasiano viceroy of Navarra and Guipuscoa, an honour never previously bestowed upon any single individual, still less upon an Italian[226]. This was enough to change Vespasiano's mind for the time being; in a letter of 1572, he is unequivocal:

> I have let it be known for many days that I do not wish to leave this service, and much less so now that His Majesty has given me this extraordinary honour, nor would I for the world give up this task[227].

His newly elevated status appears also to have revived in Vespasiano the hope of military glory. Evidently stirred by the chivalric associations evoked by a visit to Ronceval (scene of the ambush and death of Roland)[228] it occurred to him that he should invade French Navarra and kidnap Queen Joanna in Bayonne, thereby simultaneously removing a powerful protestant sympathiser and pre-empting any possible separatist move by the combined provinces.

> Having taken these two strongholds [Bayonne and Dax], the whole of Navarra is taken, since the people of these cities will support us because the majority are catholics who will band together against the heretics and do anything necessary so as to be able to practise the divine offices in freedom. These three taken, we can capture Béarne, the county of Foix, that of Arminacé and Bigorre and, finally, the whole territory on this side of the Garonne between Bordeaux and Toulouse, as there is no force there which can resist three days and with such a motive there would not be a single catholic who would not want to be there first.[229]

This ambitious project - the effective annexation to the kingdom of Spain, on the pretext of a religious mission, of a large part of south-western France - was evidently prepared upon the basis of carefully gathered intelligence and with the implicit support of the king[230]. Vespasiano's spies could not, however, let him into a more significant and better-kept secret: on a tip-off from the Spanish ambassador in Paris, Philip took steps to 'calm down his Viceroy' and twenty days later, the protestant cause in France was dealt a more devastating blow with the St Bartholomew's Day massacre[231].

225. J.R.Hale, The Civilization of Europe in the Renaissance, London, 1994, p.89.
226. I.Affò, Vita di Vespasiano Gonzaga, p.44.
227. Ibid. p.45.
228. L.Sarzi Amadè, Il Duca di Sabbioneta - Guerre e amori di un Europeo del XVI Secolo, (Cit.) p.194ff.
229. Letter of Vespasiano Gonzaga to king Philip II, 31st July, 1572, quoted in R.Tamalio, Op. Cit., P.133 and N.42.
230. Ibid. Notes 42 & 45.
231. See L.S.Amadè, Op. Cit., p.204, and also R.Tamalio, Op.Cit., p.133.

Having completed the up-grading of Navarra's defences and being restrained from further military adventures, Vespasiano seems to have become bored, restless and homesick as viceroy and started to ask for leave again, requesting 'at least six months absence' and complaining about the cold air which came down from the mountains and made him unwell. The only result of repeated letters to the king was that he was sent to Tunisia (where Don John of Austria was getting all the limelight campaigning against the infidel while failing adequately to secure his conquests), and given the job of fortifying Oran. Even in this comparatively menial role, his advice was compromised (he wanted to demolish the fortress at Oran and strengthen that at Mers-el Kebir) and was obliged to work again with his rival Antonelli. Another letter to the king contains an uncharacteristic outburst of angry frustration:

> In my opinion Giovan Battista Antonelli, by leaving out two bastions and casemates, is proposing a fortress of too narrow girth for this location; clearly, it is right that the art of construction should be adapted to respect the natural accidents of the site, but an engineer ought to know how to fortify without bastions or casemates and he ought to know how to use a compass.
> This Antonelli, in his design, keeps at a distance from the sea, leaving a good strip of land for the enemy; if he intends to make a moat, it would cost a fortune and still not be as good as the sea; if, on the other hand, he wants to do without a moat and just slope the ground down to the water, that, too, would be very expensive since the rock is hard and it's a large area; and if he doesn't slope the ground or make a moat, he will be leaving a place where enemy warships can hide themselves, where they can get close to the cliff and prevent us from putting to sea if we need help [….] and, what's more, the cross-lines [of fire] don't reach as far as the pincer form of my project, as anyone can verify if they use a ruler and compass[232].

Vespasiano's eventual reward was not the leave which he desperately wanted, but a further promotion, over the heads of high-ranking Spanish nobility, to the post of viceroy, lieutenant and captain-general of the kingdom of Valencia. In this highly (though sporadically) paid and eminently prestigious position, Vespasiano's last four years as a military commander were undoubtedly his least glorious. Aside from a supposed threat of insurgence by the Moriscos, the only demand on his warlike abilities was a protracted game of cat and mouse with the Turkish and Berber pirates, in which the object was to take as many prisoners as possible while losing as few as possible on one's own side; the prisoners were then traded for ransom, this being the only source of cash available to either side. In 1575, King Philip was declared bankrupt (when the Genoese bankers who had been tiding him over a protracted delay in gold shipments cut off further credit); neither the troops nor, indeed, Vespasiano himself, were getting paid, and the cannon which had been ordered never arrived. In the year of 1577, Vespasiano took forty Turkish prisoners for the loss of only six Christians[233].

Knowing that the pirates could not remain for long at sea without supplies of fresh water, Vespasiano took care to prevent their access to any source close to the coast. At Peñiscola, he made this a pretext for some architecture, redirecting the course of a spring to a well-guarded fountain, decorated with the inscription:

232. Dated 23rd December 1574 Quoted in R. Tamalio, Op. Cit., p.137.
233. R.Tamalio, Op. Cit., p.138.

GONZAGA, THE HERO TRIUMPHANT NO LESS IN ART
THAN IN FORCE OF ARMS, FORTIFIED THIS CLIFF WITH LABORIOUS
SKILL. HERE HE GROUND AWAY THE ROCK AND TURNED THE STONES
TO LIQUID, FROM A HIGH PLATEAU HE CHANNELLED THESE SWEET
WATERS AND WITH HIS GENIUS HE OVERCAME FOES NEVER BEFORE
VANQUISHED. THUS BY HIS MERIT HE HAS COMMANDED BOTH THE
LAND AND THE WATER. ANNO 1578.[234]

234. Quoted in L..Sarzi Amadè,
Il Duca di Sabbioneta, cit.,
p.239.

Composed in the year that Alessandro Farnese, son of his close friend and fourteen years Vespasiano's junior, embarked upon a series of military exploits which, for many years to come, were to reverse the Spanish humiliation in the Netherlands, the hyperbole of this epitaph to Vespasiano's Spanish military career can hardly have been intended without irony. When, a few months later and on the pretext of his rapidly deteriorating health, Vespasiano was allowed to return to Italy, he was, in reality, of no further use to Philip, and Philip was, himself, of little further use to Vespasiano.

Vespasiano's own sonnet records a world of opportunity which had eluded him:

> These calves with gilded horns, in homage due,
> Wisest Minerva and proud Mars, receive
> From one whose waning years remain to live
> But trumpet's sound has called to arms anew,
> Since France, with squadrons armed aims to pursue
> The path of war, what art he can conceive,
> In happier chronicles his name to leave,
> He learns again, his valour to renew.
> And now sets off, the field's fair green to cover
> With red French blood, or otherwise to find
> An honourable, glorious death at least;
> The spark of mortal life is quickly over,
> And in so vile a bond our soul's confined,
> He has good fortune who is first released.[235]

It was noted at the beginning of the last chapter that Vespasiano's education was, in many respects, insufficient to prepare him for the circumstances in which his working life was to be played out. That he was, in the event, able to adapt to a new political environment and to master a new science in the conduct of warfare can clearly be taken as evidence of a flexible and responsive intelligence. One might, perhaps, go further, suggesting that his ability to shape himself unobtrusively to his surroundings was the product of an almost unnatural objectivity, a frequently ironic detachment behind which, for most of the time, he managed to conceal what we will increasingly find to have been a passionate and tormented nature. If, as his biographer, Alessandro Lisca, tells us, "even in anger - astonishing but true - he never said what he might later regret", he might, nevertheless, have had reason on occasion to regret that he had not said what he really felt. He was, it would seem, incapable of making the flamboyant impression which, though it could have ruined his career, could also have projected him into the memorable and glorious roles to which his ancestry and upbringing inclined him to aspire.

If the career which, during so much of Vespasiano's life, kept him away from his personal territory of Sabbioneta kept him, therefore, away from his only dependable vehicle of self-expression, then it is worth remembering that the project of Sabbioneta was not a reaction, after the event, to the frustration of his more conventional ambitions but an enterprise already begun while his career was still in its infancy. It is as though he knew that he was going to need it.

235. Quoted in Affò, Vita di Vespasiano Gonzaga, cit., p.68. Queste vitelle con dorate corna Ti dà, saggia Minerva, e fiero Marte, Colui, che perso avea la miglior parte, Ed ora ad arme, e a trombe ne ritorna, Or che la Francia le campagne adorna D'armate squadre, e pone studio, et arte, Acciò suo nome in più felici carte Viva; ed ardita ai vecchi acquisti torna. E va per far vermiglio il verde campo Di sangue Gallo, ovvero a trovar modo Di qualche onesta, e gloriosa morte; Poichè la mortal vita è un breve lampo, E nostro spirito lega in sì vil nodo, Che chi pria se ne scioglie, ha ben gran sorte.

Pt 3

~5)

Conversations I.
Religious dissent, pan-sophism and coded architectural references. Critical and historical self-consciousness, women and entrepreneurs in the arts; the idea of a collection and its display.

Men make their own history but they do not make it just as they please; they do not make it under circumstances chosen by themselves, but under circumstances directly encountered, given and transmitted from the past.[236]

The intellectual world in which Vespasiano Gonzaga moved, in relation to which his ideas were shaped and his choices conditioned, was extensive both in its physical and its conceptual topography. To the extent that it can be reconstructed at all, its reconstruction will be the accumulation of fragments, traces, echoes, inferences and, in a few cases records (though not necessarily accurate ones) of actual conversations; encounters in which Vespasiano was directly involved, and others whose indirect effects are to be discovered in his subsequent actions. Few of the individuals whom we shall be meeting in this chapter are, in any sense, household names in the canon of Renaissance Studies but, cumulatively, they constitute a network through which ideas of permanent significance were transmitted. Vespasiano was close to many of the most pregnant cultural evolutions of his day and seems to have chosen for company people who would enrich his own mental life. As we have already come to know him and in the glimpses which follow, Vespasiano was constantly on the look-out for thoughts with which to exercise his restless mind. We must begin, however, with a conversation in which Vespasiano was not involved but which is critical to the understanding of the individual who was largely responsible for his education and personal formation: his remarkable aunt, Giulia Gonzaga.

In 1535 the Capuchin friar, Bernardino Ochino of Siena, one of the most famous preachers of his time in Italy, enraptured the great and the good of Naples with a sermon which, to judge from its effect, made a direct appeal to the personal religious commitment of each of his listeners. He was expressing the prevailing religious mood of his time, the spirit of *devotio moderna* and the late humanist project of a 'Christian renaissance' in which an increasingly literate, thoughtful and self-conscious laity would frame its religious practices within a revitalized universal Church. These aspirations were broadly shared by the intellectual leadership of the Church and lay behind the memorandum of 1537, submitted by a commission set up by Pope Paul III in a first, abortive attempt to clarify the Church's position in relation to a generally accepted need for ecclesiastical reform. Seven years later, Ochino was summoned to appear before the newly reactivated papal Inquisition in Rome. For some time he prevaricated, remaining in the republic of Venice, hoping, it seems, that the trouble would blow over but finally, seeing his position increasingly untenable, he left Italy for the Calvinist state of Geneva. Evidently uncomfortable, also, with the doctrinal rigidity which he encountered in Geneva, Ochino finally arrived, via England, Zurich and Poland, in Moravia, where, in 1564, he died in the house of the anabaptist Nicolò Paruta.[237] The hardening of attitudes which, during this very short space of time, had forced individuals, whatever their real inclination might have been, to define themselves as either Catholic or Protestant, was the product, not so much of doctrinal polarisation, as of papal anxiety to fend off any encroachment upon the authority of the Holy See either from within or outside the organisation of the Church. The effects of this 'essentially' political intransigence of the papacy, at a critical moment in its history (an intransigence which was fully matched on the opposite side), are violently visible in the world even today.

236. Karl Marx, The Eighteenth Brumaire of Louis Bonaparte, quoted in John Allen, Lubetkin, London, 1992, p.130.
237. See Delio Cantimori, Eretici italiani del Cinquecento, Turin, 1992, p.305 and for a highly illuminating account of religious dissent in sixteenth century Italy.

Amongst the congregation which heard Ochino preach was Giulia Gonzaga, the famously beautiful (and evidently virgin) widow of Vespasiano Colonna, who was soon afterwards to be made responsible for the upbringing of her nephew, the four-year-old Vespasiano Gonzaga. In Giulia's company, listening to Ochino, was an emaciated Spaniard, Juan de Valdès, brother of an influential courtier of Charles V, who had recently arrived in Italy, escaping the too close attention of the Spanish Inquisition but entrusted with an imperial mission in connection with a dispute between Giulia Gonzaga and her sister-in-law, young Vespasiano's mother. Giulia had made an immediate and powerful impression upon de Valdès:

> *I have been for a day at Fondi with this lady and it is a great misfortune that she is not Queen of the whole world, since I believe that God would have wished that all we poor mortals should have the benefit of her divine discourse and grace which are in no way inferior to her beauty.*[238]

Giulia was in her early twenties when de Valdès arrived in Italy, at the height of her fame and beauty, and she had been a widow for seven years; the marriage which had been arranged for her at the age of fourteen, by Isabella d'Este, marchioness of Mantua, to the forty-year old, lame and crippled Vespasiano Colonna, had ended a year later with the latter's death, leaving her with a considerable fortune. Her residence (Fig. 5.1) at Fondi, on the Via Appia, was a coveted stopover for distinguished travellers between Rome and Naples and people would go to considerable lengths to obtain a letter of introduction. Among her many unsuccessful suitors were the cardinal Ippolito de' Medici, nephew of Pope Clement VII and Don Pedro de Toledo, governor of Naples. Ariosto celebrated her in *Orlando Furioso*:

> *....and look!*
>
> *There is the one whose lovely countenance*
>
> *And grace deserve all fame that ever was.*
> *All women, past and present, she outdoes.*
>
> *Julia Gonzaga is this lady's name.*
> *Where'er she walks, where'er she turns her eyes,*
> *To beauty other women yield their claim.*
> *As if she were a goddess from the skies,*
> *They look at her amazed...*[239]

When Sebastiano del Piombo was sent by Ippolito de' Medici to paint Giulia's portrait there was widespread excitement; poets wrote verses urging him to make it worthy of her and copies of the painting circulated throughout Europe[240]. The marauding expedition of Khair-Eddin-Barbarossa, admiral to the Turkish Sultan, during which Fondi was attacked, was generally assumed to be an attempt to kidnap Giulia on his master's behalf, and increasingly fanciful versions of her midnight escape (only in her night shirt, obliged to take refuge with bandits, etc.) continued to appear in narrative verse up to the eighteenth century.

238. Letter to Cardinal Ercole Gonzaga quoted in Siro Attilio Nulli, Giulia Gonzaga, Milan, 1938, p.43. This, surprisingly the only book dedicated to that remarkable woman, is the source for much of what follows.
239. Ludovico Ariosto, Orlando Furioso, cit., XLVI, 7 & 8.
240. The original has not been positively identified.

Giulia appears to have remained calm (even, Nulli suggests in his biography, a little bored) in the midst of so much adulation; she refused admission to a sculptor who had been sent from Rome to make a medallion in her likeness and disingenuously parried suggestions that she should remarry on the grounds that "if I were to take a new husband, I would always be afraid of losing him, as I did before, so that I don't want to put myself at risk." High-minded and serious, Giulia seems, nevertheless, to have taken great pleasure in the company of talented people: Annibale Caro, academician and minor poet from Rome, having obtained an introduction through Francesco Maria Molza, was plied, during his first meeting with her, with questions: "Does Molza triumph? Is he creating a sensation? What antics has he been up to?" (She might well ask: Molza was noted for the extreme dissoluteness of his life, having abandoned wife and family in Modena to join the far from saintly court of Ippolito de' Medici, but he was a poet of some distinction.) Caro was struck, during this conversation, by Giulia's Lombard accent.

Giulia was not herself highly educated (she knew no Latin) but her childhood tutor, Giovanni Buonavoglia, had noted, with perhaps a little sincerity beyond the obvious motive of flattery, that:

> *Giulia by far excelled all the other sisters, with a ready and acute intelligence, serious, thoughtful and modest, she had a natural gift for musical harmony and feminine occupations and she could portray with a skilled and creative hand that which nature creates directly with the variety of colours.* [241]

There is no other record of Giulia's artistic talent, but she did, during her teens, correspond with Federico, first duke of Mantua, on the subject of music, obtaining and sending him copies of motets by a composer in Casalmaggiore. While there is no evidence that she held views such as would today be called feminist, it is equally clear that Giulia did not feel inclined to spend her own life in the shadow of any man. Writing of the deceased countess of Mirandola "who has for some time taken care of her state and shown the world that women can do anything well, contrary to the opinion of some men who have made up their own rules", the direction of her sympathies is clear[242].

Previous to her encounter with Juan de Valdès, there is little to suggest that Giulia took a particular interest in matters of religion but, returning home, on the day of Ochino's sermon, her life seems to have taken a new direction; by the account of Valdès, they were in such a state of 'inebriation' that they stayed up all night talking about it. The fruit of this night's conversation was Juan de Valdès' *Christian Alphabet*, written in the form of a dialogue between himself and Giulia which, while it cannot be taken as an accurate or literal record of their conversation, is nevertheless likely to convey the spirit of it[243]. The dialogue begins with Giulia's expression of a state of confusion created in her by the ideal which the preacher had held up and "whether there is any way, either by consent or by persuasion, that it can be achieved, because in no way can it last long in this storm of emotions, appetites, imaginings and contradictory impulses" As the discussion proceeds, it becomes clear that Giulia's problem is not to do with carnal appetites but with her fear of becoming a bore:

> *It is really hard for me to have to give up those conversations in which I have taken pleasure and those curious things with which I pass the time, because I fear that if I give up those things I will fall into a state of melancholy and my life will be permanently insipid.*

*241. From his Latin poem, Gonzagium monumentum, quoted by Nulli, Op. Cit. p.7.
242. Ibid., p.176.
243. Juan de Valdès, Alfabeto Cristiano, (first published Venice, 1545, with the author's name concealed in an anagram) ed. And Intro. By Adriano Prosperi, Rome, 1988. Nulli (Op. Cit.) is perhaps a little overinclined to take the dialogue as literal conversation, reading Giulia's impetuous nature into some of her interjections.*

She doesn't want her friends to notice the change in her. Valdès is quick to reassure her that the commitment she will make does not pertain to those whose spirit is "base, plebeian and servile" but that the confusion she feels is, for one with "a lofty, generous and courageous soul such as God has given you". He will show her a way to conduct a new spiritual life which will be invisible to the outside world. For the 'base, plebeian and servile' it is only the fear of hell which turns them, out of self interest, to love paradise and obey the 'law'. By 'law', of course, he is describing a view that the quality of religious life can be measured in terms of actions or 'works'. Valdès' argument is carefully phrased: if there were no 'law' there would be no conscience and sin would not be recognised, and if sin were not recognised we would not humble ourselves; if we did not humble ourselves, we would not achieve grace, and if we do not achieve grace we cannot be justified; if we are not justified, we are not saved. But "St Paul says that the 'law' is like a teacher or ruler who guides us towards Christ, whereas it is through faith that we are justified."[244]

Justification by faith, then, in the valdesian doctrine, is a higher form of religious belief suitable for the noble and the educated but unsuitable for the lower orders who need to be given a law to follow. The spiritual life of such superior persons is a private and personal matter not to be demonstrated in the world by "excessive ceremonies", "penitential superstitions" or "false devotion". If, in this respect, the *Christian Alphabet* can be seen as proposing a form of Lutheranism for the upper classes, there are many other respects in which its propositions clearly contradict the orthodoxy of the Catholic Church. Valdès is clear from the outset that man-made doctrine cannot be taken as a true guide to the faith but that one must go to the Scriptures; all of his citations are either from the Psalms or from the New Testament and he promises to give Giulia a copy of the New Testament in the vernacular. He is emphatic that members of religious orders have only the same claim as any other to Christian perfection, if they have faith and love for God, "and not a carat more". On the subject of trans-substantiation, his words are again carefully chosen, but his implication is clear: one should go to Communion in the right frame of mind, full of faith "in such a way that you resolutely believe that beneath this appearance there is the real body and blood of our Lord Jesus Christ. You should think that He left this here in the world so that whenever the appearance is represented to our bodily eyes, it will be renewed in our hearts."[245] Although he recommends going to Mass ('use it as a source of religious thoughts') and confession ('confess your affects, your defects need only be confessed to God'), Valdès assigns no essential role to the institutional Church. It is hardly surprising that, within two years of its publication, the *Christian Alphabet* was placed on the Index, forbidden reading for orthodox catholics.

In its general tone, however, the *Christian Alphabet* has much in common with the mood and, indeed some of the detailed suggestions of Ignatius Loyola's *Spiritual Exercises*, from which the injunction to examine one's actions of the previous day, from start to finish, before going to sleep, seems to be directly taken. And his slightly morbid insistence that one should have always in mind the image of Christ crucified is a sentiment by no means alien to the spirit of the Counter-Reformation.

244. Ibid. p.35.
245. Ibid. p.118.

When Valdès died in 1541 ('only with a fraction of his mind did he govern his feeble and wasted body'), Giulia Gonzaga's household in Naples had become the centre of an extensive circle of variously reformist intellectuals. She organised discussion groups and corresponded with like-minded individuals and groups both within and beyond Italy; she gave financial support to members of the 'movement' who were in difficulty (including one Isabella Brisegna who, in 1552, left her husband and went to join the protestants in Switzerland and who received 100 scudi a year from Giulia). She was closely in touch with the circle of Vittoria Colonna (Michelangelo's platonically intimate friend) whose 'bella scuola' at Viterbo was frequented not only by the likes of Bernardino Ochino before his flight to Geneva but also by senior churchmen including the English cardinal Reginald Pole and Cardinal Morone, a participant in the Council of Trent. It still seemed that the outcome of the Council's deliberations might show a softening of official doctrinal positions, particularly in relation to justification by faith. It was, after all, under pressure from the emperor that the Council had finally been summoned, and the emperor was anxious that it should include Protestant representation, seeking to reach an agreement which both sides could accept.

Already, however, in 1553, the hard-line cardinals Juan Alvarez de Toledo and Carrafa (subsequently Paul IV) had begun to take an interest in Giulia's activities. She appears to have been unaware of (or indifferent to) the danger of her position and in a letter to her cousin, Don Ferrante Gonzaga, governor of Milan (who was also in some trouble, accused of showing insufficient zeal in protecting the interests of the Church), she is defiant:

> As for the things they have said and are saying about me, if there were respect and charity rather than malice, I think it would make better sense to look at the life I lead and not at the imaginings of others [....] you know well that if you are looking for [scandal] any occasion will serve: but since God knows the truth I am not all that upset about it.[246]

Upon the death of Giulia Gonzaga in 1566 and on the pretext that they were needed in order to establish the detail of Vespasiano's inheritance, Giulia's papers were handed over to the pope, Pius V, who is said to have exclaimed: "If these had been in my hands before her death, that most noble Gonzaga would not have escaped the punishment she deserved, to be burned alive."

When she moved from Fondi to Naples in 1535, Giulia set up her household in the annexe of the convent of San Francesco alle monache; the arrangement was analogous to a modern *pension* and the living conditions were by no means conventual though the constant ringing of bells, the droning of plainchant and the whiff of incense must have been conspicuous in the environment. In this 'home', the young Vespasiano was to spend the next ten years of his life. The only child in a cultivated and high-minded entourage, without siblings or companions of his own age, Vespasiano can have had little choice but to become precociously adult, repressing playful or light-hearted impulses, unable to communicate childish thoughts. There can be no doubt, however, that the education which Giulia provided for her young charge was thorough and well rounded, far surpassing her own; by the time, at the age of fifteen, that he was sent to serve the emperor as page boy to the future King Philip of Spain, Vespasiano could read and write in Latin, Greek and Tuscan, knew some mathematics, had learned horsemanship and the use of arms. The adult company around him was of a high intellectual calibre and there is nothing to suggest that Giulia had become, as she feared she might, 'permanently insipid'.

246. *Quoted in Nulli, Op. Cit.* p.134.

Even though it might seem highly probable that, as his 'tutor and governess', Giulia would have instructed the young Vespasiano according to the religious beliefs to which she adhered so vehemently, we have no direct way of knowing what Vespasiano himself thought about these matters. At all times during his life, he was reticent upon the subject of religion but it seems likely that he would, at least, have absorbed the idea that, for an educated member of the nobility, religious belief was a private and personal matter. There is no discernible pattern in his choice of intellectual companionship which, on the contrary, seems to have covered the whole spectrum of permissible religious inclinations. He was on friendly terms with Carlo Borromeo, archbishop of Milan, subsequently canonised as the leading spirit of counter-reformation theology (a relative, through marriage, of his third wife, Margherita Gonzaga), who celebrated mass in the parish church at Sabbioneta in the summer of 1582[247]; the church was planned according to the approved model of the Gesù at Rome. At the same time, he was protecting the Jewish publishing establishment at Sabbioneta which the Church authorities wanted to close down. While his friend Bernardino Baldi became increasingly influential in orthodox counter-reformation circles, Vespasiano must have been aware that the views of the man whom he placed in charge of his Academy, Mario Nizolio, on the matter of literal and metaphorical speech, had powerfully subversive (and evidently intentional) implications with regard to the doctrine of transubstantiation[248]. The scarcity of Christian iconography in the decorative programmes at Sabbioneta has been regularly noted but, at moments of particular personal stress, we find Vespaiano seeking the solace of religion; after the death of his second wife, Anna of Aragona, he spent a month in the seclusion of a monastery[249]. On the evidence, Vespasiano's attitude was tolerant upon the subject of religion; like many of his contemporaries, he might have regarded its institutions as too important in the maintenance of the social order to allow the expression of personal belief to place that order at risk. The compromise agreed at the Diet of Augsburg in 1555 (and tacitly supported by Charles V), "cuius regio eius religio", might appear a cynical device to paper over cracks when those cracks were already too wide to be disguised, but for one who, like Vespasiano, placed a high value upon the stability and continuity of political institutions, it was a formula which offered what little hope there was. In any case, the practice of 'dissimulation' had become an accepted part of public behaviour during the sixteenth century, a necessary defensive tactic at a time when a growing mood of intolerance as well as an increasing sophistication in the gathering of political intelligence would inevitably drive sincerity underground[250]. On the subject of religion, Vespasiano kept his opinions to himself.

Pt 3 ~5

110

247. de Dondi, Op. Cit., p.318.
248. This point is raised by Quirinius Breen in his introduction to Nizolio's De Veris Principiis, cit., p. LVI: "The connections of Nizolius with Celio Curione Secondo and with Basilio Zanchi ..... may be of small importance here, for the fact of Protestant propaganda in Italy is large enough to account for so prominent an idea to be well known."
249. Affò, Vita di Vespasiano Gonzaga, cit., p.37.
250. See, for instance, Henry Kamen, Philip of Spain, Newhaven and London, 1997, p.225 and, more specifically in relation to religious belief, Watson, Op. Cit.. p.43.

Vespasiano does appear, however, to have left an architectural clue as to his personal sympathies, in the design of his ducal palace at Sabbioneta. Amongst those with whom Giulia Gonzaga was in close contact subsequent to her 'conversion' by Juan de Valdès was Marcantonio Flaminio (1498 - 1550), a humanist intellectual and poet whose career was launched under the protection of Pope Leo X. Flaminio was also associated with the group around Vittoria Colonna and was, for a time, secretary to Cardinal Pole. In the judicious words of the *Enciclopedia Italiana*, "he associated himself with those catholics who, wishing, on the one hand, to remain faithful to the Church, were nevertheless not insensible to certain theoretical principles of protestantism and, in particular, that of justification by faith." A lifelong friend and one-time colleague of Flaminio was Achille Bocchi (1488 - 1562), a nobleman of Bologna, organist to the cathedral and for many years lecturer in rhetoric at the Studio of that city as well as being the city's official historian. During the early 1540s, Bocchi began raising funds in order to realize his major ambition, the foundation of his own Academia Bocchiana. Academies of this kind flourished all over Italy during the sixteenth century, being centres for scholarly, literary and artistic investigation, the presentation and exchange of ideas outside the more restricting environment of official universities.

On the subject of religion, Bocchi (although he did protect the 'openly heretical ex-Franciscan' Camillo Renato[251]) remained non-commital. The Academia Bocchiana had its own printing press but the only work known to have been produced on this was Bocchi's own *Symbolicarum Quaestionum de universo genere quas serio ludebat libri quinque*. This consists of one hundred and fifty-one epigrams, each dedicated to a person known (or known of) by Bocchi and illustrated with arcanely emblematic images which clearly indicate the preoccupations around which his academy was centred. They fall unmistakably within the tradition of Ficino and Pico della Mirandola which might, broadly, be characterized as the attempted recovery of a universal system of knowledge which, since its first appearance, had become fragmented, scattered and lost. In the words of Elizabeth See Watson:

> *For their sources the Renaissance pansophists turned to Neoplatonic, Cabalistic, and Hermetic compilations and to the scattered fragments of proverbs, Pythagorean symbola, Orphica, and Egyptian hieroglyphs embedded in Greek and Roman texts. These seekers pushed back the boundaries of wisdom from the time of Moses and Hermes Trismegistus (Ficino) to Noah and Janus (Annio of Viterbo) and back to Adam. They extended the frontiers of wisdom to encompass Egyptian, Persian, Arabic, and Celtic realms as well as Hebrew and Graeco-Roman ones.*[252]

Within the broad spectrum of intellectual currents which might fall under the general description of 'pansophism', Bocchi's academy was probably at the more conservative end, a long way from the projected magical systems of Cornelius Agrippa or Giordano Bruno but nevertheless clearly distinct from the mainstream of erasmian humanism. As Frances Yates has pointed out, pure humanism was not compatible with neoplatonic magic though the two might overlap in a common concern with hieroglyphs and emblems.[253] It is at this point of overlap that Bocchi's academy seems to have been located.

251. *Watson, Op. Cit., pp.23-50, is right to resist the assumption that Bocchi would have heretical leanings just because he knew others who might have done, but one is more concerned, here, with a mood which was widespread in Italy at this time than with the technical question or strict orthodoxy.*
252. *Ibid., p.37.*
253. *Frances A. Yates, Giordano Bruno and the Hermetic Tradition, London, 1964, p.163.*

In the heady and dangerous atmosphere of intellectual life during the first half of the sixteenth century, the shades of distinction between those who were pushing for personal autonomy in spiritual matters and those who were seeking to construct a transcendent body of wisdom could easily become blurred and it is clear that the two tendencies did frequently coalesce in the pattern of associations formed among individuals. It could be as dangerous to adhere to the latter as to the former. Bocchi's book was authorized and underwritten by Pope Julius III (the least doctrinaire and probably the most cultured, if also the least abstemious, holder of that office after the sack of Rome; his own Villa Giulia in Rome is itself a monument to the ideals of 'pansophy') and was never placed on the Index although many of its dedicatees (they included Marcantonio Flaminio and Mario Nizolio) were far from orthodox.

Bocchi was anxious that his academy should have a permanent home and soon after 1540 he commissioned a design, evidently from the young Jacopo Barozzi, generally known as Vignola[254]. Of the first and of an amended version of the design for the façade of the Palazzo Bocchi engravings were made in 1545 and 1555 respectively and these played an important role in publicizing the institution of the academy. So effectively, indeed, did the image come to stand for the idea of an academy that this original, rather than the much reduced and modified version that was eventually built, continued to be revived even in the eighteenth century[255]. In the words of a contemporary:

> He has put up a building so well composed that it could be included among his Symbols as the example of a perfect Academy.[256]

The resemblance of Vespasiano's ducal palace to Vignola's first project for Palazzo Bocchi is not immediately obvious (Fig. 5.2): in the first place, the building in Sabbioneta, as we can see it today has no attic storey. According to Umberto Maffezzoli[57], however, there was, in fact, an attic at Sabbioneta, containing the private living quarters, but this was demolished during the eighteenth century following a serious fire. We know from de Dondi's diary[258] that 'pinnacles' were added at the corners of the palace roof which could well have resembled the obelisks at the corners in the second Vignola design. The central altana at Sabbioneta has been greatly increased in scale (in Vignola's version, the figures standing in the street, presumably intended to indicate the scale of the proposal, could barely have stood up in this top structure) and the composition of serliana and recessed panels is transposed from the attic to the altana where it can be clearly seen without visual interference from the balcony projection; in these respects, Vespasiano's design considerably improves the original. The mezzanine windows on the first floor in the Palazzo Bocchi elevations are replaced at Sabbioneta by busts on brackets, but these are set against painted panels which reproduce the form of Vignola's openings, and the detailing at Sabbioneta (whether for reasons of cost or of taste) is generally simplified and refined. Though it is known that Vespasiano's palace had, over the balcony, a baldachino of bronze, there is no equivalent feature in either engraving, but the heavy projection of the cornice with console-like brackets is similar in Vignola's and Vespasiano's designs.

254. It is hard to see why Watson (Ibid., p64) wants to argue for Sebastiano Serlio as author of this design. The evidence supporting attribution to Vignola in Anna Maria Orazi, Jacopo Barozzi da Vignola 1528-1550, Rome, 1982, seems convincing enough.
255. Anna Maria Orazi, Op. Cit., p.236.
256. G.B.Pigna, quoted in Watson, Op.Cit., p67.
257. Umberto Maffezzoli, Sabbioneta, piccola reggia padana, Modena, 1994, p.21.
258. de Dondi, Op. Cit., p.348. I think Chiara Tellini Perina (Sabbioneta, cit., p.20) is right in interpreting Dondi's 'torresini' as 'pinnacoli'. Dondi was frequently vague in his use of architectural terms. On the other hand, there is no reason to assume, as she does, that alternate triangular and segmental aedicules over the windows of the piano nobile were only added after 1577 (when Sabbioneta became a dukedom) since the inscriptions which refer to the dukedom could easily have been carved at a later date.

Absent from the ducal palace at Sabbioneta are the emblematic animal heads carved between the brackets of the main cornice, and which so strongly contribute to the character of Vignola's project. A very similar frieze is, however, to be found elsewhere at Sabbioneta in the wooden entablature which crowns the otherwise quite rustically plain Palazzo Giardino. It is perfectly possible that this was originally part of the ducal palace but that such a light-weight wooden component, looking out of place in a building otherwise of solid (or, at least, of simulated) masonry construction, was subsequently removed by Vespasiano to its present location where, though unexpected, it looks innocently charming. We shall see, in a later chapter, that the powerful brackets which now support the cornice of the ducal palace are, in themselves, important signifiers within the architectural vocabulary of Sabbioneta.[259]

This leaves one of the most distinctive features of the Palazzo Bocchi designs which is conspicuously absent from the ducal palace at Sabbioneta: its battered and rusticated ground floor. The ground floor of Vespasiano's palace presents an open arcaded loggia (similar, in many respects, to Giulio Romano's Pescherie at Mantua) and it is presumably because of this that Hanno-Walter Kruft places the building at Sabbioneta 'in the tradition of the palazzo ducale at Pesaro'[260] which it resembles in no other way. An open ground floor might seem to have the opposite implication to the fiercely exclusive suggestion of the battered wall of palazzo Bocchi; as Jacob Burckhardt pointed out, "The open colonnade is an expressive indication that the building in question is public property"[261]. Some such thought could well have been in Vespasiano's mind, anxious, as we have already seen him, to blur the distinction between his household and his city; but he did not entirely abandon his reference to Palazzo Bocchi. Vignola's ground floor does appear, slid, as it were, sideways, on the facade of the liutenant's house, the building next door; as in Vignola's design, the arch of the central opening springs from the level of the top of this base, while the windows start immediately above the same line. The peruzzian frames to the mezzanine windows, with their horizontally projecting 'ears', which appear on both main levels of the palazzo Bocchi design, appear only at the upper level in the lieutenant's house and in a simplified form. Such processes of 'displacement' (the term is deliberately borrowed from Sigmund Freud in relation to the formation of dreams) can be found recurrently, as we shall see, in the way that Vespasiano (consciously or unconsciously) worked a variety of references and readings into his architecture, his poetry and his iconographic choices. In the case of the ducal palace, he has found a way that the architecture need not be 'either, or' so much as 'both, and': both an extension of the public space of the city and the image of an ideal, pansophic academy.

If the conversations, recorded and unrecorded, which took place between Giulia Gonzaga and her circle of religious and intellectual 'dissidents' may seem to have spread ripples which could have reached as far as Vespasiano's choice of the Palazzo Bocchi image as a source for his own ducal palace, it is equally clear that Vespasiano's major preoccupations were very different from those in which his aunt was absorbed during the last thirty years of her life. Whatever he may, in private, have thought on the subject of religion, Vespasiano's passionate interest in cultural and artistic matters was by no means a private concern. In what follows, we shall be attempting to trace a few of Vespasiano's interactions with contemporaries variously involved in the production, the criticism or the distribution of art and literature: 'conversations', in general, more implicit than literally recorded, recoverable through the effects which they produced in the cultural choices which Vespasiano made. We shall discover that Vespasiano, though not in any sense a 'professional' in the world of the arts, was by no means out of touch with the most advanced ideas and practices with respect to literature, architecture and painting.

259. According to Puerari, Sabioneta, Cit., (unpaginated) commentary to plate 4, the entablature of the ducal palace was originally of wood with brackets of oak, this being replaced with the present construction during the seventeenth century. No other writer, so far as I am aware, has corroborated this claim, for which Puerari does not indicate his source. It seems unlikely, however, that he would have made it up. If the second part of his assertion is correct, some revision might be required in the section of Chapter 7 which deals with the subject of the palace's exaggerated brackets, though the general thesis there proposed is not overturned. The incremental module of the large brackets on the garden palace (there are four smaller ones between each of these) is 3.28M; applied to the facade of the ducal palace, which measures 23.71M overall, seven such modules, at 22.96M, would leave 0.75M for the width of the bracket plus a margin at the corner similar to that in the Vignola elevation. The imposition of a seven-bay cornice above a five-bay elevation would have been somewhat uncouth, a possible reason for its replacement.
C.Yriarte, (Op. Cit., p.9) also refers, writing of the ducal palace, to "l'ample corniche de bois sculpté qui la couronnait".
260. H-W Kruft, Städte in Utopia, cit., p.40.
261. Jacob Burckhardt, The Architecture of the Italian Renaissance, tr. J. Palmes, ed. P. Murray, London, 1985, p.150.

On the successful conclusion, in 1557, of the campaign against Paul IV which had left him wounded in the upper lip and in need of rest and recuperation, Vespasiano stayed for a while with his mother in Naples where he seems to have passed some time in conversation with three cultivated young gentlemen, Ferrante Carrafa, Angelo Costanzo and Bernardino Rota, all natives of the region, and the somewhat older clergyman, Antonio Minturno. Minturno's treatise, *L'Arte Poetica*, which was published in Venice in 1563, purports to recall these conversations. The first book is written as a 'dialogue' between Minturno and Vespasiano; if this was in any way an accurate record of a conversation which actually took place, one would have to concede that Vespasiano is hardly allowed to get a word in edgeways. Apart from interjections of the sort: "Yes, please do tell me about the three requirements of imitation", inserted to sustain the impression that Minturno was not just talking to himself, Vespasiano's own independent expressions of thought are extremely rare; on the other hand, it seems improbable that Minturno would have attributed to him thoughts which were alien to his way of thinking and we may, therefore, be able to catch, in these rare contributions, a glimpse of Vespasiano's attitudes towards poetry and art in general against the background of what is, in itself, quite a conventional piece of critical writing. It is worth noting, also, that, throughout this 'dialogue', Vespasiano shows himself to be deeply read and informed in both classical and modern literature.

Minturno's general position is almost entirely derived from Aristotle and Horace and, if his work has any claim at all to originality, this would reside in the fact that these classical views are applied critically to the work of modern authors. Like Vasari, writing at approximately the same time, he constructs an historical account of the decline of poetry with the collapse of the Roman empire and its revival by Dante and Petrarch, leading to its further development and flowering in the splendid courts of Naples, Florence, Urbino, Siena and Como. (Rome, Venice, Milan, Bologna, to name only the most obvious, are omitted from this patently partisan list.) Romance, in Minturno's view, cannot be classified as real poetry because it comes from Spain and Provence, where Latin has become debased. Vespasiano, however, is not prepared to accept that Ariosto, "nobilissimo scrittore de' Romanzi", must not be allowed the name of a poet, but Minturno sticks to his academic position, arguing that, had Homer treated the theme of *Orlando Furioso*, he would have stressed the idea that the Moors would have been unable to attack Charlemagne if Orlando had not gone mad, whereas, in Ariosto's version, Orlando's madness has no structural relation to the major events recounted. Vespasiano's response to this is to point out that what Ariosto was doing was to demonstrate the superiority of Ruggiero, founder of his patron's dynasty (the Estense duke Alfonso of Ferrara), "whom it was his intention to praise."[262]

262. *Antonio Minturno, L'Arte Poetica, Venice, 1563, p.28.*

That Vespasiano should have dropped into the conversation this observation about Ariosto's motive should, perhaps, be noted by those modern historians who appear to believe that, in uncovering such a relation between art and patronage in the sixteenth century, they are making an important discovery. Vespasiano does not suggest that the pleasure which he (or even, for that matter, Alfonso d'Este) would take in reading Ariosto's poetry is pleasure simply in the glorification of a fictive ancestor; he is merely observing the circumstances in which courtly art was, at that time, produced.

Minturno's exposition grinds on relentlessly: types of plot are classified (dangerous beginning, happy ending; happy start, sad conclusion; mixed happiness and misery for one or the other); 'character' is to be distinguished from 'passion' - 'the one endures, the other passes'; and the determination of 'character' by age, by class, by nationality, by natural inclination (e.g. quarrelsome, amorous, etc.) by profession or by parentage. Again, Vespasiano seems to have found this complacent catalogue of stereotypes hard to take: what about war-like women? he asks. With the trite observation that, though women have, on occasion, achieved distinction in 'male' activities, it is unreasonable to expect this of them, Minturno proceeds to treat of the passions one by one, basing his account of each on an appropriate passage from Petrarch. To the extent, then, that Vespasiano is allowed any identifiable role in this discussion, he appears as critical of a rigidly academic view of poetry, anxious to broaden, rather than to restrict, the scope of the art.

Evidently, there had also been conversation about architecture, since, without any apparent reason in the context of the dialogue, Minturno makes the following observation:

> ....the whole effort of Art is devoted to the imitation of Nature and the better it is done, the closer it gets. This can be held as a guiding principle in every sort of work. On the one hand is the Idea through whose action nature is reflected: on the other, the form in which art contemplates its own mastery. Architecture has a rule to which it must always return, however much individual buildings may differ. [263]

Curiously suspended between medieval scholastic thought on the one hand and, on the other, the idealism implicit in much Enlightenment theory, this formulation is nevertheless interesting in two respects:

1   It locates architecture quite firmly in the same cultural bracket as poetry or any other art, not because it has the authority of a classical text but because it is founded in an Idea.

2   It stresses that architecture, as an idea, is logically prior to and independent of the individual forms in which it manifests itself. It must always return to a rule, not to a set of rules.

Though thoughts of this sort may be latent in the treatises of Alberti, who wants to trace the idea of beauty back to principles which can apply in the other arts, and even, perhaps, of Filarete "building is nothing more than a voluptuous pleasure"[264] it does appear that Minturno (prompted, perhaps, by Vespasiano) was prepared to detach architecture more radically from its basis in recoverable knowledge of precedent than were the 'professionals' who wrote upon the subject.

263. Ibid. p.33.
264. Filarete, Op. Cit., p16.

It may be worth noting, in this context, that Mario Nizolio (who was Pt 3 ~5 to be appointed, five years after Vespasiano's conversation with Minturno, as head of the Academy at Sabbioneta) had already, in his *De Veris Principiis*, published four years before that conversation, used an argument which, though driven by a very different agenda, carried a similar implication:

> *Therefore, in defining the various arts, we say that Medicine is the art of*   116
> *healing well, not of understanding what is appropriate to healing: Architecture*
> *is the art of building well, not of understanding what is necessary for building:*
> *and warfare is the art of conducting war successfully, not of seeing what is*
> *apposite to the conduct of war.*
> *Wherefore Rhetoric too should be defined in the same way, that it fulfills its*
> *role not in understanding and knowing, but in doing and making and that*
> *speaking is an art not of understanding or knowing what, in a certain case,*
> *could be persuasive, but of speaking well on all matters. In this way, it must be*
> *essential in all the arts that they contain an element of action and production,*
> *not just knowledge and understanding.* [265]

Nizolio is here defending the independence (and, in his view, the priority) of rhetoric against the claims of a narrowly applied philosophy, but Vespasiano could still find in this passage, as he could in Minturno's observations on architecture, a reply to those theoretical writers on architecture whose agenda was, on the contrary, to claim architecture as their own territory upon the basis of their 'professional' knowledge of it. There is no evidence that Vespasiano discussed architecture with people who might, retrospectively, be described as professionals in the field; indeed, when Vincenzo Scamozzi was commissioned to design the theatre at Sabbioneta, his initial briefing was carried out by 'ministers' because Vespasiano was away[266].

With his friend Bernardino Baldi, however, Vespasiano talked not only about mathematics and astronomy (we have previously noted their project to construct some sort of a clock with a fifteen feet tall gnomon) but also, at length, about architecture. Baldi's *Scamilli impares Vitruviani nova ratione explicati, refutatis priorum interpretum Guliemi Philandri, Danielis Barbari, Baptistae Bertani sententiis*, which was published at Augsburg in 1612, seems to have resulted from conversations at Sabbioneta. The purpose of the work was to refute current interpretations of a particularly obscure passage in Vitruvius and it has earned for Baldi the sharp censure of later scholars, not because it is wrong but because it borrowed, without acknowledgement, from an observation in Francesco Colonna's *Hypnerotomachia Poliphili* . Plagiarism of this sort was by no means uncommon amongst writers of the Renaissance and the righteous indignation of later commentators is probably based upon a misunderstanding of the intentions as well as the conventions which lay behind such writing. In any case, from our own position, we might be less interested in the intellectual ownership of early Vitruvian interpretation than in the evidence that the *Hypnerotomachia* was being read and discussed in this way by Vespasiano and a close associate.

265. Nizolio, Op.Cit., Book III, p.23.
266. Affò, Vita di Vespasiano Gonzaga, cit. p.55.

Though not published until several years after Vespasiano's death, Baldi's *Descrizione del Palazzo Ducale d'Urbino* was evidently written while he was still living, since the fulsome testimonial, in its introduction, to Vespasiano's discernment in matters of architecture (which we have quoted previously in relation to the use of wooden ornament in the ducal palace at Sabbioneta) refers to Vespasiano in the present tense. It is a remarkable document in many ways, indicating an historical and critical self-consciousness nowhere to be found in the writings of the *trattatisti*. One could say that it was the first architectural monograph devoted to a single building - a fact which Baldi seems to have recognised in his unconvincing attempt to adduce precedents:

> This type of history, on the subject of notable buildings, is not new, nor do I speak only of such things inserted in the body of other Histories, such as the account of the tower of Babylon, of Noah's Ark, of the arrangements of the temple....[267]

Baldi's *Descrizione*, around 10,000 words in all, is divided into seventeen chapters, the order and the range of topics which he considers bearing a striking resemblance to those to be found in the building studies published in modern architectural journals. First, he deals with the question of attribution: dismissing suggestions that the palace might have been the work of Alberti or Brunelleschi, he is inclined to think (as more recent historians would generally confirm) that it was begun by Luciano Laurana, predating, as he observes in a later chapter, Bramante's supposed achievement in restoring architecture to "la buona maniera dell' architettura antica"[268].

The second chapter deals with the palace's relation to its site, noting with approval the way that an entrance has been arranged at the upper level while service quarters are embedded in a substructure which extends this level as the ground falls away towards the west. In Chapter three, Baldi gives an overall account of the ordering of the spaces: the apartments in proportion to the whole palace, the principal rooms to the apartments, ante-rooms to the principal rooms and the private chambers to the ante-rooms and, in the private rooms, the height proportioned to the length and width. For the principal salone, he gives a length of one hundred urbinate feet, a width between forty-three and forty-five and a height estimated at fifty feet. Curiously, he does not bother to remind his reader that these are albertian ratios of 4:9 and 1:2 though, as we have noted earlier, this point would not have been lost on Vespasiano. (The use of Alberti's preferred ratios seems to disqualify Francesco di Giorgio as architect for at least this part of the palace). Baldi notes, here, the comparative lack of colour and stucco decoration, supposing that Duke Federigo was looking for 'essential beauty', another concept almost absent from the treatises.

In Chapters four to eleven, Baldi goes through the main components of the palace, the substructure and stables, the cortile, the stairs, the upper floors and sala, individual apartments, library and studiolo, the towers and the garden. He praises the way that the third level in the cortile is set back:

> making the view open up and avoiding the defect of excessive height which produces courtyards which are dark, narrow, deep, gloomy and damp like a cistern.

267. The full text of the Introduction is in the version included in Memorie concernenti la Città di Urbino, Rome, 1724 (dedicated to James III of England) Other citations are from the version appended to Castiglione's Il Cortegiano, Ed. Rigutini, Florence, 1889.
268. Ibid., p.315. "The true style of ancient architecture".

Returning to the sparse ornamentation of the principal salone, Baldi writes as one for whom the revival of ancient architecture is taken for granted but for whom the exercise of taste, discriminating within an established body of production, has become a major issue:

> *The walls and ceiling are plastered and painted white, with no other ornament than that which we have mentioned [false doorways to balance the real ones]: from this it results, in part due to the marvellous scale and proportion and in part to the purity of the decoration, that one feels, on entering, a pleasure which is not outlandish and deceitful but genuinely natural, accompanied by a certain majesty in the pleasing severity of the overall effect.*

Later (in Chapter XIV), when writing on the ornament of the palace, Baldi points out that when it was built the stuccoed decoration of Roman architecture (most importantly, at Hadrian's villa) had not been discovered. He is able to look at the architecture of the Renaissance as having, already, a history and for him, unlike Giorgio Vasari (to whom he refers on a number of occasions), this history is not interpreted in terms of a sustained progress from hesitant beginnings to the near perfection of his own day. Indeed, many of the qualities which he finds admirable in Duke Federigo's palace are, in his view, sadly absent from much work of his own day:

> *....nevertheless, it must be understood that one does not find here that licentious style with which the buildings of our times are so full, in which, while the architects profess that they are imitators of antiquity, they don't realize that they are depraving it. One does not find here, I say, those capriciously broken architraves, those festooned panels, masks, mixtures of rough and smooth, and other things so frequently to be seen in modern buildings: and this, in my view, is partly because they had not then learned, on the authority of Michelangelo Buonarroti, the values of caprice rather than of rule; which would have been fine if they had all had minds of the quality of his, and avoided what was monstrous and deformed: and partly it was because they had not then discovered all the works of the ancients, nor used the example of their licence, to justify their own misplaced applications.*

Clearly, Baldi would not have thought much of Vignola's project for the Palazzo Bocchi [269]. One does not have to assume that he and Vespasiano were of one mind on every matter; our interest is in the range of topics they seem to have discussed.

Concluding his review of the various parts of the palace, Baldi has a section on those parts which either were not finished or were never started. On the evidence of old inhabitants, he claims that a further courtyard was projected to the south of the present structures; the duke had bought up property to be demolished, making way for this. In the space between the two structures, there was to have been a circular temple,

> *....which, being in a high-up, free and open situation, would have made a most beautiful view in the distance. The fabric of this was to have been very rich and by no means inconvenient to the rest of the buildings; so that the nearer one came, the more one would recognise the perfect magnificence of the prince. Nor am I just guessing at its beauty; because there is still preserved a model of it in the duke's wardrobe, from whose miniature form and the ornament which it shows, it is easy to visualize beauty, grandeur and perfection.*

269. Giorgio Vasari's view, Lives of the Artists, tr. George Bull, London, 1987, Vol. 1, p.366, is, of course, entirely different: The licence he Michelangelo. allowed himself has served as a great encouragement to others to follow his example; and subsequently we have seen the creation of new kinds of fantastic ornamentation containing more of the grotesque than of rule or reason. Thus all artists are under a great and permanent obligation to Michelangelo, seeing that he broke the bonds and chains that had previously confined them to the creation of traditional forms.

Baldi had seen, in model form, the architectural image which had haunted the urban landscapes of so many artists associated with Urbino: Francesco di Giorgio, Piero della Francesca, Raphael and Bramante, the last of whom was finally to realize it in his Tempietto at San Pietro in Montorio in Rome. Many art historians of later times would have given a lot for a look into the ducal wardrobe. If Vespasiano had been given, in conversation with Baldi, a more detailed description of the 'ideal' circular temple projected at Urbino, in his own version of this theme, the church of the Incoronata at Sabbioneta, he seems to have felt himself under no obligation to copy it.

The last three chapters of the *Descrizione* deal, respectively, with the materials available locally and which were used in the palazzo (he particularly admired the external brickwork "rubbed down so as to make the wall appear as a single piece and beautiful to see"), notable technical achievements (chimneys which didn't smoke and a system for supplying carefully stored rainwater to a fountain in the garden, for special occasions) and finally a reply to some objections (should the main entrance have been central in the façade?). It has seemed worthwhile devoting some space to the *Descrizione* because it can give us an insight to the way in which architecture was being discussed in Vespasiano's circle. Four specific points are worth noting:

1   It assumes a familiarity with up-to-date critical sources; Vasari is cited, as we have seen, and Serlio is 'corrected' over the birthplace of 'our' Bramante.

2   It sees modern architectural practice as founded in well-informed and critical observation of antique precedent, no longer dependent upon the written testimony of Vitruvius.

3   It implies a critical evaluation of architectural practice in the Renaissance framed within a self-conscious historical perspective. Recourse to antique precedent is no longer sufficient in itself to validate a modern design, nor is 'modernity' to be necessarily associated with good taste.

4   It recognises 'contextual' issues of architectural response to conditions of the site, integration of existing structures and respect for the architectural presence of earlier structures as critical to the task of an architect.

That the architecture of Sabbioneta is informed by similar thoughts has been already and will be further suggested.

The only painter of more than local reputation to whom paintings at Sabbioneta can confidently be ascribed is Bernardino Campi, one of a number of artists of that family name who were active in and around Cremona, then part of the duchy of Milan. Campi had been trained by Ippolito Costa, of the school of Giulio Romano at Mantua, and may have worked there in the Palazzo Té, though Venetian influence is perhaps more decisive in the formation of his own style. He belonged to a generation of painters for whom the emphasis of their art had shifted from the category of visual 'research' such as had culminated in the work of Leonardo da Vinci, Raphael and Titian towards the deployment of an assumed technical mastery of perspective, colour and light as a means to render the themes of counter-reformation religious instruction, as well as the portrayal of individuals, in a way that was immediate, realistic and accessible. From a lesser master, such as Campi, it was expected that he could reproduce a variety of styles and work within a tightly delineated brief.

Despite the conformist pressures of the counter-reformation (of which Milan was the intellectual epicentre) the cultural climate in the northern parts of Italy might, in relation to the standards of that time, deserve to be described as 'progressive'. Barriers excluding members of the lesser urban nobility from commercial or professional activity were less effective in these regions than elsewhere, and the position of women, within this more open framework, showed signs of a transformation which was evidently visible to contemporaries. In the section of his *Civile Conversation* which deals with the upbringing of daughters, the distinction is clearly noted by Stefano Guazzo:

> ....*some will have them [daughters] taught to write and reade, and to have skill in Poetry, musicke, and painting: others will have them learne nothing but to spinne with the distaffe and governe the house.*
> ....*If she bee to bee married into a more free country, such as Piedmont is, or our Montferrat, the father must somewhat slake the bridle hand, and give her more liberty, that she may be as fit for that life which the wives there leade, and not taken for a foole and a clowne.*

Guazzo personally disapproved of the new habit of the women of his native Casale to walk in the streets, blaming this on the influence of women from Mantua. He saw the progress of artistically talented women as inappropriate in normal circumstances:

> I sawe about the Frenche Queene certayn meane Gentlewomen, enter into such credit, onely by some one of those good partes by you rehearsed, that they are now come to be maryed to the cheefe Gentlemen in Fraunce, without any peny given them in dowrye by their father: but a private Gentleman hath no neede in his house of singing or daunsing.[270]

No doubt, in Cremona also, many private gentlemen had no need in thier houses for singing and daunsing but there were women in and around that city who were evidently not inclined to leave the matter for their husbands to decide. Parlenia Gallerati, writer and scholar, who lived in Cremona, in a letter to Ginevra Scatileia in 1540, is altogether more ambitious:

> We must have the courage to raise ourselves from the ground and, by the merit which, up to now, men have reserved for themselves only, overtake them. All our effort must be directed towards one end, which is that we persist and particularly that you, who have already shown such merit, following the example of Camilla Valenti of Mantua, who can never be praised too much, incite, exhort, inflame and instruct your compatriots so that we can be equal with men in numbers also.[271]

When, in 1546, Sofonisba, eldest daughter of Amilcare Anguissola (an eminent but impoverished nobleman of Cremona), declared at the age of fourteen that she wished to become a painter, she and her younger sister were sent to be instructed at the household (not, strictly, in the studio, where nude male models were employed) of Bernardino Campi. Campi seems to have taken his role as teacher seriously and during the three years that she studied with him, Sofonisba's command of the techniques of painting progressed rapidly. In 1549, however, Campi was summoned to Milan by the wife of Don Ferrante Gonzaga (Vespasiano's guardian and mentor, who had become governor there in 1546) and must have spoken highly of his young pupil since, in the same year, Sofonisba was also invited to Milan. This, incidentally, was the year in which Don Ferrante was arranging the marriage of Vespasiano to his son's ex-fiancée, Diana di Cardona, a union which was shortly to end in tears. After another two or three years during which she studied with Bernardino Gatti (everyone seems to have been called Bernardino at that time), Amilcare Anguissola was able to arrange an introduction for his daughter to Michelangelo in Rome. Short of formal instruction, Michelangelo seems to have given her encouragement and advice; upon his suggestion that it would be a greater challenge for her to draw a child crying than one smiling, she made a splendid drawing of her young brother, Asdrubale, in the moment that his finger had been nipped by a crab. This drawing, sent as a token of gratitude to Michelangelo, earned her, in return, his drawing of the head of Cleopatra. It seems[272] that Sofonisba's introduction to Michelangelo was effected by Annibale Caro, a friend of the Anguissola family and the same whom we have previously encountered when he was struck, at their first meeting, by Giulia Gonzaga's northern accent.

270. Stefano Guazzo, Civile Conversation, cit., pp.74-78.
271. Quoted in Valerio Guazzoni, "Donna, pittrice e gentildonna. La nascita di un mito femminile del Cinquecento" in Various Authors, Sofonisba Anguissola e le sue Sorelle, Cremona, 1994, p.61.
272. Ilya Sandra Perlingieri, Sofonisba Anguissola, The First Great Woman Artist of the Renaissance, New York, 1992, pp.67-72. Amilcare's letters to Michelangelo are reproduced in the appendix to Sofonisba Anguissola e le sue Sorelle, cit.

The paths of Sofonisba and Vespasiano continued to intersect on a regular basis during the following sixteen years, with only one piece of positive evidence that they met or knew one another. In 1558, Sofonisba's independent reputation as a painter was such that she was was called to work in Milan by the Duke of Alva, whose portrait she painted in that year; the Duke of Alva had replaced Don Ferrante as governor there in 1554, and it was in his service that Vespasiano had been active in the Roman campaign against Paul IV, ending with his wounding at the siege of Ostia. In 1559, Sofonisba left Milan to serve at the court in Spain as lady-in-waiting to the new queen, Isabella de Valois. (Convention did not allow that a woman could be explicitly employed as a painter, though it was almost entirely in this capacity that she worked at the Spanish court.) Nine years later, Vespasiano was to make the same journey, by which time, following the death of Queen Isabella, Sofonisba was retained as governess to Isabella's two daughters. For three years, prior to his posting to Navarra, Vespasiano spent most of his time at court and it was during this time that King Philip decided that it was time for Sofonisba to be fixed up with a husband. Upon Sofonisba's polite but firm statement that she would prefer, if she must marry, that it be 'in Italy', discreet enquiries were put out as a result of which Diego de Cordova, advised by a certain Broccardo Persico who was a friend of the Anguissola in Milan, wrote to Cardinal Espinosa:

> With regard to your correspondence of last night concerning the business about Sofonisba, I can tell you (and I am quite sure) that Ercole Visconti, who is here with Vespasiano Gonzaga, is the cousin of Vespasiano and owner of two good estates, one in the state of Milan and one in Piacenza, and was once interested in Sofonisba but not any longer, so there is no need to arrange a marriage, as I understand it from Vespasiano.[273]

Visconti was Vespasiano's right-hand man, shortly to be sent back to Italy as governor of Sabbioneta during Vespasiano's prolonged absence. This was, as we shall discover, not the only instance of Vespasiano's concern to see his cousin respectably married; Ercole's romantic inclinations evidently ran counter to social pressures upon him to settle down.

In the event, Sofonisba (now thirty-nine years old) was married to Fabrizio de Moncarda, an undistinguished representative of the Sicilian nobility who was unable to keep himself from being pushed around by his more powerful relatives. Some time before 1578, on his way by sea to Spain where he hoped to plead his case at court, Fabrizio 'disappeared', said to have been killed by pirates. Sofonisba set off from Palermo soon afterwards, evidently with the intention of returning to Lombardy, but 'fell in love' and, in 1580, was married (without the approval either of her family or of King Philip) to Orazio Lomellini, captain of the ship on which she sailed. With Lomellini, who was generally at sea, plying between Genoa and Palermo (like her first, this marriage remained childless), she set up home in Genoa and resumed her career as a painter, turning increasingly to religious subjects until, her eyesight having almost completely failed, she had to stop. In 1620, she and Orazio moved to Palermo. Sofonisba's reputation was by now such that Van Dyck made the journey to visit her there in 1624, recorded by a sketch of the ninety-two year old Sofonisba in his notebook. She died in the following year.

273. The letter is reproduced in Sofonisba Anguissola e le sue Sorelle, cit., p. 373.

Had the project of Sofonisba's marriage with Ercole Visconti been realized, the artistic scene at Sabbioneta would have been enriched by one of the more significant painters of her time. Quite possibly in Cremona or Milan during the '50s and certainly in Spain during the early '70s, Vespasiano was in contact, through Sofonisba, with some of the most progressive tendencies in portraiture. Much has been made of Sofonisba's precocious experiments in 'genre' painting - intimate family scenes which capture the fleeting dynamics of a moment in time. Her memorable image of 'Bernardino Campi painting the portrait of Sofonisba Anguissola' (Fig. 5.3)- he, turned towards his invisible sitter, she, portrayed, looking out at the spectator, throwing into complex uncertainty the issues of subject, object and representation- indicates a speculative engagement in the nature of her art which goes far beyond mere technical skill. Both in her numerous self-portraits and in those of family groups and individuals, there is life, sympathy and, often, a touch of humour which sets them apart from the 'official' representation of dignitaries prevalent at the Spanish court. Contrasting Sofonisba's portrait painting with that of other leading artists working at the same time in Spain, Maria Kusche points out that, while borrowing from Antonis Mor his use of 'props' to stress attributes of the subject, his sumptuous contrasts of dark colours with reds and gold, his blurring of the outline of the body in deep shadow, Sofonisba concentrated light upon faces and hands, dissolving the background and combined in her presentation of her subjects their private with their public personality, putting them in the presence of the spectator.

> *While Mor suppresses the conflict, stressing the lofty public status of his subjects and Sánchez Coello shows the dignity of his subjects leaving the tension to be discovered, Sofonisba balances the official with the intimate [....] In a word, Sofonisba extends the scope of the official portrait, conferring upon her subjects greater bodily weight, greater beauty, feeling and personal narrative.*[274]

Allowing that this has been written in a context where it was desirable to identify in Sofonisba's work those characteristics which would set it apart from the norm of contemporary practice and that similar characteristics might, in reality, be found in some works by other artists of the time, it seems, nevertheless, a convincing account of the special qualities which Sofonisba brought to her work. One feels that one would be able to recognise a work in which these particular features were evident. Any such conviction quickly evaporates, however, when a particular work, of uncertain attribution, comes up for consideration.

274. Maria Kusch, "Sofonisba e il ritratto di rappresentanza ufficiale nella corte spagnola" in Ibid, p.150.

The painting in the Civic Museum at Como (illustrated at the head of this chapter), now safely identified as a portrait of Vespasiano Gonzaga[275], has been (and was, before the identification of its subject) attributed to the distinguished Dutch painter and official portraitist at the Spanish court, Antonis Mor. The date 1559 appears as though etched onto the surface of his armour. In relation to this portrait, however, we have an instance of the fragility of the base upon which the history of art must often be constructed. Two learned writers, Ugo Bazzotti and Leandro Ventura[276], have based their argument upon a statement in Affò[277] that, in 1558, Vespasiano went to Brussels in order to pay homage to King Philip (he came away well rewarded, being made a Grandee of the Spanish court; the portrait could have been a celebration of this event). Mor could, then, have made a sketch while Vespasiano was in Flanders and finished the portrait in the following year - except that, from about 1554 to 1559, Mor appears to have been in Spain. When, in the latter year, he returned to Flanders, he evidently did so under something of a cloud (possibly connected with suspicions about his religious orthodoxy) and settled inconspicuously at Antwerp[278]. Conjecture seems, in this case, to have been stretched beyond the point that a safe attribution of the portrait can be put forward, particularly in view of the skill which many painters of the time displayed in copying the style of, or, frequently, entire paintings by their contemporaries.

In the light of Maria Kusche's distinctions, one might easily see in this portrait of Vespasiano precisely that fusion of the official and the intimate which she sees as having characterized work of the Lombard school and of Sofonisba in particular. It would be convenient to dispense with the hypothesis of a sketch and later completion; one could simply say that the painting was done in Italy in 1559, either by Sofonisba, just before her departure for Spain, or by Bernardino Campi[279] (though, on the evidence of what little remains from Campi's extensive output of portraiture during the '50s, it is hard to imagine that Campi would have produced a work as forceful as this), or by another Lombard painter. But the very fact that a substantial group of artists in the second half of the sixteenth century did portraits which are, in so many cases, almost impossible to attribute with any certainty, can be taken as a measure of the extent to whch these painters were working towards a shared objective, each absorbing and reinterpreting aspects of the others' achievement. It is unlikely that the artistic project of a portraiture which sought, increasingly, to represent its subjects in terms, not of what they symbolized but of who they individually were, could have been driven solely by motives peculiar to the community of painters; more probable that the project was a collective response to an emerging appetite amongst those who commissioned the work. Paradoxically, in the same generation for which religious intolerance had enforced an outward reserve and in whose political life the practice of dissimulation had become an accepted mode of expression (we have seen how, in his comments upon the progress of his own affairs, Vespasiano seldom said what he was really thinking: more often, the opposite), in the art of portraiture it was, precisely, the psychologically 'truthful' presentation of its subjects which had come to dominate the agenda.

In relation to Vespasiano's supposed conversations with Bernardino Baldi, as they are reflected in Baldi's *Descrizione*, we noted the appearance of a notion of architectural history, not frozen in mythical time and symbolic form but embodied in specific forms and in real time. Such a 'modern' notion of history was a space which, through the medium of portraiture, Vespasiano and others in his generation were evidently eager to inhabit.

275. See Ugo Bazzotti, "Nobilis Cicatrix - Un Nuovo Ritratto e una nota impresa di Vespasiano Gonzaga" in Civiltà Mantovana, 12, 1986, pp.9-22. The scar on his upper lip, together with his personal emblem of a winged thunderbolt which is engraved upon the breastplate, can leave little doubt that it is a portrait of Vespasiano.
276. Ibid. And L.Ventura, "Vespasiano Gonzaga Colonna (1531 - 1591) Alcuni appunti in margine alla mostra iconografica nel quarto centenario della morte" in Civiltà Mantovana, 3rd series, No 1, 1991.
277. Irene Affò, Vita di Vespasiano Gonzaga, cit., p.24.
278. Georges Marlier, Anthonis Mor Van Dashorst, Brussels, 1934, p.15.
279. Marco Tanzi, writing in Mondo Padano, 16th Sept. 1991, is quoted (Ibid. N.5, p.87) as believing Campi was the author, supporting this theory with the evidence of A.Lamo, Cremona, 1584, that Campi painted a portrait of Vespasiano. This would place the association of Vespasiano with Campi and his circle a long time before Campi came to work at Sabbioneta.

Among the commissions received by Bernardino Campi was the task of completing the set of twelve 'portraits' of Roman emperors for the Gabinetto dei Cesari in the ducal palace at Mantua, of which eleven had been executed by Titian. Campi was then commissioned to make copies of the entire set which were sent to Vienna for the collection of the emperor Ferdinand I; these transactions were arranged by Jacopo Strada who, though he was not the first individual to make a living by what would today be called the 'art trade', was, nevertheless, the first to do so on an international scale and in the service of Europe's leading collectors of the day.[280] Strada, born in Mantua in 1515, could claim nobility of birth and had the resources to finance a wide range of entrepreneurial activities. Though he was not a man of profound learning, he had an extensive working knowledge of contemporary and antique art, enjoying a widespread reputation as the leading antiquarian of his time. Strada worked not only for three successive Holy Roman emperors but also for Hans Jacob Fugger (his first patron) whose collection was scientific, rather than artistic, in its main emphasis. He also worked for the emperor's brother-in-law, Duke Albrecht V of Bavaria, whose art collection was the most important north of the Alps. As a middleman, in a position to obtain lucrative commissions, Strada's services were also sought by important artists; as his reward for delivering samples of his work to Duke Albrecht and Fugger, Titian painted Strada's splendid portrait. For his transalpine patrons, Strada compiled inventories of Italian art collections; for the duke of Bavaria he arranged the production of a complete set of drawings and a model of the Palazzo del Té in Mantua as well as important modern buildings in Rome. For these patrons, Strada would procure almost anything; he evidently procured his own daughter, Katharina, for the emperor Rudolf II[281].

Strada's entrepreneurial activities in the province of Mantua were cut short in 1567 when, still protesting the orthodoxy of his belief, he was forced to absent himself under threat from the Inquisition; fourteen years later, in that city, he was burned in effigy as a confirmed heretic.

Like an itinerant bee, cross-pollinating the cultural centres of Europe, Jacopo Strada played a significant role in the dissemination of knowledge and ideas across a continent in which demand for intellectual and artistic acquisition was insatiable. He worked on a project to publish Leandro Alberti's *Descrittione di tutta Italia*, a comprehensive 'catalogue' of recent italian art and architecture; at the time of his death (1588) he was engaged in producing a dictionary in eleven languages[282], and his son published, posthumously, Strada's book of mechanical milling devices which, though lacking applicable technical value, was aimed at aristocratic readers who felt that they should, in principle, possess knowledge of this sort[283]. Of more permanent significance, however, was the role which Strada played in the development of a new type of architectural space for the exhibition of the varied collections which he helped his patrons to accumulate. Of even more far reaching consequence in the history of architecture was the purchase by Strada, in 1553, from Sebastiano Serlio, of his sixth, seventh and eighth Books of architecture and the publication of the seventh in Frankfurt, in 1575.

280. See Dirk Jacob Jansen: "Jacopo Strada et le commerce d'art", in La Revue de l'art, 77, 1987.
281. See R.J.W.Evans, Rudolf II and his World, Oxford, 1973, p.49.
282. J.R.Hale, The Civilization of Europe in the Renaissance, London, 1994, p.159.
283. Georges Comet, "Un intermédiaire culturel: l'artiste-ingénieur, l'exemple de Strada de Rosberg" in Histoire et Societé, Vol.IV, Aix en Provence, 1992.

Strada's italian activities are only known with any degree of precision for a period during the late 'sixties during which his rival, Niccolò Stoppio, was sending regular reports back to Hans Jacob Fugger in an attempt to establish his own superior qualification to work as his agent. During this time, Strada is known to have had dealings with Don Cesare Gonzaga (ex-fiancé of Vespasiano's first wife) and a number of other 'near misses' are to be found in the record. The most substantial record of a connection between Strada and Vespasiano himself is the fact that Strada's son Paolo was awarded a benefice in the territory of Sabbioneta with effect from 1568; though not conclusive, this seems to suggest something more than a casual acquaintance.

It is far from clear to what extent Strada can be said to have worked as an architect, rather than as an adviser to his patrons in matters of architecture; his first employment with Ferdinand I seems to have been of an architectural nature and his name is associated with the design, for Maximilian II, of the Neugebäude, an extravagant garden and pavilion outside Vienna which was started in 1569[284]. Strada was almost certainly involved in the design of the magnificent 'Antiquarium' in the ducal Residenz at Munich, started in the same year. Both are emphatically linear structures (the Neugebäude some two hundred metres long, three linear spaces strung together in line) formed by the repetition of a single bay design and similar, in this respect, to certain medieval forms associated with use as libraries, dormitories and hospitals[285]. A more immediate precedent for such long rooms was to be found in France, where the late medieval practice of building 'galleries' was noted by Serlio in his seventh Book: "Above a loggia, there shall be a room which is known in France as a gallery for walking".[286] If Serlio's description can only apply in a very general sense to the two 'galleries' with which Jacopo Strada is associated, it corresponds very closely to the Corridor Grande which Vespasiano Gonzaga built to house his collections at Sabbioneta. (Fig. 5.4)

The composition of repetitive, linear buildings (comparable, in some respects, to the stoas of hellenistic and roman antiquity, as well as the markets and basilicas whose descendants are the bazaars of the Middle East) is a type of plan in which every part is expressed architecturally as being of equal status and in which any hierarchy of position is explicitly suppressed. It is neutral with respect to its contents in the same way that a list arranged alphabetically is neutral, the product of a state of mind radically different from that in which most architecture of the high Renaissance was conceived and in which centrality or bi-axiality is celebrated at a level of principle. As an element of urban composition, it represents the diametric opposite of the circular or polygonal 'temple' whose almost uncanny stillness was a theme of so much art emanating from Urbino (where Baldi had seen the model of a circular temple in the duke's wardrobe); where the latter aims to fix an ideal object in a contained space, the form of the stoa seems to project perspective into unlimited distance, offering no point of rest. From the second quarter of the sixteenth century, such stoa-like buildings begin to appear quite regularly in response to building programmes where the non-hierarchical representation of their contents might be appropriate. Sansovino's library at Venice, of 1537, Vasari's Uffizi at Florence, from 1560, the Portico dei Banchi at Bologna, also started in 1560, following a design by Vignola, can be seen, in this sense, as belonging to a 'family' in which Vespasiano's Corridor Grande was a comparative late-comer. As a single, acutely elongated room raised above a continuous open arcade, however, the reference of Vespasiano's building to a pre-Renaissance french prototype (a room for walking), adapted to the very 'modern' purpose of putting his collections on display, seems to combine an up-to-date knowledge of contemporary practice with an apparently self-conscious attitude to historical precedent. Here, as we shall also find in other buildings at Sabbioneta, Vespasiano gave a modern 'spin' to a range of apparently archaic architectural references.

284. Dirk Jacob Jansen, "Jacopo Strada editore del Settimo Libro" in C. Thoenes (Ed.) Sebastiano Serlio: Sesto Seminario, Milan, 1989, pp. 208 & 211. No such association is recognised by Rupert Feuchtmüller, Das Neugebäude, Vienna/Hamburg, 1976.
285. See Nikolaus Pevsner, A History of Building Types, Cit., pp.139ff.
286. Sebastiano Serlio, Tutte l'opere d'architettura et prospettiva, Venice, 1619, Book VII, p.42.
287. I.Affò, Vita di Vespasiano Gonzaga, cit., p.47. Affò and, following him, Carli seem to have taken this to be a description of the Corridor Grande. This is strange, particularly in the case of Carli, since he claims to have seen drawings sent to Visconti from Spain in which the building should, presumably, have been recognisable.
288. H-W Kruft, Städte in Utopia, cit., p.46, refers to an earlier 'gallery' "of which we know nothing."
289. Ugo Bazzotti, "La Galleria degli Antichi di Sabbioneta: Questioni cronologiche, attributive e iconografiche" in Atti del Convegno, cit., p. 376.

The Corridor Grande was evidently not the first linear space constructed by Vespasiano for the purpose of exhibiting his collections. The Galleria delle Città which appears, at one time, to have occupied a large part of the northern wing of the ducal palace was evidently a room of this type, some 25 - 30 metres in length and with a width of about 5 metres. This room is described in a letter from Ercole Visconti to Vespasiano in Spain, apparently nearing completion around 1573:

> The Galleria has been brought to a good state, but the stucco urns have not been done because they would have been more ornate than the rest of the Gallery, and they go with it all very well, being recessed into the wall and painted with bronze, as are also the consoles which support the frames. The rest of the frieze and other paintings are done in bright colours, the frames in off-white stone. The cities depicted are these, and they come off very well: Naples, Rome, Florence, Genoa, Constantinople, Venice, Augsburg and Antwerp. At the top end, where there is not much available space, Sabbioneta has been done and at the far end Mirandola [....] The fireplace in the Galleria, in red Verona marble, is quite lovely. [287]

In a first-floor room of the ducal palace, now known as the Sala delle Città, there are frescoed representations of Genoa and Constantinople and it is reasonable to suppose that this is what now remains of the 'gallery' described by Visconti, prior to the major reconstruction of this part of the palace which was subsequently carried out by Vespasiano. If that is the case, then the room in which eight, rather than just two cities were represented, would have been three or four times as long. [288] It seems, then, that Vespasiano had planned to house his collections in a 'long gallery' before he left for Spain in 1568, before the publication of Serlio's Book VII and before the Corridoio del Bertani (not, in fact, by Bertani but by Bernardino Facciotto [289]) in the ducal palace at Mantua, which dates from 1571. While it may be of some minor interest to historians that a 'long gallery' was put in hand at Sabbioneta in circumstances which strongly suggest conversations with Jacopo Strada but before the latter had (if, indeed, he did) projected similar structures at Vienna and Munich, it is nevertheless clear that, for Vespasiano, the architectural statement of his first gallery was by no means strong enough. A few years after his return from Spain, he set about the construction of the Corridor Grande and the work appears to have proceeded at astonishing speed [290]. It is almost as though Vespasiano feared that his earlier gallery, buried inconspicuously within the fabric of his ducal palace, might, for all that it was innovative in certain respects, pass unnoticed: in its new incarnation, three times the length and raised above an open loggia, condensing into a single architectural form the urban perspective interests of Sansovino, Vasari and Vignola, the late medieval French prototype referred to by Serlio and the 'objective' ordering of collected material evidently attributable to Strada, Vespasiano left no room for doubt that he meant it.

290. Most modern writers are content to accept at face value Niccolò de Dondi's entry, which appears to state that building was started in 1583 and finished in 1584. There are problems with this:
1) Dondi's entry is for the year 1583 (no day or month given) and was clearly inserted retrospectively, since he could not, otherwise, have known when the building was finished.
2) Allowing that work might have started at the very beginning of 1583 and been completed at the very end of 1584, we are still to believe that this imposing structure was completed in less than twenty-four months. Dondi gives the dates of April, 1586 for the laying of the foundation stone of the church of the Incoronata and June 1588 for its consecration, that is, twenty-six months for a considerably smaller building which might, in any case, have been consecrated when the main carcass was complete but before its decoration was in place.
The Incoronata has none of the complex brick detail required for the external formation of the Corridor, and remains, in any case, unfinished on the outside. Dondi's time-scale for the construction of the Corridor seems, on the face of it, unrealistic.
Dondi could, of course, have been mistaken (or incorrectly transcribed?) concerning the date of commencement.

There may be more to it than this. In each external pilaster of the upper Pt 3 ~5
register of the Corridor, there is placed a niche. Tending to dematerialize an element
which should, strictly speaking, be read structurally, this motif is rarely to be found in
the architecture of the high Renaissance outside of a quite limited 'family' of buildings
and projects. An early occurrence is in the Tron monument of 1473 in the Frari,
Venice, by Antonio Rizzo, a classicizing interpretation of Gothic forms frequently to
be found in that city[291]. More self-conscious is Baldassare Peruzzi's use of the motif
in his design for the facade of the chapel of San Giovanni del Duomo at Siena where
its reference to a medieval precedent, the Cappella di Piazza in Siena, is confirmed
by Peruzzi's description of the motif as 'modernaccia', that is, in the modern, as
opposed to the antique style[292]. In the published works of Sebastiano Serlio (in which
he incorporated much of the draft treatise which he inherited from Peruzzi) the
motif of a niche inserted into a pilaster makes quite frequent appearances. His design
for a palazzo del podestà in Book VI[293], (whose composition of two superimposed
arcaded storeys is also reminiscent, in many respects, of the Corridor Grande,) has
niches placed in the pilasters of the upper arcade, as they are at Sabbioneta. If this
design was a source for the Corridor, this would be confirmation that Vespasiano had
discussed the contents of Book VI with Strada, since Book VI was not printed during
Vespasiano's lifetime.

      Dating from his 'peruzzian' years, an urban perspective by Serlio shows,
in the foreground, three superimposed niches in the face of a pilaster, alternating
vertically with rectangular recessed panels. In this image, the pilaster can be read as the
returned end of a frontal façade and, in this respect, it closely resembles an incident
in the Villa Imperiale at Pesaro, built to the design of Gerolamo Genga for Eleonora
Gonzaga, duchess of Urbino, which was started in 1529. In the view of Christoph
Frommel[294], Serlio is likely to have known this design and to have borrowed from it
in his urban perspective. Genga, like Serlio, grew up strongly under the influence of
Peruzzi, from whom he seems to have learned the perspective skills which he employed
in the production of stage settings, as early as 1513, for the ducal court at Urbino[295].
While there could be reasons to see in the Villa Imperiale a prototype for important
features of the Corridor Grande - its use of plain exposed brickwork, formed into
simple panels, frames and recesses, is undoubtedly suggestive in this sense - it could
also be significant that the middle ground of Serlio's urban perspective is occupied by a
linear building evidently consisting of a single room at the upper level and raised above
a cross-vaulted open loggia at ground level. It is possible, of course, that Vespasiano
knew both the villa and Serlio's image and that his design is a condensation and a
displacement of elements from both. Or there may have been a single common origin
for all three designs in a peruzzian image which is now lost. (Fig. 5.5)

291. See John McAndrew,
Venetian Architecture of the
Early Renaissance, Cambridge
Mass. and London, 1980, p.63.
292. Christophe L. Frommel,
"Serlio e la scuola romana"
in Sebastiano Serlio: Sesto
Seminario, cit., p.42.
293. Sebastiano Serlio,
Architettura Civile, (Eds.
A.Bruschi and P.Fiore) Milan,
1994, Tav. 61.
294. Op. Cit., p.46.
295. See Antonio Pinelli and
Orietta Rossi, Genga Architetto,
aspetti della cultura urbinate
del primo 500, Rome, 1971,
pp.107 ff.

The motif of a niche placed in a pilaster can also, however, be found in two other buildings, mentioned earlier, which belong to the 'family' of stoa-like structures: it is present on the ground floor of Vasari's Uffizi in Florence and it appears as a feature of the interior of Strada's Antiquarium in Munich. Why, one might ask (other than by sheer coincidence, which cannot be ruled out), does this uncommon motif, evidently carrying the association of medieval overtones, attach itself to buildings of a linear, repetitive order and, in at least two cases, buildings destined for the display of artistic, archeological or scientific collections? Of all medieval building types, that which most forcefully develops the perspective effect of stoa-like repetition is, of course, the gothic cathedral. Like the early 'museum' structures of the Renaissance, gothic cathedrals were intended to encapsulate a comprehensive system of knowledge. In the words of Erwin Panofsky:

> In its imagery, the High Gothic cathedral sought to embody the whole of Christian knowledge, theological, moral, natural, and historical, with everything in its place and that which no longer found its place, suppressed.

And a little further on,

> The second requirement of Scholastic writing, "arrangement according to a system of homologous parts and parts of parts," is most graphically expressed in the uniform division and subdivision of the whole structure.[296]

The search for an architectural metaphor with which to express the totality of human knowledge was a significant concern of the Renaissance[297] but the medieval *summa* and its expression in the architecture of cathedrals was undoubtedly, at that time, not only the original but also the dominant model for a universal classificatory system.

In the case of Vespasiano's gallery, we know that his determination to include such a building amongst his collection of buildings at Sabbioneta was independent of any precise definition of its contents. (Dondi informs us that in June, 1589, Vespasiano had removed the busts of famous military commanders, replacing them with 'certain horns of various animals' which had been sent from Prague[298].) The collection may well have included, in addition to a large quantity of ancient coins, medals and works of art, the mathematical instruments purchased for Vespasiano at Mantua in 1575[299]. In this respect, Vespasiano would have been by no means untypical; the state of mind in which such collections were assembled and displayed was not primarily aesthetic, but driven by a desire to appropriate all available forms of knowledge and to objectify them as potential sites of study. One can suppose that the pilaster niches on the outside of the Corridor Grande were intended to contain (or, at least, to imply the possibility of) sculpture and that this, ordered in a linear, non-hierarchical sequence, would, in a sense, symbolize the collected exhibits. Occupying, (usurping, one might say), the space of the structural markers in the "uniform division and subdivision" of the architecture, the exhibits become, themselves, the structuring element of the composition in the same way that biblical figures and saints became, in the built theology of Gothic architecture, the metaphorical 'structure' of the church. This feature, as it happens, is particularly evident in the interior of the Stephansdom at Vienna, site of Strada's first involvement in stoa-like architecture for the display of a modern collection. It seems, then, that Vespasiano's 'conversations' with Jacopo Strada bore fruit in the formulation of a new type of building: a Cathedral of Modern Knowledge. (Fig. 5.6)

296. *Erwin Panofsky, Gothic Architecture and Scholasticism, London and New York, 1957, p.44.*
297. *Documented, memorably, by Frances A Yates in The Art of Memory, London, 1966. Astrologically derived concentric 'theatres' figured largely in these investigations.*
298. *de Dondi, Op. Cit., p.348.*
299. *Marzio Dall'Acqua, Op. Cit. In Atti del Convegno, p.39.*

There is another building at Sabbioneta in which Vespasiano seems to have played with the idea of a 'cathedral of learning' and this is the 'public' library which occupied the upper floor of the southern wing of the Servite convent of the Incoronata. Though rather less than a third of the length of the Corridor Grande, it was, at some thirty metres, a distinctly 'long' room by normal standards. At either end of this space (there is no particular reason to suppose that it was originally subdivided) there is a quite literally gothic window, an arched opening split into two subsidiary pointed arches with a central column such as are to be found in countless Italian buildings of the late middle ages. (Fig. 5.7) In the window which faces the small piazza, the column, though it is a correct version of the Ionic order, is bizarrely rotated through ninety degrees so that a volute is presented side-on to the frontal view. As is frequently the case at Sabbioneta, this improbable motif is made to appear, in its urban context, so natural that its patently ironic intent has entirely escaped attention. We do not know, of course, the nature or the extent of the collection of books which Vespasiano chose to make available to his subjects but we can infer something of his attitude to their mental improvement: not for them the dangerously progressive speculations which, at the start of this chapter, we saw condoned by Juan de Valdès in the case of Vespasiano's aunt Giulia, possessor of "a lofty, generous and courageous soul."

131

~6)

Conversations II.
Stefano Guazzo's *Civile
Conversation*, Vespasiano's
part in it and Shakespeare's
reading of it. The mood
of imperial Prague.

Machiavel, in the eighth book of his Florentine History, gives this note of Cosmus Medices, the wisest and gravest man of his time in Italy, that he would "now and then play the most egregious fool in his carrriage, and was so much given to jesters, players and childish sports, to make himself merry, that he that should but consider his gravity on the one part, his folly and lightness on the other, would surely say, there were two distinct persons in him." Now methinks he did well in it. [300]

The tone of renaissance life was by no means inevitably serious and it was not considered inconsistent with the dignity of a prince that he would, on occasion, let his hair down and enter into the spirit of light-hearted banter. If our interest in the recorded or reconstructed 'conversations' which made up the last chapter was to locate Vespasiano Gonzaga, intellectually, within a variety of current discourses, we are fortunate in possessing, also, the record of a conversation held, simply, for conversation's sake and in which we are able to form a picture of Vespasiano as a social being: to observe the nature of his interactions with other people in terms of their style rather than their significant content.

In Chapter 3, we encountered Vespasiano in the role of governor of the city of Casale in Monferrato, where his job was to settle the population in subjection to the rule of his cousin, Duke Guglielmo of Mantua. This was in the aftermath of a potentially violent confrontation as the citizens of Casale sought to hold on to their traditional liberties. Vespasiano's evident aim, in carrying out this assignment, was to do so in such a way that, while the sovereignty which he represented could in no way be called in question, the quality of life remaining for the citizens of Casale should suffer no more than was necessary. Not unnaturally, the nobility of the city were anxious that, in this latter respect, Vespasiano should receive all the encouragement which they could give him and it was in this connection that a series of banquets was instituted with the intention that their governor might come to regard Casale's leading citizens in an atmosphere of personal friendship. The conversation supposed to have taken place at one of these banquets was evidently considered to have been exemplary and became the matter of the fourth book[301] of Stefano Guazzo's *Civile Conversation* (parts of which we have, in other connections, quoted earlier).

Stefano Guazzo (1530 - 1593) was a member of the minor nobility of Casale, the leading light of a modest literary academy there and a person who made himself useful, in various secretarial or diplomatic capacities, to the Gonzaga dukes of Mantua. His brother, Guglielmo, who appears as a protagonist in the dialogue of the first three books of the *Civile Conversation*, was employed in the service of the Gonzaga duke of Nevers, and the culture represented in the first three, as well as the final book, though it is not courtly like that proposed by Castiglione, is by no means provincial. The *Civile Conversation* was written in Guazzo's semi-retirement and its purpose was to demonstrate "....that civile conversation is an honest commendable and virtuous kinde of living in the world."

300. Robert Burton, The Anatomy of Melancholy (first published 1621) New York, 2001, p.121.
301. Stefano Guazzo, Civile Conversation, ed. Sir Edward Sullivan, Bart, London and New York, 1925. Book Four was omitted from Pettie's translation of the Civile Conversation published in 1581 "for that it contayneth muche triflyng matter in it" and was published in its first English translation by Bartholomew Young in 1586.

While it would be unwise to assume that Guazzo's account is a complete and accurate record of so long and rambling a discourse as he describes (he does not explicitly record his own participation), it is equally clear that the dialogue is constructed on the basis of things which were indeed said by those people on this or some similar occasion and that the 'character' with which he invests each of the guests is not purely Guazzo's invention. There is a freshness and a life-like quality about this fourth book which is conspicuously lacking in the 'dialogue' of the earlier books. Guazzo was writing about people whom he knew well and the frequently inconsequential shifts from one topic to another (unlike the rigidly pre-ordained progression of topics in Castiglione's *Book of the Courtier*), has the ring of truth about it. The quotations in what follows are from Bartholomew Young's Elizabethan translation, from which an English reader may hear, with greater authenticity, the voice of those times.

On a winter's night in 1567, a company assembled at the house of Caterina Sacca del Ponte: Lelia San Giorgio, Francesca Guazzo (wife of the author), Gianna and her husband, Bernardino Bobba, Giovanni Cane, Cuglielmo Cavagliate and Cavallero Bottazzo. Vespasiano was invited as guest of honour and, with him, his cousin Ercole Visconti. It was evidently considered unusual that a couple, husband and wife, should attend such an occasion together, as it is observed that Gianna and Bernardino Bobba "who by force and vertue of matrimonie, are but one person," should be counted as only one guest, thereby maintaining the ideal number of nine, corresponding to the nine Muses. On the contrary, the notion that women should participate at such occasions independently and in their own right seems to have surprised nobody. In the light of the political circumstances, of which all the party must have been very conscious, it is hardly surprising that the conversation got off to a sticky start:

> ....*whereuppon at the sight of Lord Vespasian, all the companie rising up, and offering him the place, he commaunded them to sitte downe againe, which done, they all kepte such silence for a good space, that they gave Lord Vespasian occasion to saie, that he thought, he was fallen into such a companie, that would have passed the time in some manner of devising, and discourses, but now perceaved himselfe to be rather in a solitarie and silent place.*
>
> *At which wordes one looking uppon an other, and everie one holding his peace, he rose up to departe, and with a curteous conge, take his leave of the Lordes and Ladies....*

Bit by bit, the conversation gets under way, exploring the thought that there should only be nine present - should Giovanni Cane ("Lord John") be thrown out, since his surname makes him a dog? - and Cavallero Bottazzo suggests that if there are nine Muses, Apollo should also be present and "represent his Majestie", a role eminently suited to Vespasiano.

> *No, no, said L. Vespasian, Imagine that all my titles are left at home, and that amongst you here, Seignor Vespasian is but a private man, like anie other. And therefore let us make a triall, to whose Lot it shall befall to beare the swaie and Principalitie amongst us, and so, willed that everie one should cast Lots: And taking up a Petrarq, which lay upon the table, he devised, that everie one should choose a verse of the first Sonet, which in opening of the Booke, should apeare to him on the right side thereof, and that he or she, to whom anie one verse of that Sonet, more properlie touching regiment or seignorie, then anie other might befal, should be by general consent created King or Queene.*

Gianna Bobba ("Ladie Jane") is duly elected, "Whereupon all the companie rejoyced not a little". By means of this ritual, Vespasiano has put them at their ease. The conversation which develops from this point might be described as something between a constituted official 'meeting', with a chair and a largely improvised agenda, and a children's birthday party in which the consumption of smarties is restrained by the interposition of guessing games. For their first 'manner of devising' Vespasiano and Cavallero Botazzo are appointed as judges while, taking up Vespasiano's earlier comment that he seemed to have come to a 'solitarie and silent place', the rest are invited to make 'some pretie sporte of solitarinesse', naming, each in turn, a place where they would choose to be solitary and matching it with a proverb. For instance:

> *Then Lord Hercules said, Because I must honour my Misteres as well with my pen and papers, as with my tongue and heart, I will shut my selfe up in a solitarie studie, where I will so spende my time in secret studie, that praysed She shall be (if I live) in more then thousand bookes.*

When it comes to the judging, Cavallero Bottazzo says that they ought not to make a hasty decision, 'but chew it well in our mindes before' and this gives Vespasiano the opportunity to suggest that supper should be brought in, but that none of the contestants can have any until they have redeemed themselves from their solitude by answering a riddle.

> *When this sport was ended, the Queene asked if it were time to goe to supper?*

But another six pages of conversation intervenes:

> *And while they were thus arguing, the table cloathes wer spread and furnished with sundrie sorts of Viandes, wherfore, after they had washed their hands, and given thanks to God, the Queene first placed her self, and after her everie one according to her commaundment, and so supper began, which was enterchangeablie relished with sundrie sweet and pleasant speeches.*

It becomes very clear that the guests, whether or not they were looking forward to the meal itself, were at some pains to avoid any suggestion that it had been the prospect of good food which had brought them together. Lady Caterine feels obliged to apologise for the small quantity which is placed before them, but this is immediately countered with protestations that they are not particularly hungry. "For here be not (I thinke) anie ravening woulves, neither have we anie cause to be afraid of the dog, who is both olde and toothlesse, and whom a little meate can suffice", and there is general agreement that a modest diet is healthier than heavy eating:

> ....that poet was a good fellow, who commended so highlie a slight banquet, meaning of those kindes of meats, which put not the teeth to anie paine in grinding them, but are easily swallowed down, as good Potage, tarts, Milke, Honie, whitepots, grated cheese, jellies, and such like. It may be also (said L.John) called a light banquet, not having respect to the quantitie of the meate, but to the qualitie of the stomacke, which receiving but a little meate, makes easy and speedy digestion. Howsoever it be, said Cavallero, a spare diet was ever commended, and all the delightes of this supper shall not depend on the sweete tasts of meates, but of the pleasant discourses of this worthie assemblie.

Though we are not given any details of the dishes which were served at Lady Caterine's supper, it is evident that the style of the entertainment tended towards the *nouvelle cuisine* which had been spreading into western Europe from France during the fifteenth and sixteenth centuries. In the words of Massimo Montanari:

> .... the flood of spices and flavourings which overran Europe in the fifteenth century soon led to boredom. Now that everyone could make use of ginger, cinnamon and every sort of 'rare spice', the rich looked elsewhere for a mark of distinction. For the same reason, the highly spiced, fat-free cuisine of the old Europe at a certain point changed its character. Specifically, people reverted to indigenous and to some extent 'rural ' products: in the sixteenth century the élites of France abandoned spices, substituting chives, shalots, mushrooms, capers, anchovies... More delicate flavours and tastes, better adapted, certainly, to the oil or butter-based cuisine which was becoming established at the time; but there was also the pleasure of those who, from the vantage-point of their wealth, permit themselves the rediscovery of 'poor' foods: a sentiment which - fortunately - we know so well today. [302]

Though a direct comparison of the two banquets would clearly be inappropriate, in view of their authors' entirely divergent interests and intentions, it is nonetheless instructive to note the transformation in gastronomic values which seems to separate Francesco Colonna's *Hypnerotomachia Poliphili*, published in 1499 from the supper party at Casale in 1567:

> When this fourth rich course was removed, the table was relaid for the fifth with a crimson silk cloth, and the nymphs clothed in the same. The flowers were yellow, white, and amethystine Cairo roses; the food consisted of eight morsels of the choisest roast pheasant meat, and as many pieces of a light white bread. The sauce was thus: fresh egg yolks with pine nuts, orange water, pomegranate juice, Colossine sugar and cinnamon. The dishes were of emerald, and so was the table of the sublime Queen. [303]

302. Massimo Montanari, La Fame e l'abbondanza, Rome/ Bari,1997, p.148.
303. Francesco Colonna, Hypnerotomachia Poliphili trans. Joscelyn Godwin, London 1999, p.109.

In none of the thirteen pages devoted to Colonna's description of this astonishing banquet is there any suggestion that conversation had a place in it. By any standards, his is a different world from that where the guests were received into a room with a copy of Petrarch on the table and distinctly remote from the austerity of Vespasiano's observation:

> *Truelie, if we would but accustome our selves to tast the Lacedemonians sawce, with a more hongerie and savorie appetite (their labours I meane travell, taking of paines, running, honger and thirst), wee should not so much trouble our poore Cookes, in devising dailie such sondrie sorts of dishes and sawces, neither should we neede so manie napkins to make cleane our fingers: but we have, by reason of ydlenesse, and want of exercise, made our appetites so dull and drowsie, that to sharpen and awake them, we send messengers, some to this countrie, and some to that, sparing for no cost, to bring us home divers daintie and strange sortes of meates and fruites.*

Considering that Lady Caterine might have made a considerable effort to entertain her guests to a high standard, Vespasiano's comments could seem to have been a little churlish. When it comes to the drinking of wine, however (and this, like the serving of food, has to arise out of a 'spontaneous' development in the conversation), the tone is not so moralistic; the women water their wine, but show no enthusiasm for abstinence, while the men set about drinking with evident relish. Lord John, when it is his turn:

> *....pawsed twise, or thrise, to tast the wine the better: to whom L. Lelia said, Me thinks L. John, you eate your wine, in stede of drinking of it. So must he doe, said he, who would suck out the quintessence of it. Do you not know the proverbe: Three things are ill handled. Byrdes in boyes hands, Young men in olde mens hands, And wine in Germains hands, who do not drinke it, but swallow it downe at a gulp, and breaks the neck of it in pouring it down as into a Tonne, and so they breake (said L. Vesp.) often times their own necks.*

Alleged excesses of the Germans are a convenient cover for the supposedly more decorous drinking habits of the Italians. Towards the end of the meal, when another two rounds have been consumed with the accompaniment of suitable banter, the arrival of the last course is taken as the pretext for one more:

> *I have expected (said L. Lelia) that all these amorous speeches should have ben converted in the end to drinking, and so saying, the table was furnished with other daintie cates, amongst the which there was the foresaid Tart, and many kindes of delicate fruits, wherupon L. Caterine looking towards L. John, said, Behold, now I have kept my promise with you, as touching that morsell which shall make you drinke once againe.*

In its conduct and presentation, we get the impression that Lady
Caterine's dinner party was unpretentious and homely and that Vespasiano was sincere
in his appreciation of this. Guazzo's account lends credence to Alessandro Lisca's
comment (quoted at the start of our Introduction) that Vespasiano was happy to
eat the same food as his soldiers. By modern standards, the conversation may seem
brittle, excessively allusive and often contrived but the formality of its tone was clearly
not an obstacle to an easy interchange of ideas within a comparatively broad range,
encompassing flirtatious banter with the occasional moment of quite serious reflection
as well as a wealth of anecdote, sometimes risqué (the ladies, it seems, were not caused
to blush or complain at this) but often genuinely entertaining. The meal is brought
to an end with the arrival of a musician who sounds his harp as a sign that the guests
should stop talking and then sings a song of egregious flattery to Vespasiano:

> *To sing of all your worthie deedes,*
> *your honours great and hie,*
> *My humble voice (thrise noble Lord)*
> *cannot it selfe applie.*
>
> *Orpheus must retourne againe*
> *who with his stile divine,*
> *Must praise you, and your vertues rare,*
> *which like the Sunne doe shine.*
>
> *For you are he whome Monferrata*
> *Hills doe still adore,*
> *In cleering of those cloudie daies,*
> *in which we livde of yore.*

And so on for another thirteen verses. Vespasiano's embarrassment may well have been genuine, but he is persuaded to accept these praises rather than to offend Lady Caterine:

> *I will content my selfe, saide Lord Vespasian, at this time, and when so soveraigne a commaunder as you, good Ladie, doth will mee to accept of them (although contrarie to natural reason, as also to please all parties) I will beleeve that black is white.*

The song (or, possibly, the general relief at its being over) becomes another pretext for a round of drinking,

> *and so the table clothes being taken awaie, and thanks geven to God, supper was ended.*

Guazzo interrupts his narrative at this point in order to deliver his own judgement upon the quality of the conversation, and to stress that dinnertime conversation was not always thus:

> *....menne should learne to avoyde confused disorder and ryotte, used commonlie in Banquettes, in the which there is nothing more followed, then filthie dronkennesse, and nothing so much embraced, as sensuall concupiscence, whereuppon the fumes ascending up into the braine, doe binde and dull the understanding, and seeme as spurres to the tongue, to contentious quarrelinge, insolent speeches, rashe dealinge, slaunderous backbytinge, and to dishonest and beastlie talke, and oppresse the mynde with ydle thoughts, wanton cogitations, vile and barbarous pretences.*

Obviously, the occasion demanded that all the guests should be on their best behaviour. After the meal, it was left to Vespasiano to restart the conversation and one might detect in his choice of topic a reference to the unspoken agenda of the evening. From the observation that entertainments such as they were enjoying were a welcome antidote to melancholy, he embarks upon a homily on the importance of being content with what one has rather than falling prey to "odious and wicked comparisons", unrealistic ambition and envy of those better off, which can only lead to anguish and disappointment. None of them can disagree with the suggestion that a meal and a conversation such as they have been enjoying ought to prevent anyone from becoming depressed and it is decided that Cavallero Bottazzo (who raises the question) should entertain them all on the following evening. This settled, the Queen rises from the table and leads them over to the fire and Lord Hercules is given the task of inventing a new game for them to play. The new 'sport' is that each in turn shall imagine something which is compounded of two other things as, for example, a fish taken by a hook and a bait 'conversing together'.

Heerat the Ladies objected and sayde, that the sport was too difficult for them to devise uppon a sodaine. Nothing at all (sayde Lorde Hercules) for while the men propowned their conceites, you (faire Ladies) may have time to premeditate and thinke on yours. [This is the only instance of an unequal treatment of women as participants in the conversation: in the event, the ladies' misgivings are evidently unfounded.] *And hee tourning towards the Queene, first of all sayde:*

I present you (sweete Ladie) a wound, which your beautie and vertue conversing together, doth make in the hearts of mortall men.

LordVespasian said to Ladie Caterine:

I present you a confusion, which hope and feare conversing together, have engendered in my breast.

Lord Bernardine said to Ladie Lelia:

I present you a snare, which your hand and mine conversing together have wrapped about my heart.

Cavallero said to Ladie Frances:

I present you a Prisoner taken in a net of Golde, which love and your hair conversing together, have woven.

Then the Queene said to Lord Hercules:

I present you a stalke of flowers, which the Earth and the Sunne conversing together have brought forth.

Ladie Caterine said to LordVespasian:

I present you a crown, which learning and warre conversing together have compacted.

Ladie Lelia said to Lord Bernardine:

I present you a Chamblet, which needle and silke conversing together have wrought.

Ladie Fraunces said to Cavallero:

I present you a letter full of my secrets, which penne and ynke conversing together, have written.

The Queen and Vespasiano are judged "most fitlie and finelie" to have expressed their thoughts. After three more eliminating rounds, it is Lord Hercules who is left out on his own. Showered with reproaches and made "to stand on his feete aparte from the rest", he must answer a riddle from each of them on pain of being suspended from the group for the remainder of the season. Not surprisingly, his "suddaine and prettie aunsweres" are generally applauded and Lord Hercules is allowed to sit down again. As the evening progresses, it becomes increasingly clear that it is Vespasiano's cousin who can rise to the occasion, "play the most egregious fool" and make himself the life and soul of the party. His open admission that he is 'in love' and longs for the company of his mistress provides the basis for much of the remaining conversation, tending to provoke a sceptical response from the other men and some motherly concern from the women. It leads to a lengthy debate whether it is through the eyes or by the tongue that amorous impulses are most forcefully transmitted:

> *....the eyes [....] do openly disclose the hidden and secrete passions of our heartes [....] but often times, they seeme to demaund and promise something, and as messengers from the heart, and give also the most apparent tokens. ....yet the tongue neverthelesse is bestowed upon us as a keie, to open the secret thoughts of our minde. [....] So that I think, that the eies are great dissemblers, and greater than the tongue, because the tongue dare not tell a lie, without the help and counsell of the eie.*

Eventually, Lord Hercules is persuaded to address Lady Lelia with an amorous 'complaint' which he performs to the great mirth of all the company. Following a crescendo of clichés, his speech concludes:

> *I beseech thee (faire ladie) that in recompence of these long and great paines which hetherto by concealing, and by continual death I have sustained, thou wouldst not denie me at the least, to laie thy daintie mouth to mine, and with a sweet breath sucke out this poore soule, and send it to his former home, entering into the which, who can tell? If it may not with the vertue of some sparkle of the divine spirit, which shal be conjoyned with it, minister both a livelie pulse and substance to my fainting members, and preserve them also a little longer, onelie for thy service and sweet sake....*

Lady Lelia assures him that she would certainly have allowed him a kiss if his life had, indeed, been in danger,

> *But because I percieve that this your infirmitie is not mortall, I will therefore keep it a little time longer with myself for my own comfort.*

Inevitably, from the insincerity of those who protest love in exaggerated terms, the subject of infidelity comes up, coupled with the idea (it is getting late and the company beginning to feel tired) that while lovers find it difficult to sleep at night, those who are settled in marriage can sleep soundly, even when they are being deceived. This leads to discussion of Lord Hercules' sleepless, restless and unsettled condition, prompting the women (the Queen, in particular, who is there as part of a 'couple') to ply him with advice how he may find "an honest and vertuous wife" and he, clearly at ease finding himself the centre of so much female attention, puts forward a string of hypothetical objections:

> *She may be faire (said Lorde Hercules) and yet may cause me to depart from her side.*
> *You will never rise from her, saide she againe, if you will take her to be faire in my sence, that is faire of minde, because if she be such a one, she will not faile to comfort you in your adversities, and wilbe as carefull for you as she may bee, and so beeing free from all thoughts, and sleeping upon her owne eyes, you shall spend all the night in sweete and pleasant rest.*

Lord Hercules, it may be remembered, is the same Ercole Visconti who first thought that he would, but then decided not to marry the painter, Sofonisba Anguissola (from all that one knows of her, eminently 'faire of minde'). Vespasiano's ongoing problem with his cousin, in this respect, appears in his comment:

> *All this talke, said Lord Vespasian, will inferre nothing else, but to set Lord Hercules free from his amorous passions which hold him in continual and vigilant paine, if not, then we must seeke out some honest and wel disposed wife for him, which might perhaps procure him to sleepe.*

But if the picture which we can form of Vespasiano's cousin, Ercole Visconti is that of an easy-going, evidently charming extrovert, skilled at sweet-talking the opposite sex, unruffled at finding himself the butt of inconsequential jokes and endowed with that effortless grace of manner which figures so highly among the attributes required by Castiglione in his *Book of the Courtier*, Guazzo's account shows Vespasiano to have been distinctly ill at ease in circumstances where all that was required was pleasant small-talk. Too much concerned to say what was right, too passionate in his beliefs, too candid in the expression of private thoughts and feelings, Vespasiano's contributions in the conversation seem, repeatedly, to strike a note out of tune with the general mood. His "confusion, which hope and feare conversing together, have engendered in my breast" seems to offer a gratuitously intimate revelation of his inner state while the vehemence with which he condemns those who lack appetite through lack of exercise goes beyond the normal requirements of party conversation. When the Queen raises a question why people may "lament, not onlie for sorrow, but oftentimes for joy", Vespasiano's reply might, for him, have been 'correct' but its tone is needlessly pedantic in the circumstances:

> *Griefe for example on the one side, said L. Vesp., which doth naturallie refrigerate and binde up the veines, whereupon the humour hidden amongst them is expressed and issueth forth by the eies. And joy on the other side, whose property is, to calcefy, and to dilate the porosities, so that the humors hidden within, doe easilie come forth.*

In the discussion which follows Lord Hercules' amorous 'lamentation', it is the general consensus that while there may be foolish and vain women "(nay rather gyrles)" who are likely to fall for the antics of "these effeminate and unbearded youths", to be seen in church and elsewhere "like wilde and unbridled colts, with such a licencious kinde of languages, ridiculous gesture in their countenances and foolish motions of their bodies", sensible women will pay no attention to the insincere ranting of those who claim to be in love. It is Vespasiano who wants to argue the other side:

> But Ladie Fraunces, offereth wrong, in not agreeing, that lovers should not be beleeved, who cannot feigne, when they would verie faine, but the more they are in love, the more they tell things that are not apparentlie credible, and yet are most true....

and at the very point that the conversation is drifting towards the subject of infidelity, it is Vespasiano, again, who interjects a note of oddly discordant idealism:

> But let us now saie once againe [....] that wher ther is love, ther is faith, and where this mutual love is, ther all deceit and falsehoods are taken quite awaie.

For a modern English reader, some of the interest in Guazzo's text might lie in the probability that Shakespeare would have read it.[304] The book was an immediate success in Italy and became, in the English translation from which we have been quoting, and in the words of Professor M.P.Tilley[305]: "next to Castiglione's *Courtier* [.....] probably the best known Italian book in England during the Elizabethan period". Traces of Guazzo's text have been found in *Hamlet*[306] and the wealth of proverbs with which the *Civile Conversation* is strewn is evident in Shakespeare's writing as it is in that of many other writers both then and since. Neither Guazzo nor Shakespeare is, however, the subject of our present investigations and if there is any way in which Shakespeare's knowledge of the text could illuminate this, it would be in the possibility that a 'shakespearian' insight could be brought to bear upon the character of Vespasiano Gonzaga.

In exploring the associative content and references which Vespasiano embedded in his architecture, we have repeatedly uncovered an 'over-determination', the condensation of a wide variety of thoughts, memories and associations into an architectural synthesis whose apparent unity belies the disparate nature of its constituent impulses. The discourse of psychoanalysis and, in particular, the categories introduced by Sigmund Freud in *The Interpretation of Dreams* have made it possible to examine creative processes in a new light. Similarly, in the case of Shakespeare's writing, Kenneth Muir can say:

> Shakespeare thus combined a variety of different sources in the texture of his verse, and the process, in most cases, was unconscious. [....] so it would be possible, if we had a complete knowledge of Shakespeare's reading, to show that words, phrases and images coalesce in his poetry [....] Two or more passages became linked in his mind if they had a common factor, although the resultant phrase might not include that factor.[307]

304. See my "Vespasiano Gonzaga and Shakespeare's imagined Italy" in Temenos Academy Review No.4, London, 2001.
305. M.P.Tilley: English Proverb Lore in Lyly's "Eupheus" and in Pettie's "Petite Palace" N.Y. 1926, quoted in J.L. Lievsay: Stefano Guazzo and the English Renaissance, North Carolina, 1961, p.55.
306. e.g. K.Muir: Shakespeare's Sources London, 1957, p.122. "...the attack on cosmetics in Hamlet. resembles a passage in Guazzo's Civile Conversation (II, pp 10 - 13)"and Harold Jenkins (ed) The Arden Shakespeare: Hamlet, Methuen, London and New York, 1982, p. 497, notes the same parallel between Hamlet III i 144 and Guazzo ii 13: "A woman taking away and changing the colour and complexion which God hath given her taketh unto her that which belongeth to a harlot."
307. K.Muir: Op.cit,, p.15.

We can look, then, for continuities of thought in Shakespeare's writing which might contain material (words or thoughts) which are not continuous in the text (or texts) where he found them. We can look for thoughts and associations in the source which, in Shakespeare's reformulation, become displaced and coalesced with material from other sources. And we can look for the construction, in Shakespeare's syntheses, of complete, complex and believable human characters where, in the fragments which he brought together in forming them, such unity was either absent or barely perceptible.

As the guests are releasing themselves, in turn, from the state of 'solitariness' in which the first game had placed them, Lord William, the last to do so, is asked:

> *Who were more in number, men living, or dead men? To whom he aunswered, Men living, because the dead men are not at all. [….] But in the meane while, Cavallero did not surcease to replie to L. William's aunswere: viz. That the dead are not at all, with saying thus, This aunswer of yours L. William, is more litterall, then substanciall, but yet I think that according to your meaning and the bare words, it may stand with reason, that there are not more dead men, but rather more living, because Plato was wont to say, that during this present life, we are as dead men, and that our bodies are our owne sepulchres, meaning to inferre thereby, that we begin to live, when we dye. Whereupon, according to this construction, we that are living must be accompted dead, and those that are dead, must be thought as living, the which graunted, most true it is, that ther are in number more living men, then dead.*

Light-hearted though the context may be, this passage renders problematic the notions of being and not being. Discussion of dead men leads (steered, needless to say, by Lord Hercules) to men who are killed by the cruelty of their mistresses:

> *These speeches did give the Queene some occasion to tell him [Vespasiano], that shee did infallablie perceave, by so apparant blaming of women that some Ladie or other was at open defiance, and war with him. Ah Madame (said he) I would it pleased love, that the matter were brought to such a passe, because at some one time, I might come face to face with armes and blowes to ende all my sorrows at once.*

At the end of the party, when conversation has turned light heartedly to the subject of sleep, Lord John quotes a proverb:

> *The high Almaine drinkes out his sorrow.*
> *The French man singes his out.*
> *The Spaniard consumes his in lamentations.*
> *And the Italian sleeps his out.*

> *Truelie, added Lorde Vespasian, I finde that sleepe is a great lightening and asswaging of sorrowfull thoughts, and therefore by great reason, and good consideration, it is called cosin German to Death, because it doth so neere participate with hir qualities and naturall effectes.*

It seems improbable that so observant a person as Shakespeare would have failed to recognise in Vespasiano, as he appears in Guazzo's account, the character of one of his own social misfits: a man in a state of uncertainty whether he belongs with the living or the dead, who wishes that he could "come face to face with armes and blowes to end all my sorrows at once", who seeks comfort in the death-like "naturall effectes" of sleep. He understood such a human condition famously well:

> *To be or not to be, - that is the question: -*
> *Whether 'tis nobler in the mind to suffer*
> *The slings and arrows of outrageous fortune,*
> *Or to take arms against a sea of troubles*
> *And by opposing end them? - To die - to sleep -*
> *No more; and by a sleep to say we end*
> *The heart-ache, and the thousand natural shocks*
> *That flesh is heir to.…*

The word 'natural', though displaced in its literal meaning, seems to echo a common substructure in the thoughts which both passages express.

We need only note, in drawing attention to this parallel, that Vespasiano did say some strikingly Hamlet-like things and that, conversely, Shakespeare's play can give us a way of seeing Vespasiano which would not have been evident to the majority of their contemporaries. Hamlet, quintessentially, represents the complexities and internal conflicts of an emerging 'early modern' man and Vespasiano's words are evidence that such a man did not come into being because Shakespeare wrote *Hamlet*: more precisely, Shakespeare wrote *Hamlet* because he knew that such men were beginning to exist in the world.

In the light of the Shakespearian resonances which we may have found in Guazzo's account of the supper party at Casale, it is perhaps worth recording that probably the worst 'shakespearian' speech ever committed to paper was put into the mouth of Vespasiano Gonzaga. *Sabbioneta - a Drama in Three Acts*, was performed at the Bijou Theatre in London on 9th September 1896, of which the following brief extract must suffice:

> *(Vespasiano soliloquises). Oh, thou flaming cresset that swing'st harmoniously i' the ordering o' the laws of nature, 'tis easier to stay thy progress i' the amethystine air, than for that frail creation the heart of woman to pulsate with one throb of honesty.* [308]

308. L.C. Falbe, Sabbioneta, A Drama in Three Acts, London, 1907. Act II, Scene 3.

There is one further 'conversation' worthy of some brief attention, although it can be reconstructed only by inference and by virtue of the influence which it seems to have exerted upon Vespasiano. In 1588, a diet was convened in Prague, intended to sort out the embarrassing situation created when Maximilian, brother of the emperor Rudolf II, was elected king of Poland and attempted unsuccessfully to take the kingdom by force from its incumbent ruler, Sigismond, by whom he was taken prisoner. At Rudolf's instigation, Vespasiano, along with two other notables, was asked to attend as representatives of King Philip. Setting off from Sabbioneta in June, 1588 and returning in April, 1589, Vespasiano must have spent something like six months at Rudolf's court in Prague. Rudolf and Vespasiano had been acquainted since Rudolf's boyhood in Spain and it was Rudolf who had elevated Sabbioneta to the status of an independent dukedom.

From those historians who like to see their kings and emperors strong, orthodox and uncomplicated, Rudolf has had a bad press. Intelligent enough to see quite clearly that Europe was on the brink of crisis, not only on account of internal conflicts fuelled by the advance of protestantism and the rivalry of France and Spain but also under immediate threat from Turkish forces poised on the Empire's eastern borders, Rudolf chose to do as little about any of this as possible. Abandoning his excessively exposed capital of Vienna, he established at Prague (a city of whose population only ten percent were Catholic) a retreat from the tormented world outside, in which every form of unorthodox intellectual enquiry and artistic experiment was allowed to flourish. Significant scientific research (Kepler succeeded Tycho Brahe in 1600; Clusius, the botanist, had already worked for Maximilian II) progressed alongside urgent but inconclusive magical and alchemical projects; while Spranger was painting perversely erotic scenes of classical mythology, Roelant Savery was opening up new artistic avenues with his studies of flowers and landscape and Archimboldo was making his 'composed' portraits, heads made from vegetables and fruit. John Dee, the English Rosicrucian, and Giordano Bruno were active in Rudolf's Prague. Emblematists, antiquarians (we have already encountered Jacopo Strada), poets, (including the English poetess, Elizabeth Jane Weston) found protection there.[309]

To speak of an 'influence' upon Vespasiano, resulting from his six-month stay at the court of Prague, would be to impose an oversimplified model in the absence of any evidence to indicate with which, if any, of the diverse (and often contradictory) intellectual currents which were to be found there, he may have been in contact. It seems more to the point, in any case, that Vespasiano could have encountered circles where attitudes and preoccupations similar to his own were entertained and the evolving priorities of his final years reflected and confirmed. The visit to Prague seems, at least, to have reinforced a change of mood which was already evident during the preceding years. Two months after his return, as we have noted earlier, Vespasiano took down the busts of famous generals which had decorated his Corridor Grande, replacing them with the horns of various animals and other naturalia, much of it sent from Prague. Such an interest in 'scientific' knowledge was not new to Vespasiano (he was building his giant sundial, with Bernardino Baldi, already in 1583) but the contemplation, part philosophical and part aesthetic, of natural objects had acquired the stamp of external authority. Baldi's epigram is evidence that he (and thus, one must imagine, Vespasiano) was aware of the implications of recent advances in scientific knowledge:

> If venerable Ptolemy could have used
> The glass which Galileo has introduced,
> From Atlas' height he could have told with ease
> Stars, fishes, grass, flowers, birds and trees. [310]

309. For a thorough account of Rudolf's entourage, see R.J.W. Evans, Rudolf II and his World, Oxford, 1973. Western European coverage of the subject is disappointingly sparse.
310. Quoted in the Introduction to Bernardino Baldi, Le Vite de' Matematici, Ed. Elio Nenci, Milan, 1988.

At Prague, such proto-scientific interests were not constrained within the permissible bounds of orthodox ideology but constituted the driving force behind Rudolf's various enterprises.

For all that the pretext of Vespasiano's journey to Prague had been political, it marked the end of his involvement in any form of external political activity and a progressive withdrawal of interest even in the domestic affairs of Sabbioneta. Vespasiano's attention turned increasingly to his 'country retreat' at Villa Pasquali, a hamlet no more than a kilometre from Sabbioneta.[311] At La Grangia (the name may recall a similarly named rural hermitage near Segovia which was frequented by Philip II), there was a depot for the collection of agricultural and horticultural goods, payment in kind for smallholdings rented out by Vespasiano. Towards the end of 1589, work was started to improve the canal which linked Villa Pasquali with Sabbioneta, not only facilitating the transport of produce but also enabling Vespasiano to travel to his retreat by boat.

Even after its adaptation as a country villa, Vespasiano's house at Villa Pasquali (of which hardly anything remains) was extremely modest in its provision, sufficient only for a minimal household: a loggia with five arches, opening to an androne, a kitchen and two other rooms on the ground floor with a tiled staircase leading to three partitioned rooms and a granaio above. The columns of the loggia appear to have been recycled from some other building although the fireplaces were of elegant design *alla francese*. The androne was decorated with olympian deities, the so-called 'gardener's room' had pastoral scenes framed between lion-headed atlante while the saletta had a fictive, painted loggia of three columns and, in a medallion, the portrait of Rudolf II.

Surrounding the house were, to the west, a courtyard containing thirteen pomegranate trees and, to the east, a large garden (to which the loggia opened) separated by a wall from a small one; to the south was a system of fish-ponds connected, via a grove of nut trees, to the canal. The large garden contained a hundred trees - pears, apples, nuts, chestnuts, plums, figs, mulberries and medlars as well as vines and roses; here, also, there was a fountain with a basin of red marble upon a white marble base. In the small garden were twenty fruit and ornamental trees and an arched pavilion with columns and seats of marble, wooden shutters: the whole decorated with vines and jasmine. Above the fish-ponds there was a portico and a bridge with a dove-cote over it. There were, in addition, stables and a stall for calves.

The scene which is evoked by this reconstruction is one in which Nature is celebrated not so much for the decorative and sensuous qualities which are the theme of so many urbane gardens of the time, as for the fecundity, the productivity of the earth, the water and the air. These are the qualities which give to the Lombard plain its very particular atmosphere, and it seems that Vespasiano wanted, in his rustic retirement, to enjoy the most essential character of the place. He was under no material pressure to ensure a supply of the edible produce of his dominion (his properties in the south provided wine and olive oil and, as we have noted, Vespasiano's culinary tastes were quite frugal) but the sight of such natural fertility seems to have moved him. The 'solitarie and silent place' chosen by Vespasiano in the last years of his life was, nevertheless, one in which the life-giving work of Nature was unequivocally affirmed.

311. See Enrico Rossi and Roberto Marchini, "La Corte della 'Grangia' a Villa Pasquale: Residenza suburbana di Vespasiano Gonzaga" in Civiltà Mantovana, No. 107, Nov. 1988. Their reconstruction is largely based upon inventories and other written sources.

Pt 4

~7)

The Name of the Fathers.
The ancestral talisman and its
architectural redeployment
at Sabbioneta. Rome, ancient
and modern, and its place
in Sabbioneta's virtual history.

The father, the Name-of-the-father, sustains the structure of desire with the structure of the law - but the inheritance of the father is that which Kierkegaard designates for us, namely, his sin.[312]

To a modern reader of psychoanalysis, it might seem an original, even a shocking thought that, in assuming the paternal name, an individual assumes an identity and a place within the social institutions of language and law, substituting a socially constituted for an autonomous enactment of desire. For an aristocrat of the sixteenth century, on the other hand, it would have been hard to imagine any more self-evident truth. In the world inhabited by Vespasiano Gonzaga, a family name was only one amongst many 'linguistic' structures - legal and territorial, heraldic or associative - by which an individual became inserted into a theoretically limitless continuity of ancestors and descendants. The Name-of-the-father, the emblems and the titles which passed through the generations were not the 'property' of any individual but, like a relay runner's baton, tokens of a collective enterprise and a binding force which was undiminished by temporal distance. So crushingly impersonal a vehicle of identity could not, however, coexist easily with the demands of individual self-discovery and expression which, on another reading, one might see as the distinctive characteristic of the Renaissance. The tensions, ambiguities and contradictions inherent in such a predicament are well illustrated in the case of Vespasiano Gonzaga.

Already in 1556, Vespasiano had started to collect portraits of his ancestors, and in his private study and library, at the heart of his ducal palace, the upper part of the walls is composed of a frieze with relief portraits of twelve generations of ancestors (and their wives) and including his own son, Luigi. It seems that he took some trouble to base these portraits on what evidence could be found as to the actual appearance of those persons. Evidently not content with this display of dynastic piety, ten life-size equestrian figures of painted wood were ordered from Venice and, in 1589, placed one behind another along the walls of the salone of the ducal palace: nine generations of the Gonzaga with Vespasiano, riding out together in blue and gold armour. Only four of these figures have survived, so that the effect of their relentless perspective can only be imagined, but one can still feel the power of their presence in the space of the palace. To have embodied these ancestral spirits so forcibly in his 'official' residence might lead one to suppose that Vespasiano had more in mind than merely to assert his hereditary standing and that in part, at least, the display might be seen as an act of propitiation.

In surrounding himself with images of his ancestors, Vespasiano may have been more thorough, in the collection of authentic detail and more forcefully dramatic, in their presentation, than would have been normal in his day, but these actions would not, in themselves, have seemed at all strange to his contemporaries. Less commonplace, perhaps, was the architectural dialogue with his ancestors into which Vespasiano seems to have entered. A family of motifs is to be found in Vespasiano's architecture which had, already, an extensive history - very specific to the Gonzaga dynasty - a history of which Vespasiano was clearly conscious. Re-enacted at Sabbioneta, that history is collapsed and its chronology dissolved. To illustrate this requires a detour.

312. Jacques Lacan,
The Four Fundamental
Concepts of Psychoanalysis,
Harmondsworth, 1979. p.34.

The entablature which crowns Vespasiano's ducal palace (and which may have been substituted for an earlier version more closely referring to Vignola's Palazzo Bocchi) consists, (Fig. 7.4) in accordance with the classical canon, of three superimposed elements: lowest, the architrave (literally, 'main beam') which, in each of the 'orders', stands for the primary element spanning between a pair of columns. Above this, the 'frieze' was the space in which beams running away, perpendicular to the façade, would lie and in the Doric order the ends of these beams are represented in the form of 'triglyphs'. Projecting above the frieze, the cornice stood for the secondary construction of the roof itself and frequently included an array of 'dentils', small blocks which could be understood as the ends of rafters. As a point of principle, if the composition of the entablature was to recall an ideal carpentry construction (as Vitruvius had said that it should), the largest beam would support smaller beams which would, in turn, carry still lighter components:

> .....*if that which in the original must be placed above the principal rafters, is put in the copy below them, the result will be a work constructed on false principles.* [313]

By this definition, the entablature of the ducal palace at Sabbioneta is constructed on false principles: the space of the frieze is filled with enormous brackets which cannot, in any way, be understood as the ends of secondary beams. The zone which they occupy is disproportionate to the whole and the effect is distinctly unclassical. It is not that brackets placed in the frieze are, in themselves, a shocking innovation: they appear at the topmost level of the Colosseum in Rome and were taken up, during the Renaissance, by a number of architects including Alberti (Palazzo Rucellai, Florence) and Bramante (cloister of Sta. Maria della Pace, Rome) and, later, by Peruzzi and Serlio. It is their exaggerated size and the evident determination, at Sabbioneta, not to resemble any classical prototype which seems to call for further explanation.

313. Vitruvius, The Ten Books on Architecture, tr. M.Hickey Morgan, Dover, New York, 1960. Book IV, Cap. 3, p.109.

314. *According to Vasari, Le Vite dei piu celebre Pittori, scultori e Architetti,, Florence, 9125, p.304 (life of Filippo Brunelleschi), Fancelli was in charge of the first phase of construction of the Pitti Palace: "Fu esecutore di questo palazzo Luca Fancelli, architetto Fiorentino, che fece per Filippo molte fabbriche, e per Leon Batista Alberti la cappella maggiore della Nunziata di Firenze, a Lodovico Gonzaga." Vasari is hardly to be relied upon in this case, as in others where he had no direct knowledge of the subject.*

315. *Ibid. p.579. Burckhardt's observation (Burckhardt, J., The Architecture of the Italian Renaissance, tr. J. Palmes, Ed. P. Murray, London, 1985, p.43) is interesting: "the Florentine cornice had a predecessor in the embattled parapet carried on strongly projecting consoles.." To make sense, this would have to refer to Palazzo Medici Ricardi and not, as the text implies, to Palazzo Strozzi.*

316. *Jim Law, in Chambers and Martineau, Op. Cit., catalogue item 34, p. 124, notes the anomaly: However, the original military purpose of the building is evident in the towers and crenellations of thoroughly Lombard flavour ..... Local building practice was yet to form a true partnership with the imported classicising style. But there is no evidence that a literally military imperative lay behind this feature of the palace.*

317. *In the Palazzo del Podestà in Mantua, in rural mansions at Motteggiana and San Michele in Bosco as well, on the evidence of surviving correspondence, as parts of the Castello at Gonzaga. See Vasic Vatovec, C., Luca Fancelli - Architetto, Epistolario Gonzaghesco, Florence, 1979, p.273.*

To trace the origin of Vespasiano's aberrant entablature design, we must look back rather more than a century, to 1451, when Luca Fancelli was put in charge, by Lodovico Gonzaga (second marquis of Mantua, Vespasiano's great-great-grandfather) of the design and construction of his provincial palace at Révere, on the south bank of the Po. Insofar as he is recognised by architectural history, Fancelli is, of course, primarily known as the technical expert to whom was entrusted the realization of Alberti's two mantuan churches, San Sebastiano and Sant'Andrea. His arrival at the Gonzaga court appears to have been in 1450, nine years before Alberti's first known visit; he had been summoned by Lodovico II on the recommendation of Cosimo de' Medici, having previously worked in Florence on projects associated with Brunelleschi and, possibly, Alberti[314]. The 'palazzo' at Révere, on which work had already started, was, in effect, a substantial country villa destined for use by members of the Gonzaga family as a place for hunting, entertaining and, quite often, avoiding the plague. If there was any florentine precedent for such a building (Michelozzo's Villa Medici at Fiesole was only started in 1451) it seems that Fancelli, in his first independent commission, chose to ignore it. (Fig. 7.1) The façade, though symmetrically ordered, is extremely plain; its only use of an order al'antica is in the half columns of the pedimented doorway and the tall rectangular shape of the windows, framed only by a slender architrave, has nothing in common with the arched double windows of contemporary florentine palaces. The displacement of the windows towards the centre or to the extremities of the façade was to become a recurrent feature in lombard and venetian architecture. The most striking element of the facade is, however, the array of blind, non-functional, ghibelline crenellation which crowns the composition: very un-florentine, very un-renaissance.

It seems likely that, during the 1450's, there were numerous cases where an array of ghibelline crenellation had been walled-in as its function in military defence had slipped into disuse; no doubt Fancelli and his patron would have seen them. What was remarkable in the palazzo at Révere was that the device should be introduced self-consciously as an architectural motif in a building which had, in any case, no specific defensive purpose. It is equally surprising that a young artist, trained in the architectural culture of the florentine Renaissance, should have allowed himself to be responsible for a design which, though clearly advanced (one cannot say 'modern' since, in the parlance of the Renaissance, this would have been understood as Gothic, as opposed to 'antique') in relation to either florentine or lombard architectural traditions, should give such emphatic prominence to a feature evidently adapted from medieval precedent. In the case of a contemporary florentine palace, it would have been in the design of its crowning entablature that its architect's command of antique precedent would particularly have been demonstrated (it was for this feature of his Palazzo Strozzi that la Cronaca was especially praised[315]).

Certainly, the architectural effect of Fancelli's 'crowning' is uncomfortable to the eye of anyone accustomed to the formal language of the high Renaissance[316], but the motif reappears in subsequent works of a non-military nature with which Fancelli is known to have been involved[317]. With two rather strange exceptions to which we shall return, the motif of blind ghibelline crenellations dropped out of use after Fancelli's death in 1495.

One can only guess at the circumstances which could have led to the adoption of so clumsy a device for the crowning of the palace at Révere. It is most improbable that the idea came from Luca Fancelli, who would have been anxious to show off his florentine refinement, so one must suppose that it was done at the patron's instigation. Lodovico Gonzaga was, by the standards of his time and social position, a very well educated person (a pupil of Vittorino da Feltre's famous school at Mantua, which Lodovico's father had established), eager to exhibit an up-to-date cultural orientation, and whose court at Mantua was amongst the most brilliant in Italy. The architectural references available to him were, nevertheless, quite strictly limited: no treatise had yet been published in the '50s and the handful of partially completed works by Brunelleschi or Michelozzo which Lodovico might have seen in Florence could offer him no guidance as to the appropriate external appearance of a rural palace. One can easily imagine, then, that for Lodovico, at this early stage of his engagement with architecture, it was not yet possible to conceive of a palatial facade which was not finished off with crenellation. Quite simply, for him, that was how palaces were. One can also imagine that as time went by, as Lodovico's visual training in the new florentine manner progressed, he would have come to realize that blind ghibelline crenellations were not the proper answer; that they simply didn't look right.

There is indirect corroboration for this (and an indication that Vespasiano would have been aware of the issue) in a passage in Baldi's *Descrizione* of the ducal palace at Urbino:

> *Regarding that embellishment of the roof, which is almost like the crown and perfection of the entire façade, it should be known that instead of those large cornices which run round the inside, outside there are projecting modillions of carved wood, between which, forming a soffite, there is left a square which, edged with a moulding, leaves space for a very large rosette and this, accompanied by other ornaments, produces a very beautiful effect. This decoration was added when the eaves of the roof were made to project; since, as can be seen with crenellations whose gaps have been walled in, there was a plan to ring the whole building with crenellations in the style of a castle so as to match the design of the old building which, instead of a roof, had crenellations of this sort: but judging that this would be neither useful nor elegant, it was decided to make the roof project with the ornament which can be seen today.*[318]

Unlike his friend the duke of Urbino, Lodovico was evidently unwilling to abandon altogether the idea that his palaces should appear in military dress (the 'domus nova', safely within the fortified enclosure of the ducal palace at Mantua, was a different matter) and either he or Fancelli soon hit upon a much happier formula. Freestanding in front of the palazzo at Révere is a surviving fragment of the earlier medieval fortezza. (Fig. 7.1) It is similar to many defensive structures in this area dating from the thirteenth and fourteenth centuries and is ringed by machicolations which support a gallery from which defenders could drop boiling oil or pitch onto the heads of their enemies. Towers such as this are clearly functional, rather than decorative, both in conception and execution and their function, like that of crenellations, was, by the middle of the fifteenth century, falling into disuse. Symbolically (and, indeed, visually), however, they were still highly charged objects and it was to objects such as these that Lodovico (or Fancelli, or both) seem, now, to have turned their attention.

318. Bernardino Baldi, *Descrizione del Palazzo Ducale d'Urbino, cit., p. 319.*

Although Fancelli is known to have worked on a number of provincial residences, these buildings have almost entirely disappeared. Of particular interest, therefore, is the remaining gateway tower at Gonzaga. (Fig. 7.2) This highly self-confident composition recalls the clock-tower at Mantua[319], with its pedimented gable, its obelisks and tripartite articulation. The façade facing inwards towards the town has the base of its pediment broken by a tall arched opening, possibly echoing that of Alberti's San Sebastiano façade. What is striking and evidently original about the design is, however, the entablature below the pediment in which the frieze is occupied by brackets of precisely the form which we have noted on the ducal palace at Sabbioneta. Either here, or about the same time in a work which has subsequently disappeared, Fancelli seems to have produced a motif which solved the double problem of sustaining a military effect while serving the architectural purpose of a classical entablature.[320]

The scarcity of physical remains testifying to Fancelli's work for the Gonzaga in their provincial centres is, from an historian's point of view, more than compensated by the wealth of correspondence which has been preserved[321]. The Marchese, Lodovico II, appears in his letters as a patron who took a deep personal interest in many aspects of the design and execution of these projects, even taking on the design itself at Saviola, describing himself as Fancelli's 'disciple' and seeking his detailed advice on the 'correct' way of proceeding. Of the architectural features to which specific reference is made, none was the subject of such recurrent interest as was the 'crowning': in August, 1468, for instance, we find Lodovico requesting that the cornice in the 'first' courtyard be similar to that in the 'cortile delle don[n]e'. While we can have no sure way of knowing what either of these was like in this case, there seems to be a clue in relation to the works at Gonzaga, where there are two references to 'ciuffi' as part of the ornament of the 'coronamento' and to the fact that they would involve raising the height of the wall: 'ciuffo' means, literally, 'forelock' and it is tempting to believe (though impossible to establish) that this metaphor, evidently private to Lodovico and his architect, was a reference to the pendant form of brackets such as those which survive in the gateway tower.

That Lodovico Gonzaga and his architect appear, in this correspondence, to be using a private - and, to architectural historians, baffling - term to describe an architectural motif related to the entablature suggests that 'ciuffi' were the fruit of lengthy previous discussion and that they were the architectural resolution of a very particular requirement of the patron. The buildings which were required to manifest Gonzaga power in its provincial centres were those where it would be appropriate to present a military and, to some extent, archaic image such as the formalised representation of machicolation would have evoked. Beyond the requirements of propaganda, however, one might glimpse the trace of a more superstitiously atavistic attachment to the architectural forms of Lodovico's ancestors. In a postscript to a letter to Andrea Mantegna of 1459, Lodovico refers to the anxiety which attended the partial demolition of the Castello San Giorgio:

> We have no need of astrologers now and if you were to go by what they would have predicted to our illustrious father, that the castello of Mantua would be ruined, you would not have guessed that we have half demolished it, as we have done, and that you can expect to live to see the new one standing.[322]

319. Though loosely associated with Alberti, the clock tower seems to have been largely built to Fancelli's design from 1462; the bracketed entablature which surrounds it below the attic storey was probably added later by Bertani.

320. Again, from Urbino, there is evidence that parallel thoughts were in the air. Francesco di Giorgio's sketches for turrets (produced at some time between 1470 and 1490), though they are still terminated with apparently functional crenellations, show these supported by a variety of brackets which, in one case, quite closely resemble those which were introduced by Fancelli at Gonzaga. In no executed work known to be by Francesco di Giorgio is the motif developed, as it was in the Gonzaga territory, but its appearance in the treatise is evidence that, in the architectural culture of Urbino, as in that of Mantua, there was perceived to be an architectural problem in the 'crowning' of dynastic structures.

321. This correspondence is reproduced and summarised in Vasic, op.cit.

322. Ibid., p.184.

Behind the bluster is an implicit acknowledgement of the potency of the old magic still associated in Lodovico's mind with the forms of military architecture so that one might see the perpetuation of archaic motifs by the Gonzaga as evidence that they were unwilling to abandon such forms just in case it was upon their magically protective influence that the continuing fortune of the dynasty depended.

With the arrival of Giulio Romano, to be court painter and architect at Mantua, in 1524, that city was firmly placed on the map as a centre of the most up-to-date visual culture. At the age of twenty-five, Giulio's 'training' in the studio of Raphael was complete but his development as a mature and independent artist took place during the following twenty years in the context of Lombardy and its preexistent artistic and building procedures. Though it is known that he was active as an architect throughout the province, there is hardly a single case, outside the city of Mantua itself (aside from the abbey at San Benedetto Po), in which his hand can be positively identified. There are, however, two locations[323] at which Giulio's involvement is on record, even if in neither case is it certain which parts of the architecture should be attributed to him: at Corte Spinosa and at Casàtico. At both, the motif of exaggerated brackets in the frieze is prominent and in one they appear directly confronting the earlier fancellian motif of filled-in ghibelline crenellations. (Fig. 7.3)

In the last year of his life, Giulio provided a design to extend and upgrade the fortified villa at Casàtico; his client (to use the word 'patron' would be inappropriate in this case) was Camillo Castiglioni, son of Baldassare, author of *The Book of the Courtier*. Baldassare was a close personal friend of Giulio - was, indeed, instrumental in persuading him to move from Rome to Mantua - and it is not unreasonable to assume that the design for these works would reflect an unusual degree of mutual understanding between the architect and his client. The bizarre form of the two gateways which frame the entry sequence to the villa and which clearly belong to this phase of building seems to have escaped critical attention. The outer gateway is crowned by a fancellian blind ghibelline crenellation (a reduced version of which crowns much of the earlier phase of building) while the inner gateway, seen beyond, has paired brackets in the frieze of its 'entablature' which seem directly to quote those of Fancelli's tower at Gonzaga. The juxtaposition of two such archaic references was the sort of 'conceit' which would particularly appeal to an aristocrat with literary, rather than specifically visual leanings. And for an architect whose works were characterised by his contemporary Aretino as "anticamente moderni e modernamente antichi", a double-take of this kind would be not in the least out of character: Fancelli's first and second versions of the formalisation of archaic motifs now held up for ironic inspection.

In its subsequent architectural history, the motif of oversized brackets was to become absorbed into the repertoire of mainstream Mannerism, devoid of any particular dynastic overtones[324]. In works directly connected with the Gonzaga dynasty, however, the fancellian bracket continued to be employed with more earnest intent. Bertani's campanile of the church of Santa Barbara in the ducal palace at Mantua, begun in 1564, brought the family 'badge' into the heart of Gonzaga power while the entablature which he added to the clock tower at Mantua (if it was he who did so) paid Fancelli a compliment which the latter would surely have appreciated. Don Ferrante Gonzaga, Vespasiano's mentor in many respects, initiated a series of urban projects by junior members of the family when, in 1549, he commissioned Domenico Giunti to make a plan for the town of Guastalla. Here, in the ducal palace which dominates the main square, the Gonzaga presence is emphatically stamped on the palace's façade in the form of its heavily bracketed entablature. Again, between 1587 and 1590, Vespasiano's cousin, Giulio Cesare Gonzaga, created a new piazza at Isola Dovarese where the political dominance of the Palazzo Ducale is established through the 'sign' of its bracketed crown.

323. There is also the interesting, proto-palladian Villa Zani at Villimpenta of which Paolo Carpeggiani has written in (Various authors), Corti e Dimore del Contado Mantovano, Florence, 1969: "Un documento dell'architettura di Giulio Romano LA VILLA ZANI DI VILLIMPENTA", pp.49-62.

324. Peruzzi (who might also have seen examples of fancellian brackets during the twenties, when he was working in Bologna) took up the idea while, at the same time, reclaiming it for a more erudite classicism by incising onto the face of large (but quite slim) brackets the triglyph pattern of the Doric order. This version which, through the medium of Serlio's copy books, became widely adopted, served to (re)diffuse (and defuse) the form, now entirely stripped of its original meaning, into commonplace architectural practice.

It seems, then, that, in crowning his ducal palace with a heavily bracketed entablature, Vespasiano was doing nothing out of the ordinary: he was using a sign which, to many people in his day, would have been well understood and this would, indeed, be a disappointing conclusion at the end of so lengthy a digression. That Vespasiano found the motif of particular interest, however, and that he was aware of its history may be confirmed by the appearance, in a painted city view between the windows of the Sala dei Circhi in the garden palace at Sabbioneta, of a structure closely resembling Fancelli's gateway at Gonzaga[325]. (Fig. 7.2) The 'crowning' of the Corridor Grande was evidently the result of further reflection: Caroline Elam[326] refers to its 'crowning fortifications' - wrongly, but one can see why. Here, indeed, the motif of the bracketed cornice would appear to have gone full-circle, to have returned to its atavistic roots; the brackets support semi-circular arches exactly as they had done in the tower at Révere. Before its demolition, the Castello, the fortress of Vespasiano's forebears, formed the opposite side of the piazza. Its fortification had been upgraded by Vespasiano's father, Luigi, who was evidently also responsible for the turreted gateways at Rivarolo and it is not unreasonable to suppose that the architecture of the Castello would have been similar - almost certainly it would have been of exposed brickwork and there would be machicolations. (Fig. 7.4) In responding to a context heavily suffused with the spirit of his ancestors, Vespasiano evidently persisted where the builders of the ducal palace at Urbino had had second thoughts, managing, this time, to invent a crown that was not only useful (in projecting the roof) but also, if not exactly elegant, nevertheless sufficiently classical and powerfully convincing.

If, then, with the design for the crowning of his Corridor Grande, Vespasiano seems to have gone further than his contemporaries in seeking to sustain (even to amplify) the 'linguistic', as opposed to the merely allusive or stylistic resonance of an ancestral motif, this understanding might also illuminate the case of one of his other more puzzling productions. At Commessaggio, where the road from Mantua crossed the Delmona canal (part of the irrigation system supplied by the Oglio, which marked the boundary of the dominion of Sabbioneta), Vespasiano built a bridge and, beside it, a tower which still remains. (Fig. 7.4) This tower, which was built in 1583, appears to be a direct copy of those of the Castello San Giorgio in the ducal palace at Mantua which date from the end of the fourteenth century. Unlike these, however, its crenellations are blind in the fancellian manner. But if the walls and gateways which he built at Sabbioneta were in the most up-to-date manner and could have been effective defensively in the conditions of sixteenth century warfare, Vespasiano, of all people, would be aware that his tower at Commessaggio was both technically and architecturally obsolete and that no potential assailant would pay serious attention to it. The inscription at its base: "Vespasiano, by the grace of God first duke of Sabbioneta, placed this tower to be visible by the river and erected a bridge at the interruption of the road in the year of Our Lord, 1583" suggests that it was intended more as a marker than for any specific military purpose, and its position implies that it was a marker directed towards Mantua. We have seen how ruthlessly Vespasiano had to pursue his claim (just or otherwise) to Commessaggio against his cousins of San Martino dall'Argine, and Vespasiano had more than enough experience of the acquisitive territorial ambitions of his kinsman, Duke Guglielmo whose motives towards Sabbioneta he was fully justified in suspecting. In Vespasiano's mind, the ancestral covenant which he invoked, through the architectural medium of blind ghibelline crenellations, seems to have carried a force undiminished by the transformations of more than a hundred intervening years.

325. The decoration of this room, in which are represented also the reconstructed Circus Maximus and Circus Flaminius, is cited by Kurt Forster (From Rocca to Civitas, Cit., p.27) as an invitation to see the Piazza d'Armi (visible from the window of this room) as "an imagined Palatine" where the architecture of the Corridor Grande seems to echo that of the Circus. We seem to have, here, another case of the 'over-determination' which is characteristic of Vespasiano's productions.
326. Caroline Elam, "Sabbioneta" in AA Files, No.18.

If the symbolic weight of his ancestry seems to have pressed with exceptional force upon Vespasiano, the biographical reality of his circumstances ran starkly contrary to the symbolic ideal. The personal disgrace implicit in the gradual realization, during the last twenty years of his life, that his was likely to be the weak link in the continuity of succession was evidently a reality to which the conventional forms of his time could give no public expression, and it seems that the more certain it became that the male succession was to end in the person of Vespasiano, the more obstinately did Vespasiano reassert, in his public actions, the mythical ideal. As early as 1572, when Luigi, Vespasiano's only son, barely seven years old, was brought to join his father in Spain, it is clear that his health was a constant source of anxiety. In his letter of that year to Ottavio Farnese (from which we have already quoted) one has the impression that Vespasiano was already preparing himself for the outcome which he most dreaded:

> ....both for his education and also from the natural inclinations of a father, I have ordered that my son Don Luis be sent to me in Spain, if his health holds up, with the next sailing and I will keep him with me until he is a bit bigger and then, if we are both alive, I intend to place him in the service of the prince of Spain, being already received by the King as his domestic page. However, in these things, men propose and God disposes.

Luigi's eventual death in 1580 has been the subject (largely fuelled by the graphic but unsubstantiated account - possibly founded in local tradition - of Antonio Racheli[327]) of much morbid speculation, according to which Luigi died three weeks after Vespasiano, in a fit of anger, had kicked him in the groin[328]. However, Vespasiano's letter to Ottavio Farnese shortly after the tragedy of his son's death, suggests that his friend had been kept up-to-date in the development of an illness whose outcome was known to be only a matter of time:

> ....Don Luis my son - it has pleased Our Lord to call him to himself, and to show great mercy to him and to me, since he has for three years been in such a terrible state that he and I have died repeatedly.

If, as is now generally believed, Luigi's death was the result of congenital syphilis, it would be hard to imagine a more bitterly ironic revelation of what the Name-of-the-father might carry with it. This thought is unlikely to have escaped Vespasiano, knowing as he did that he was, as Alessandro Lisca put it, "the cause of his son's death".[329]

327. A. Racheli, Memorie Storiche di Sabbioneta, Cit., pp. 653-4. Racheli even provides dialogue to embellish his narrative.
328. The truth or otherwise of this persistent report will probably never be established beyond doubt. Recent forensic evidence (Mallegni, Bedini & Fornacini, Analisi dei reperti umani in La Tomba di Vespasiano Gonzaga 400 anni dopo. Catalogo per una Mostra, Sabbioneta, 1991, p.100, quoted in note 115 to G. Malacarne: "Gli Stemmi di Vespasiano Gonzaga dal Ramo Cadetto di Sabbioneta" in Atti del convegne.. Cit.) subsequent upon the exhumation of Vespasiano's and Luigi's remains, has revealed no evidence of damage in the area of Luigi's groin but the authors are unable to rule out the possibility that he was kicked 'in the soft parts' It is now generally believed that Luigi died from congenital syphilis.
329. This, and the letter above, quoted Ibid., p.100. For an informative account of the impact of syphilis during the sixteenth century, see Paul Larivaille, La Vita Quotidiana delle Cortigiane nell'Italia del Rinascimento, Milan, 1989, p. 167 ff.

The history of Vespasiano Gonzaga and of Sabbioneta as it was written before the outbreak of the first World War was written by Italians (occasionally, Frenchmen) and belonged, unambiguously, to the history of Italy. In an awakened interest manifested, in 1959, by the publication of Kurt Forster's important paper, the subject has become a part of the international history of art and architecture. Whereas, in the former, one finds frequent references to Sabbioneta as a 'little Athens', in more recent writing Sabbioneta has become emphatically Roman: "both a city and the image of the city"[330]. Vespasiano, by this account, adopts the patricians of ancient Rome as his 'virtual' ancestors. The athenian metaphor was evidently intended to differentiate Sabbioneta in terms of its refined and élitist culture as well, perhaps, as its modest scale, at a time when reference to ancient Rome would have left it undifferentiated from the rest of italian culture. That the years between 1914 and 1959 had seen the emergence of town planning procedures and models in which recourse to antique precedent was, at a level of principle, rejected (perhaps, also, that Mussolini had promoted the EUR suburb of Rome as a direct challenge to both the imperial and the papal cities) could give a modern relevance to the interpretation of Sabbioneta as an intended recreation of the Eternal City. It remains an important question, however: what - aside from the obvious fact that Rome was the paradigm for almost every aspect of renaissance cultural production - might have been particular about Vespasiano's evident preoccupation with roman themes?

Leone Leoni's bronze figure of Vespasiano (illustrated at the head of Chapter 1) portrays him unequivocally in the dress and with the accoutrements of a roman dignitary. The marble column, brought from Rome by Vespasiano's father after the sack of 1527, was set up at Sabbioneta as a significant urban 'marker' (though it is Minerva, tutelary deity of Athens, as it happens, who is placed at the top of this column). The Saletta dei Cesari, a small room on the first floor of the garden palace, is given over entirely to the celebration of roman themes: in the fictive space of a colonnaded loggia, the last six of the first twelve Caesars are represented as statues while monochrome profiles of the first six appear in lunettes at the base of the vault. In the central panel of the vault is a putto clashing cymbals and in monochrome, on either side, are shown the stories of Mutius Scaevola and Horatio Cocles, two heroes of the early Republic each of whom, with reckless courage, held back the invasion of the Etruscan Lars Porsena and each of whom came out of it permanently maimed, the former having lost his right hand and the latter, one of his eyes. (These episodes are represented, also, in the subsidiary decoration of Vespasiano's studiolo as well as the Sala degli Specchi and in the Teatro all'Antico; evidently they were of special significance in Vespasiano's mind.) On the end walls are painted, respectively, Rome personified, between two vanquished barbarians, and Fame, sounding a trumpet of war. No doubt, Vespasiano wanted to recall his own military exploits within the context of this stirring evocation of roman military prowess; it is curious, however, that the scenes of superhuman bravery should be episodes in Rome's very early, republican, history, the protagonists acting in a personal, rather than an 'official' capacity, while the Caesars are no more than mute witnesses to, or inheritors of, the triumph of their city. The two republican stories appear almost consecutively in Livy's History[331], where the narrative is set in the context of an unusual state of social consensus:

330. Kurt Forster, From Rocca to Civitas, Cit., pp. 27-31. Forster suggests that Vespasiano could associate himself with the roman Imperium through his historical elevation (by the Holy Roman Emperor) to the rank of dukedom; with Jupiter and the olympian gods by virtue of the Gonzagas' territorial possession of Virgil's birthplace and, thus, the virgilian myth of Aeneas and, via his Colonna heredity, with the city of Rome itself.
Hanno Walter Kruft, (Städte in Utopia, Cit.), subtitles the lengthy section of the book devoted to Sabbioneta Ein "neues Rom". For him, even the supply, from Rome, of marble for Vespasiano's funeral monument is corroboration of such a reading.
331. Titus Livius (Livy), The History of Rome from its Foundation, Trans. Aubrey de Sélincourt, London, 1971, Vol. I, Book II, pp.115-119.

...the commons were exempted from all tolls and taxes, the loss of revenue being made up by the rich, who could afford it; the poor, it was said, made contribution enough if they reared children. These concessions proved wonderfully effective, for during the misery and privation of the subsequent blockade the city remained united - so closely, indeed, that the poorest in Rome hated the very name of 'king' as bitterly as did the great. Wise government in this crisis gave the Senate greater popularity, in the true sense of the word, than was ever won by a demagogue in after years.

If Vespasiano was thinking about Livy's text (as he is likely to have been) when he selected these two stories to represent an ideal of military dedication, and if, as we are entitled to suppose, he intended to reflect something of himself in the represented scenes, then we might detect, here, some note of irony in relation to his own career of military service under four successive emperors. For whom is the figure of Fame blowing her trumpet of war?

There is abundant evidence, then, to support a 'roman' reading of Vespasiano's intentions: at his inauguration as master of the academy at Sabbioneta, in 1562, Mario Nizolio had referred to that city as "neither more nor less than a new Rome"[332] and some lines from a sonnet addressed to Vespasiano by his friend Bernardino Rota can also be taken as evidence that such thoughts were consciously entertained among Vespasiano's contemporaries:

> *Now Janus' door is closed and peace secure,*
> *And fury, once abroad, is now chained down.*
> *A dauntless heart, strong hands and resolute*
> *Raising up walls and towers, are given to you,*
> *Son of great Remus' father, noble and brave.*[333]

The son of Remus' father was, of course, Romulus and it is reasonable to assume that the reference to his brother (aside from providing a rhyme in the original) is intended to stress the idea that Remus insulted his brother with the suggestion that building fortifications was a pointless exercise. The tone of Rota's sonnet, like that of Vespasiano's, to which it is a reply, is essentially frivolous; the exchange was little more than a game and the thoughts which the sonnets contain, though they are quite elegantly expressed, are frankly inconsequential. In confirming, then, that the metaphor of Rome's foundation to characterise a building project and the identification of a sixteenth-century nobleman with the first Roman were tropes which would come readily to the minds of those with whom Vespasiano was in the habit of exchanging sonnets, Rota's lines might seem, while supporting it, to rob the 'roman' interpretation of Sabbioneta of some of its profundity. Clearly, in any case, Sabbioneta was not intended to resemble Rome in any literal sense. None of Sabbioneta's buildings seems to invite the recollection of a monument, visible in Vespasiano's day, of the ancient city: the Colosseum, for instance, the Pantheon, Theatre of Marcellus or one of the triumphal arches. Rather, one would have to say, Rome is immanent as a felt presence at Sabbioneta, reflecting its prominence in the mental landscape which Vespasiano inhabited.

332. Quoted in Antonio Paolucci and Umberto Maffezzoli, *Sabbioneta, il Teatro all'Antica*, Modena, 1993, p.19.
333. This sonnet is included, together with a number of poems by Vespasiano (of which an account will be found in the following chapter) in his *Vita di Vespasiano Gonzaga, Cit.*, pp.67-72.

In the theatre at Sabbioneta, designed in 1588 by Vincenzo Scamozzi, however, a more direct case for a 'roman' interpretation of Vespasiano's city seems to present itself. It is the only building at Sabbioneta which employs an order both externally and internally; its *cavea*, surmounted by an open colonnade, each column supporting one of twelve olympian deities, fully reproduces the spirit, if not the geometrical construction of Vitruvius' prescription. Figures of roman emperors stand painted at the back of the loggia (the emperor Vespasian directly behind the place where his namesake had his seat). More emphatically, the lateral walls are decorated to simulate triumphal arches through which are to be seen views of Rome. The fixed perspective scene which Scamozzi designed appears, in his drawing, composed of palaces and town houses not unlike those represented in Peruzzi's earlier theatrical projects (Fig. 5.7) and, in the same way that Peruzzi introduced recognizable fragments of ancient roman monuments, looming above the modern street architecture, Scamozzi shows the upper part of what appears to be Trajan's (or Marcus Aurelius') column. Scamozzi's set was destroyed during the eighteenth century and has recently been replaced with a fixed perspective in which buildings of Sabbioneta are clearly identifiable. Even without such literal reification, it is not difficult to infer an intended metaphorical reciprocity of the space of the theatre with the space of Sabbioneta, rendering Vespasiano's city itself 'roman', not just the theatre.

On the external string band above the theatre's rusticated lower floor appears the inscription:

ROMA QVANTA FVIT IPSA RVINA DOCET

"Its very ruin tells what Rome once was." This epigraph[334] (which was quoted by Scamozzi in his *L'Idea della Architettura Universale* and appears also on the title page of Serlio's sixth Book) has its origin in the *Opusculum* dedicated in 1510 to the pope Julius II by the florentine Francesco Albertini, whose purpose was to celebrate the revival of art and architecture in Rome under Julius' leadership. The spirit of its citation at Sabbioneta, as in its original context, is likely to have been far from complacent: both a statement of the challenge posed by the ancient city to its modern inheritors and a reminder of the frailty of even the most spectacular human endeavour. It should not, perhaps, be forgotten that Vespasiano's father, Luigi 'il Rodomonte', took part in the sack of Rome in 1527 (though he appears, subsequently, to have felt uneasy about this[335]) while, in 1556, Vespasiano had (without evident qualms) entered that city, in the company of the duke of Alva, to impose humiliating terms upon the recalcitrant Pope Paul IV. The papal city which Luigi left shattered and which, twenty-nine years later, Vespasiano had again forced into submission did not, aside from a small number of monumental structures quite widely dispersed, present a very impressive spectacle. That the present dereliction of Rome could be an occasion of pity, even of a certain contempt, is evident from a comment in Cardinal da Bibbiena's play *Calandria*, which was performed in Urbino in 1513, with a prologue by Baldassare Castiglione and a fixed scene by Gerolamo Genga:

> The place which you see here is Rome, which was once so ample, so spacious, so grandiose that, in its triumph, it held within itself many cities, countries and rivers; and is now become so small that, as you can see, it can easily fit into your own city. That's how the world goes. [336]

334. *A longer extract from the Opusculum is quoted in Denys Hay, The Italian Renaissance, Cambridge, 1980, Note to p.168.*
335. *See, for instance, the interesting essay of Gianna Pinotti, Un Principe del Rinascimento: La dinastia di Luigi Rodomonte Gonzaga, da Falconetto a Sabbioneta, Sabbioneta, 1996, pp.12-14.*
336. *Quoted in Antonio Pinelli and Orietta Rossi, Genga Architetto, aspetti della cultura urbinate del primo 500, Rome, 1971, p.113.*

Surprisingly, the views of Rome which appear framed in the triumphal Pt 4 ~7 arches to each side of the theatre at Sabbioneta are not views of the ancient city but show, respectively, the Castel Sant'Angelo, complete with a cluster of clearly medieval structures at the top, and, opposite, the Campidoglio with an inaccurate, though recognizable version of Michelangelo's Palace of the Conservators. (Fig. 7.6) The elliptical pavement and equestrian statue of Marcus Aurelius can also be made out. Subsidiary views show unspecific fragments of ruined ancient buildings in a predominantly rural setting populated by 'tourists' in modern dress and locals engaged in country pursuits. The fictive audience and players who look down into the theatre from a painted gallery above are dressed in the style of the 1580s. Evidently, we are invited to think about Rome as it is in Vespasiano's day rather than about its original splendour and we are invited, in particular, to think about two of its visible structures: the Castel sant'Angelo and the Palace of the Conservators. It was in the former that Pope Clement VII was imprisoned following the sack of Rome (Vespasiano's father played a significant role both in his imprisonment and in the negotiation of his subsequent release). The Conservators, whose official seat was the only completed structure of the refurbished Campidoglio, represented, at least symbolically, the legal constitution of the city, independent of papal sovereignty. By an inscription over one of the triumphal arches, this evocation of modern Rome is dedicated to the emperor Rudolf II[337].

Was the architectural - and, literally, theatrical - event which marked the culmination and the completion of Vespasiano's project at Sabbioneta an event in which the emperor was invited to revive his imperium at the site of its origin?

There are several features of Sabbioneta's architecture which are only explicable in terms of an intention that the city would look as though it had an extended history. (Fig. 7.7) The parochial church of Santa Maria Assunta, though its internal arrangements reflect fully up-to-date principles of counter reformation organization, presents itself externally with a distinctly medieval flavour (it bears a strong resemblance in general form to the similarly dedicated church at Fondi, Vespasiano's birthplace). One cannot help wondering why it was considered necessary, during the eighteenth century, to replace its main doorway with the piece of inconsequential baroque design[338] which, on the façade as it appears today, seems so out of place. Was Vespasiano's eclecticism, in this case, offensive to post-tridentine taste? Similarly, the Palazzo della Ragione, in whose unclassically wide-spaced ground floor colonnade Vespasiano appears to have reused shafts and capitals from a medieval structure, is evidently intended to evoke the architecturally naïve constructions to be found in many small towns of Lombardy.

337. DIVO. RVDOLFO II CAESARI. AVGVSTO. FOELICITER. PRINCIPANTI..
338. The present doorway, designed by Natale Tivani, dates from 1726. (Giovanni Rodella, "Sabbioneta dopo Vespasiano: Gli edifici Religiosi di Sabbioneta" in Civiltà Mantovana, No. 13, 1986, p.8.

The overtly 'gothic' windows of the 'public' library embedded in the convent of the Incoronata have been noted. One might note, also, that the 'unfinished' exterior of the octagonal church (said to have been consecrated and therefore, presumably, substantially complete in 1588), where the brick piers which carry the roof above the main walls are left as though keyed to receive some other eventual facing (as so many unfinished italian buildings of the Middle Ages and the Renaissance are), renders the architecture highly ambiguous in terms of its location in time. This, again, could have been deliberate. Unquestionably deliberate is the design of the small fragment of elevated corridor which once linked the garden palace with the Castello. Here, the exposed brickwork is made of square headers, set on the diagonal. The clear reference to roman *opus reticulatum* has been noted[339] as evidence of a humanistic interest in antique precedent but it might, more simply, have been intended to look like the denuded fragment of a pre-existing antique structure.

We have referred, in Chapter 2, to the numerous embellishments which, during the last years of Vespasiano's life, were lavished upon the Castello, rendering it evocative of the world of chivalry and romance: evidently, in constructing the city of Sabbioneta, Vespasiano was anxious that his ancestors - 'virtual', mythical or historical - would not be out of place in it.

339. E.g. Chiara Tellini Perina, *Sabbioneta, Cit., p.36*

~8)

The Mother.
The dark world of
Vespasiano's poetry.
The 'dead mother'
complex and the
myth of Aristeus.

At the end of his *Vita di Vespasiano Gonzaga*, Ireneo Affò, 'so as not to defraud the public', appended six sonnets and two longer poems by Vespasiano which he had been able to assemble from various sources, contenting himself with the comment that in this way 'our Vespasiano can, with better reason, have a place in the class of noble versifiers'. Two of the sonnets and the two longer poems fall into the general category of 'love' poetry, share a number of themes, and appear to address personal, rather than more generally social or cultural issues. At a point where the focus of our enquiry has begun to shift from Vespasiano's transactions in the political and cultural world around him towards the interior life which might have shaped and directed those transactions, this is an appropriate point at which to insert them into our text. Translated, as far as possible, so as to convey the impression of reading the original (which is printed alongside) and to preserve the sense, if not always the literal meaning, of the words, here they are:

Dunque una, ch'io ritrovo un chiaro Sole
A le tenebre mie; una, che tanto
Rivolge in meglio ogni mio interno pianto,
Che l'alma n'ha dolcezze intere, e sole;
Una, che oscura ogni altra, ch'aver suole
Di compita virtute il pregio, e 'l vanto;
Una, che col parlar saggio, e col canto
Fa ch'io conosca Dio, che l'ami, e cole:
Tu, tu folle non vuoi ch'io cerchi, e segui,
Non che pur miri? E chi farà che ancora,
Se non lei, che tu sia vago, e sereno?
Una, che in parte al suo valor s'adegui,
Mi mostra; e se non v'è, consenti almeno
Ch'io viva in lei, perch'ella in me non mora.

172

One, then, a Sun to me who with its rays
Lightens my shadows; one who can so soon
Comfort my inward sorrows, who alone
Brings perfect sweetness to the soul always;
One who obscures all others, who outweighs
All the earth holds, all virtues' paragon;
One whose sagacious words and gentle tone
Turn me to God, to love Him, and to praise:
You, madman, do you forbid me to go near,
Follow or even look? Who, if not she,
Can make you peaceful or content? Show me
One, then, even in any part her peer,
And if there be none so, at least allow me
My life in her, hers that she lives in me.

Untitled Sonnet 2.

Non sento aria giammai tranquilla, o ria,
Ch'io non dica: ecco il suono, ecco le note
Di lei, ch'or l'alma allegra, or la percote
Coi modi, che virtute, ed amor cria.
E se amor lungo il Tago ancor m'invia,
O in poggio, o in campo, o in parte al Sole ignote,
Allor veggio i bei crin, le vaghe gote,
E i cari lumi, come già solia.
Ho l'idea così fissa, e sì tenace
Il pensiero, che appena ora descrivo
Una di mille, in cui la scorgo, forme.
Oh se sapesse almen, ch'in quelle or vivo!
Fora la speme al gran desir conforme,
Ed io con più ragion forse più audace.
I never hear the wind, peaceful or shrill
But say: these sounds are hers, who now caresses,
And now abrades the soul, by turns expresses
The changing moods that virtue and love distill.
When by the Tagus, wandering at love's will,
By field, or hill, or woodland's dark recesses,
I see those fair cheeks and those lovely tresses,
The light of those dear eyes that haunts me still.
So firmly is the thought now taken hold,

Hardly, by now, have I begun to list
The myriad forms she takes before my eyes.
If she but knew that by them I exist!
Hope, then, would be more equal to the prize,
And I, with better cause, perhaps more bold.

173

Dolor d'Aristeo

Stanco omai di tacer, d'amar non sazio
L'infelice Aristeo piagato, ed arso,
E vinto alfin dal tormentoso strazio,
E del fuoco, che amor nel petto ha sparso,
Aprì le porte al duol di sì gran spazio,
Che il pianto a traboccar non fu già scarso,
Che l'ode il monte, e l'arenosa sponda,
Che il ligustico mar percote, e innonda.

L'alte querele, e que' focosi venti,
Che movea di sospiri a un freddo core,
Al cor di quella, che con gli occhi intenti
Scorgea nel fronte d'Aristeo l'ardore,
Eco sola risuona; e tu non senti,
O fredda Luna, il grave alto dolore?
E di lamenti al suon doglioso, e rauco
Triton pur pianse, Melicerta, e Glauco.

Sorrow of Aristeus

Silent too long, weary with grief untold,
Now Aristeus, burned and lacerated
With fire that in his breast has taken hold,
Yielding at last to torment unabated,
Throws open wide in outburst uncontrolled
The doors which weeping had before frustrated;
The mountains hear, and sandy beaches wide
Beaten and washed by the ligurian tide.

To high complaints that still could move a tear
From a cold heart, to breath of burning sighs,
Her heart, who clearly sees love's pain appear
In Aristeus' brow, only replies
An echo. You, cold moon, did you not hear
That wild outpouring of his miseries?
At such harsh clamour, Triton in ocean deep,
Glaucus and Melicerta too, would weep.

Lasso, dicea, s'alta cagion fur sempre
Alteri affetti, ond'alto onor s'acquista,
Alte son le mie voglie, alte le tempre,
Che move del mio Sol l'altera vista;
Alteramente ard'io, benche altri tempre
Con sì poco sperar l'altezza mista:
Ma se il mio ardor senza speranza è un giuoco,
Che sarebbe sperando il mio gran fuoco?

Per quella pura neve, ond'esce il fuoco,
Ch'ogni mia speme tra le fiamme agghiaccia,

Tanti lacci amor tende, che ben poco
Giova il fuggir, o contrastar ch'uom faccia.
Tant'amaro piacer dal casto loco
Piove, che il gran desìo perde la traccia;
Perchè attento a mirar l'alte faville
Teme d'un laccio, ed è poi colto in mille.

If noble cause a noble spirit drives
To noble deeds and honour's acquisition,
From high desires that fatal power derives
That draws me, alas, to my Sun's noble vision;
My passion's noble, though in it there lives
So little hope, mixed in such high ambition:
If, without hope, my passion's just a game,
What, hoping, would be the measure of that flame?

And I, amid those fire-bearing snows,
The flame where all my hope's in ice compacted
Caught in the nets which love so densely throws
Can by no human effort be extracted.
From that chaste spring such bitter sweetness flows
That longing from its course is soon distracted
And, in that dazzling light, so much enraptured,
Fearing just one, by a thousand snares is captured.

Oh quante volte il doloroso core
Quasi presago di futuri affanni,
Fuggi miser, dicea, fuggi l'ardore
Dolce, ed acerbo, e i dilettosi danni;
Che se il fuoco de gli occhi, armi d'Amore
Arder può l'Istro, che gelò tant'anni,
Può l'arsa Libia al più fervente cielo
Gelar del petto l'indurato gelo.

Da l'altra parte il gran desìo che scorge
L'esca de la beltà, nè vede gli anni,
Esser, dicea, non può, se il ciel ne porge
Sì vaga Dea, che non gradisca, ed ami:
Se amor per questa a tanta gloria sorge,
Ragion è ben, che tal vittoria brami:
Già prodotta non l'hanno i monti Caspi,
Non i monti Risei, non gli Arimaspi.

How often does my troubled heart lament,
As though prophetic of new miseries,
Flee, wretch, it cries, flee the entanglement
Bitter and sweet, delicious injuries;
If fire of the eyes, Love's armament,
Can boil the Danube that cold seasons freeze,
So, that hard frozen heart can turn to ice
Libia's scorched desert under flaming skies.

But, contrary, the voice of my desires,
Seeing beauty's bait, not future misery,
If Heaven provides, it says, duty requires
That you should love so rare a Deity:

175

And love which to such glorious end aspires
Gives reason to seek such a victory.
On Caspian heights her like has never been
On Arimaspi nor on Risean mountain seen.

Io, lasso, offeso dal soverchio lume,
Che aprian quegli occhi quasi duo levanti,
L'alte volgie bagnar di Lete al fiume
Tentai, non basso esempio a mille amanti,
E il gran Motor pregai giugnesse piume
A l'alma, che fuggìa lungi da' pianti;
Ma tal piacer precipitava al corso,
Che il desìo ruppe di ragione il morso.

But I, alas, suffering in the glare
Of those twin rising suns that light her eyes,
In Lethe's flood would drown my deep despair,
The remedy that many a lover tries,
And pray the great Mover give me wings to bear
My soul in flight far from my miseries;
But soon such hope of comfort falls by the way
As wild desire overthrows reason's sway.

Sopra un ritratto

Quando lontano dal fatal mio Sole
Di rividerlo il gran desio m'accende,
Verso l'alme bellezze altere, e sole
Con l'ali del pensier l'alma s'estende:
Ivi s'annida, ed indi uscir non vuole,
Che vede il volto, e le parole intende;
Ma se più oltre il pensier passa, io sento,
Che pensando al mio ben cresce il tormento.

Perchè conforme al gran piacer, che sente
Chi gode appieno il desìato bene,
E' il dolor, che un amante allor che assente
Sta dal suo caro pegno, e sol s'attiene
Al ben passato, ed al dolor presente,
Al certo affanno, a la dubbiosa spene;
E se pur col pensiero ha qualche pace,
E' più lieve che 'l vento, e più fugace.

Over a portrait

When, far away, I burn to see that face
My guiding Sun, and longing to be near,
On wings of thought my soul extends in space
Toward kindred beauties, noble, high and rare:
There will it lodge, nor will it leave the place
Wherein that visage and that voice appear.
But thought, reaching too far, I now confess,
Promising comfort, adds to our distress.

Since, equal to the joy, to counterpose,
For one who tastes in full his wanted pleasure,
The misery which every lover knows

Who, separated from his dearest treasure,
Happiness past retains, and present woes,
Faint hope, certain despair in equal measure;
And if, in thought, we find some little ease,
It stays no longer than the fugitive breeze.

Ond'io, che col pensar pace non spero
Trovar allor che il gran desìo m'infiamma,
Poichè non posso con l'obbietto vero
Smorzar del petto mio l'accesa fiamma,
Con gli occhi, con la mente, e col pensiero,
Che non ne lascio pur picciola dramma,
Miro sua bella immagine, che priva
D'ogni uman senso par pietosa, e viva.

Tosto che a gli occhi il desìato obbietto
Si mostra, ed indi poi trapassa al core,
Come tranquilla in l'arenosa letto
Il mar placato il boreal furore;
Così tranquilla in me l'ardente affetto
L'accesa voglia, e l'infiammato ardore:
E vorrei tutto trasformarmi in vista,
Tant'alta speme nel mirarla è mista.

While I, who do not hope for ease, or ending
Of longings that have set my heart on fire,
To soothe my burning fever, apprehending
The living object of my fierce desire,
With eyes intent, each faculty attending,
To the last drop, absorbing it entire,
Gaze on that likeness, tender and forgiving,
Which, lacking human senses, still seems living.

No sooner seen, the object of devotion
From eye to heart immediately passed,
As sandy shallows still the sea's commotion
And calm the fury of the north wind's blast;
So, in my breast, all turbulent emotion
And fiery thoughts are pacified at last:
Then to pure vision would I change my state,
Such high hope does that image intimate.

Perchè le narro allora i miei sospiri,
Le mie vegghiate notti, i giorni amari,
Il timor, la speranza, e que' martiri,
Che forse col morir giostran di pari;
E che lontan da lei gli eterni giri
Mi son d'ogni altro ben tenaci, e avari:
Ma narrando il mio duol, lasso, m'avveggio,
Che si finisce il mal, comincia il peggio.

Perchè tacendo lei, che nulla sente
De' miei gravi martir, de le mie pene,
La speme, che pur dianzi era presente,
O s'allontana, or tormentosa viene.
Così raddoppia il mal sì fieramente,
Che a debol filo il viver mio s'attiene;

Che la speranza, ove tradir s'è vista,
Tutto il regno d'amor turba, e contrista.

So, full of sighs, I tell her of my plight,
The sleepless nights, the day's bitter remorse,
My fears, my hopes, the miseries which fight
Even with death, perhaps, in equal force;
How, far away from her, my restless flight
Affords no comfort to relieve its course:
Alas, telling my pain, I now believe,
A worse begins with my first pain's reprieve.

She, nothing hearing of the loud lament,
Of my incessant pain, nothing replies,
And hope, which only now seemed permanent,
Now ebbs away, now back, tormenting, flies.
Doubling my anguish with so fierce intent,
My spirit's fragile bond almost unties;
And showing, now, that hope is mere illusion
Convulses love's domain in bitter confusion.

Ond'io che il mesto cor tengo tra l'onde
De gli affetti tra lor contrarj sempre,
Nè veggo poi l'amate chiome bionde,
Nè il volto, onde convien che mi distempre,
Nè scorgo, ahi lasso, que' begli occhi, d'onde
Escono i strai de le più fine tempre,
Conchiudo alfin, che l'aspra lontananza
E' quel martir, ch'ogni martire avanza.

And I, my anguished heart tossed to and fro
By swell of passions constantly at war,
See not 'beloved golden tresses' now,
Cruel occasion of my soul's uproar,
That face, alas, those lovely eyes, which throw
Beams of the purest light, I see no more.
In separation, now, I recognise,
That pain which every pain intensifies.

For a modern reader (even, perhaps, to one in Vespasiano's day), these 'love' poems must present a number of difficulties. In the first place, they are highly artificial; despite (or, possibly, because of) the hyberbole with which the emotions of joy or suffering are represented (like the exaggerated gestures represented in Mannerist painting), it is difficult to recognise them as genuine or believable. The 'loved one' is allowed no recognisable identity, age, place or even, at times, distinctive gender, being employed more like a piece of stage furniture, described in superlatives of such a conventional and general nature that it is hardly a human being at all which comes to mind. In the same way, when personages from classical mythology, places or natural phenomena are evoked, they tend to appear extraneous to the thoughts being developed, having no organic necessity in the poetic structure.

In the second place, it must be admitted that these poems appear, in many places, to lack a consistent purpose or direction, to shift uncomfortably between declamation and analysis, public rhetoric and intimate revelation, as though they had been collaged together from pieces of many and disparate compositions. Their superficial unity, which they derive from their tightly controlled metrical structure and rhyme, belies a restless iteration between possibilities of expression where each is taken up for a while, tried out and then abandoned before it has been allowed to encompass a completed poetic experience.

Thirdly, and perhaps more seriously, these poems are evidently written in a state of total self-absorption; they have no subject other than the mental condition of the writer, inhabit no landscape or imaginative territory outside of Vespasiano's agonised self-examination. They are, for this reason, extraordinarily bleak, arid and monochrome; the self-pity which seems to infect almost every line tends to alienate, rather than to attract the reader's sympathy, and the world in which we find ourselves, reading these poems, is one from which we rapidly wish to escape.

To be sure, from an aesthetic point of view, these are objections which must point to the thought that Vespasiano was not among the world's great poets. One can see, in this sense, why they have been neglected. Our present interest in these poems is not, however, purely aesthetic (although it is hoped that an aesthetic dimension will emerge in what follows) since, if nothing else, these poems must be able to tell us something about the mind of the man who wrote them, beyond the face value of the text itself. It should be clear to any reader that Vespasiano was not particularly concerned in these, as he might have been in some of his poems quoted earlier, to demonstrate wit or erudition for their own sakes. One has a strong impression that the 'love' poems are intended to convey - if only to himself - something that was of great importance to him and, furthermore, that, in committing these thoughts to the exacting discipline of metre and rhyme, he would seem to have attached a value to them as objects for aesthetic attention. We know, in any case, that Vespasiano was by no means ignorant or stupid in relation to literature, that he was deeply read in both classical and modern poetry and fully conversant with the critical discourse of his own day. Rather, then, than dismiss these poems as the work of an untalented aristocrat who believed, nevertheless, that writing poetry was among the accomplishments which a man of his class ought to display, it seems appropriate to give Vespasiano, in this case, the benefit of the doubt, trying to uncover what it was in them that made them, in his mind, worth the considerable effort of writing them. It may be that the defects of these poems turn out to be, in themselves, pointers towards the condition which lay behind them.

To begin with the most problematic: 'The Sorrows of Aristeus' exhibits to a high degree all of the defects which have been mentioned. Opening in declamatory style with the image of a being who, no longer able to contain his grief in silence, gives vent to a great howl of misery in an empty nocturnal landscape of mountains and sea coast (some of these lines are, in themselves, quite effective), the second verse ends, unconvincingly, almost comically, with the names of three maritime deities who should be moved to tears. What follows is neither believable as the uncontrolled outpouring of grief we are led to expect nor as the sort of utterance which would move anyone to tears. Instead, we are taken through a series of tightly argued positions regarding the abstract notion of love, presented as noble aspiration, as dangerous entrapment, as cause for final retreat from life itself, a play of conflicting impulses worked through with some psychological precision but also with a curious mental detatchment. The subject interrogates itself with neither pity nor partiality.

Why, in any case, are these thoughts attributed to Aristeus? Unless Vespasiano's reference is so arcane as to be inaccessible to further investigation, we must assume that the figure intended is the wandering son of Apollo and Cyrene who eventually settled and became a successful bee-keeper; who fell in love with Eurydice and, by his pursuit of her, caused her death from snake-bite and his own punishment in the loss of all his bees. Advised by his mother, he visits Proteus, holds on to him through all his self-transformations and extracts from him the cause of his predicament and the course of action which will bring back his bees. In this curiously amoral narrative[340] there is little to suggest that the distress which Aristeus suffered resulted from an unhappy love but, rather, from the loss of his economic well being. The reference appears, on the face of it, and like the seemingly random invocation of maritime deities, the ligurian sea (Aristeus is not recorded as having visited this coast, though he did get as far as Cumae) or the mountains which had not produced 'her' equal, to be little more than allusion for allusion's sake, demonstrating the poet's knowledge of classical texts without any particular poetic intent. Or was there rather more to it than that?

In 'The Sorrows of Aristeus', a theme emerges which runs, in one form or another, through all of the 'love' poems: a paralysis of the will induced by the conflicting impulses of hope and fear. We have come across this before, at Guazzo's dinner party, where Vespasiano contributes to one of the conversation games:

> *I present you a confusion, which hope and feare conversing together, have engendered in my breast.*

340. My source here is Lemprière's Classicasl Dictionary, cit., p.76. Other versions, e.g. Enciclopedia Italiana, Rome, 1934, provide much detail of the geography of Aristeus' travels and the cults devoted to him but allude only in passing to his connection with the myth of Orpheus and Eurydice.

Neither in that conversation nor in 'The Sorrows of Aristeus' is the nature of his hope nor the origin of his fear given any identifiable form or focus; he seems to indicate an existential condition rather than an externally provoked reaction. In the first Sonnet, the same thought is given a more precise definition: after an evocation of the object of his love in whose entirely conventional terms there is barely a trace of specific personal feeling, Vespasiano abruptly splits himself into two opposed voices, one that seeks for solace in the contemplation of his love and another who forbids it. Significantly, it is the voice of command or repression which is branded as a 'madman'. In the last line, we have an indication that the poem has other overtones than merely the repression of an erotic impulse: The words are lifted almost directly from Juan de Valdès' *Christian Alphabet:* "che sempre tu, Signore mio, viva in me et io viva in te."[341] Without wishing to suggest that the sonnet is intended to carry a 'coded' religious message, one might, nevertheless, take this reference as evidence that the poem addresses more complex issues than simply the state of being 'in love'.

In the second sonnet there seems, at first sight, to be more engagement with a world outside of Vespasiano's own mental condition, a world which becomes the projection of a personality apparently not his but whose mercurial nature enables him to see an aspect of her in every external object which he encounters. The last three lines, on the contrary, bring us back to the private world of his own thoughts and impulses and to the paralysing conflict of hope and fear which, it now seems, 'she' could resolve if only she could understand that his identity depends upon her projected presence in the world around him. This is a complicated and difficult thought which, though it does not exclude the obvious inference that he was, indeed, thinking about a particular person as he wandered beside the Tagus - a person with whom he may well have been in love while he was in Spain - suggests, at the same time that, in thinking about himself thinking about 'her', he was confronted, yet again, with the contradictions of his own psychological state and it is these which, once again, have become the principal subject of the poem.

The same themes are explored with devastating concentration in 'Over a Portrait', undoubtedly the most convincing poem of the four. Free from distracting and lifeless classical references on the one hand and from the awkward shifts in style or direction, on the other, which detract from the force of his other poems, 'Over a Portrait' moves with relentless precision through the stages of self-analysis. Only for a moment, in the fourth verse, are we allowed a reassuring glimpse of the outside world and this, effectively, coincides with the point in the poem where Vespasiano seems to have found some relief from his state of anguish. To remain in this happy condition, he would have to achieve a state of 'pure vision', a possibility which recedes as soon as he attempts to explain himself to her. The life which he had, for a moment, projected into the portrait, turns out to be illusory and, with the betrayal of his hope, love's domain is 'convulsed in bitter confusion'. In the final verse, he finds himself unable, any longer, to see in the portrait those ideal qualities in search of which, at the beginning, his soul had set off in flight: the words 'beloved golden tresses' have been put in parentheses because they are taken directly from Petrarch[342] and this is a clue pointing us, as we shall see, towards a very different reading of the poem.

Pt 4 ~8

180

341. *Juan de Valdès, Op. Cit. p.94. "That you, my Lord, always live in me and I in you." The line presents us with a striking case of over-determination; in his Vita di Luigi Gonzaga, which is included in the same volume as his lives of Vespasiano and Giulia Gonzaga, Affò has presented a number of poems by Vespasiano's father from which Vespasiano seems to have borrowed upon several occasions. One of these, In lode della sua Donna, (p.151) contains the lines:*
Ed io del suo calor privo morrei,
Ch'ella in me vive, ed io sol vivo in lei.
"And I, without her warmth, would die, that she lives in me and I only live in her."
We are not obliged to attribute Vespasiano's line to any single source; rather, we should note the complexity of association which characterizes his work as well as the (generally pessimistic) twist which Vespasiano gives to the thought of others.
342. *Petrarch, Rime Sparse and Other Lyrics, Ed. and Trans. Robert M. Durling, Andrew W. Mellon Foundation, USA, 1976, Poem No. 34.*

One would, of course, give a lot to know whose was the portrait which provoked in Vespasiano this fit of soul-searching. It seems to have been a woman (though, as in the well-known case of Shakespeare's 'dark lady', this can never be taken for granted), and the separation might well have been that of Spain from Italy (or vice versa). L.S.Amadè, the only writer on Vespasiano to have paid any attention at all to the poems[343], comes rather hastily, on the basis of the reference to the Tagus in the second sonnet, to the conclusion that Vespasiano fell in love when he was in Spain and, from the reference to 'beloved golden tresses', he is prepared to hazard the guess that the lady in question was a blonde. One would have to suppose, on this basis, that 'Over a Portrait' was written after Vespasiano was back at Sabbioneta and that - still more improbable - he had her portrait with him there. Portrait painting, even at the court of Philip II, was hardly an everyday activity and tended to be reserved (particularly, in the case of women) for people of considerable importance. If, as seems most probable, the poem was written while Vespasiano was in Spain, it is likely that the portrait in question was one on display in one of the residences occupied in rotation by Philip's court and this would limit, still further, the range of possible subjects. Conceivably, it could have been Vespasiano's aunt Giulia, sufficiently famed for her beauty and painted, among others, by Sebastiano del Piombo and Titian (a favourite of Philip II) and there is nothing in the poem to exclude its dedication to such a person to whom Vespasiano was undoubtedly very deeply devoted. Another tempting hypothesis would be that the picture was one of the many self-portraits made by Sofonisba Anguissola, who returned from Spain to her first marriage in Palermo, aged thirty-nine, in 1575; this was three years before Vespasiano's final departure. Of her outstanding chastity, as well as her intelligence, there can be little doubt and she emerges from the record as possessing all those extrovert qualities - vivacity, spontaneity and a light touch with people around her - in which Vespasiano seems to have found himself lacking. It might well have been that Vespasiano was more fond of her than he ever dared to admit - that the 'madman' in him forbade his approaching her. This can be (and must remain) no more than speculation and there is no evidence at all to support it.

The identity of the person whose likeness prompted Vespasiano to write 'Over a Portrait' is, in any case, of little relevance to the poem's meaning. The 'reference' to Petrarch suggests that Vespasiano wanted to locate his own experience in relation to a very specific body of poetic thought of which Petrarch, at the inception of the Renaissance, had been the supreme exponent. Petrarch's Laura, though he insists on her historical reality, naming the date, the place and the occasion of his first sight of her as well as his learning of her death, is, nevertheless, idealised as a classically reinterpreted version of the heroine of medieval chivalric poetry. This figure, Muse, Mistress, Madonna, chaste tormentress, object of unrequited erotic passion, was an established archetype of idealised femininity which could readily be adapted to the purposes of Renaissance art[344]. Painters celebrated her in countless images of the Virgin Mary. The originality of Petrarch's project is that his love poems are turned inwards, exploring his own mental state in writing them: thinking about himself thinking about Laura. Poetically, Petrarch makes no distinction between the erotic and the religious, allowing each to stand as the metaphor of the other. Laura stands for a craving, a lack, a component of the poet's spiritual existence personified as ideally feminine.

343. Luca Sarzi Amadè, Il Duca
di Sabbioneta, cit., pp.190-1
344. See, for instance, Huizinga,
Op. Cit., p.104 ff.

Vespasiano's poems do not at all resemble those of Petrarch (even though he might have intended that they should); where the latter sparkle with rich and varied imagery, both the world of the troubadours and that of classical mythology marvellously alive and the forms of nature endlessly responsive to the evolution of his mood, the landscape of Vespasiano's poetic world is, as we have noted, bleak, solitary and self-enclosed. Where Petrarch inhabits a wide spectrum of feeling, Vespasiano returns, obsessively, to the same dilemma. Nor are these four 'love' poems really similar in mood or mental structure to the majority of poetry which was being written in Italy during Vespasiano's lifetime (though they might, superficially, appear to be). In this respect, Vespasiano's poetry seems closer to that of Michelangelo (which he almost certainly did not know, since Michelangelo's poems were not published until 1623) even though, on the basis of just four poems in the one case, compared with some three hundred in the other, it is hardly surprising that the latter appear to cover a wider range of experience. Michelangelo's poems, like Vespasiano's, occupy a bleak landscape of monochrome imagery, juxtapose emotional hyperbole with dry casuistry and oscillate uncomfortably between the languages of convention and of intimacy. Benedetto Croce found them full of "improprieties, meaningless expletives, contortions and roughnesses"[345]. If Vespasiano seems trapped within the closed circuit of hope, fear and confusion, Michelangelo is unable to escape from a morbid fascination with guilt and the masochistic anticipation of punishment. Like Vespasiano, Michelangelo speaks, on occasion, with compelling authenticity. In each case, one has the impression that the Petrarchan project of self-exploration through the reinterpretation of conventional forms and imagery has been stretched beyond its potential to carry the psychological revelations which they want to express; the neat and essentially complacent catalogue of the human passions which Minturno had condensed from his reading of Petrarch was no longer adequate to articulate the psychological discoveries to which Petrarch's poetic method, ruthlessly pursued, was found to lead. Probably for this reason, the mood of both Michelangelo's and Vespasiano's poetry seems, in some ways, to anticipate that of English Metaphysical poetry in the seventeenth century by which time, with a little help from Shakespeare and others, poetic form had adapted itself to the expression of new emotions and new forms of spirituality. As Vespasiano tells us, in his state of confusion he can no longer see the 'beloved golden tresses' of idealised womanhood. He had looked into a different world.

Vespasiano's poems differ in another important respect from that of almost any of his contemporaries: they are without a trace of piety. Where Michelangelo might torture himself with the inadequacy of his religious striving, most writers of the time (including Michelangelo's platonic soul-mate, Vittoria Colonna) were explicit in assigning a reliably redemptive role to religious experience and sentiment. In the mental landscape of Vespasiano's poems, there is no such safety-net; on the contrary, he appears to be in a state of free fall. The only reference to conventional religious belief is in the first sonnet, where 'she' turns him towards God, 'to love Him and to praise' but the 'madman' forbids him access to this comfort. Neither do the poems appear to contain any attempt at the exposition of philosophical thought.

Whatever it is, then, that Vespasiano is trying to express in his poems, it is not a simple matter of being 'in love' and feeling the pangs from which lovers have so often claimed to suffer; nor is the 'love' which he describes intended as a metaphor for any conventional form of religious experience. It is about neither an object nor a belief. In order to gain a clearer view of what the poems may really be telling us, it might be instructive to look at some of the circumstances of Vespasiano's emotional life.

345. Quoted in Pierre Leyris' Introduction to his French edition: Michel-Ange Poèmes, Paris, 1983, p.13.

In his known relationships with women, Vespasiano was either very unlucky or, as one is more inclined to believe, compulsively destructive. The death of his first wife, Diana de Cardona, after ten years of marriage, has been the subject of much sensational speculation, rightly described by Kurt Forster as 'often repeated horror stories [....] lurid clichés of a *biographie romanceé* unsupported by the historical evidence'[346]. What seems fairly certain, however, is that Vespasiano was alerted by anonymous letters to his wife's infidelity (it appears, in any case, that she became pregnant) and that she was given no alternative but to take her own life. As Alessandro Lisca put it:

> It is said that her life was taken violently, because she paid insufficient regard to her virtuous reputation, and that the responsibility must fall upon Vespasiano, who often repeated the well-known saying of Caesar that the wife of a great man must be not only without blame but beyond the suspicion of blame.[347]

Officially, she died of apoplexy but no marked tomb or memorial was provided for her. More revealing, perhaps, are the circumstances of the marriage in the first place. Brought from Sicily (where he had previously been Governor) to Milan (where he was now governor) by Vespasiano's powerful uncle Ferrante Gonzaga, Diana was supposed to marry Ferrante's son Cesare with whom, according to Affò, who had seen it, she had been in 'amorous' correspondence. Instead, the engagement was abruptly broken off and, evidently following a violent quarrel between Diana and Ferrante (even her mother was not informed until later), she married the eighteen-year old Vespasiano secretly at Piacenza. Affò refers to her pregnancy at this time but gives no indication who might have been the father (could it have been Ferrante himself?), and there is no subsequent record of this pregnancy's outcome.

That Diana was uncommonly attractive is attested by 'a milanese gentleman' who recorded in one of his *Hundred Sonnets* how, when he was taking a cure in the baths at Aiqui, there was, in the company of the Countess of Somaglia (who helped him over some travel documents):

> ....the Lady Diana Cardona Duchess of Ariano, and consort at this time of the Magnanimous Signor Vespasiano Gonzaga; who, impaired in the use of her left hand, through the fault of a surgeon who had clumsily severed a nerve, meaning to bleed her, had been advised by her doctors to come to Aiqui and immerse the injured hand in the eddies of the stream there and restore it through the virtue of that sulphurous mud.

346. Kurt Forster, From Rocca to Civitas cit. Note 4. The source of many 'horror stories' concerning Vespasiano is, of course, A. Racheli's Memorie Storiche, cit.
347. Quoted in Affò, Vita di Vespasiano Gonzaga, cit., p.41. Most commentators regard this statement in Vespasiano's 'official' biography, written a year after his death, as conclusive.

In the sonnet with which this action is commemorated, an angel is come down from heaven in beautiful human semblance, the waters sound the name Diana and murmur Cardona while the hills give out the sound Ariano.[348]

The picture of Diana which emerges from this record is of an impetuous and, evidently, sexually precocious young woman already consistent with the subsequent supposition of her adultery[349]. At the age of eighteen, it would not surprising if Vespasiano should have found her hard to cope with; the marriage did not, in any case, get off to a good start, as Vespasiano almost immediately became ill (with suspected consumption) and was laid up for several months. Whether, at this time, Vespasiano loved Diana - or she, him - there is no way of knowing; it seems, however, that she willingly involved herself in his projects, organising the delivery of stone from Goito and writing to Duke Guglielmo to inform him of Vespasiano's decision to demolish the monastery adjoining the Rocca since it made a weak point in the city's defences[350], and that she wanted to be a good wife. Given that her fertility was already demonstrated and that Vespasiano's was at a later date, it is difficult to account for the lack of any offspring during the ten years of their marriage. Diana might, with some reason, have felt neglected.

Even if one may allow that the mores of sixteenth century Italy were substantially different from our own expectations of behaviour towards people close to us, it is impossible to believe that Vespasiano can have felt no bitterness, guilt or remorse over Diana's death although it could not be evident to him, as it might have become later, that these horrifying events were not isolated and fortuitous in his life but the first emergence of a pattern from which he seemed unable to free himself.

In his second marriage, five years later, Vespasiano was hardly more fortunate and, as with the first, there is evidence that, for Vespasiano, the occasion was deeply stressful; almost immediately, he became ill and had to spend three months in bed. As we have seen earlier, the match with Anna of Aragona was arranged at the command of Philip II and the wedding took place in her native Spain; by the time they left for Italy, she was already pregnant and gave birth in 1565 to twins, of whom the daughter, Isabella, survived. Less than a year after this, Luigi was born and a male succession seemed assured, but soon after this Anna began to exhibit signs of deep depression, removing herself to Rivarolo where, after thirty-six days of acute fever (she had tuberculosis), she died, leaving Vespasiano 'with such affliction as I have never felt for any other misfortune'[351].

There is no hard evidence upon which to base an explanation of Anna's condition at the time of her death, but some slight corroboration that there was more than a purely medical dimension to it in a curious item in the last testament of Giulia Gonzaga, written shortly before her own death in the previous year: "I request that the most illustrious lady, Anna of Aragona shall pray to Our Lord for me"[352]. In the same testament, no other person is requested to pray for Giulia; there is no evidence that the two would ever have met, but one must assume that there was something, known to Giulia, which would have made sense of this otherwise arbitrary nomination. It can only be an inference that Vespasiano had, consciously or not, played a part in the precipitation of her mental breakdown; he was constantly at her side during her illness (he even became ill himself) and his grief on this occasion seems to have been entirely genuine; it was to be fifteen years before he attempted another marriage, supposedly in a last desperate bid to secure a male heir but it seems doubtful that this was a serious expectation, more probable that, in the daughter of a close friend, he sought the consolation of support and friendship. Margherita Gonzaga, grand-daughter of Ferrante, Governor of Milan, seems, at least, to have given him that.

348. Anton Francesco Rainerio, Cento Sonetti, Milan, 1553, unpaginated, Sonnet No. LXV.
349. According to J.J.Jusserand, (French Ambassador to the USA) in his "A duke and his city. Vespasiano Gonzaga, duke of Sabbioneta" in The School for Ambassadors and other Essays, London, 1924, p.123, Diana was a lady "of very coquettish dispositions". Jusserand's judgements have a quite disarming way of being off the point; he describes Vespasiano, for instance, as a man of his time who "had nothing of the dreamer who thinks of the far-off future". But I am obliged to him for pointing me to Guazzo's Civile Conversation.
350. G.Malacarne, "Gli Stemmi di Vespasiano Gonzaga del Ramo Cadetto di Sabbioneta" in Atti del Convegno, pp.85-6.
351. Quoted in Ibid. p.91. As usual, Racheli's romantic elaboration of these events (that she dressed in penitent's weeds, accusing herself of every kind of guilt) must be viewed with caution, but that the illness was the culmination of a depressive condition seems clear enough.
352. Nulli, Op. Cit., p.178.

Clearly, at a time when marriages were often arranged with minimal regard for the personal preferences of the parties involved, there would be no obvious reason why Vespasiano should blame himself for two successive failures; all we can say for sure is that he never demonstrated convincingly that he was capable of enjoying a normative married condition, as many others in similar circumstances seemed able to do. He had certainly not lived up to the somewhat over-ambitious admonition of his aunt Giulia (whose brief experience of one marriage had, after all, left her disinclined to attempt a second):

> True contentment with the things of this world consists in this, that husband and wife should love one another and be at one in their desires, because in such a case everything will go well and they will live in peace and happiness. [353]

With another woman in his life, his mother, Isabella Colonna, Vespasiano was similarly denied a satisfactory relationship: even before the untimely death of his father, Isabella had begun to squabble with her sister-in-law, Giulia, over the inheritance of whom, Giulia having been married to Isabella's father shortly before her own marriage to Giulia's brother, Isabella was now deprived. Following the shock of her bereavement (there is evidence of a genuine attachment between Isabella and il Rodomonte) Isabella became very unsettled, moved first to Lombardy, where she set up home at Rivarolo, but began to quarrel with her father-in-law and soon moved back to Fondi, while the issue of who should look after the young Vespasiano became increasingly tied up in the issue of the inheritance. Shortly after this, she was remarried to the wealthy prince of Sulmona while Vespasiano remained with Giulia at Fondi. This arrangement was not legally confirmed until 1540, when Vespasiano was nine years old.

At the age of only eleven months when his father died, Vespasiano had probably no conscious memory of the circumstances of this event. It seems, however, that he was familiar with the *Eclogues* of Gerolamo Muzio, the first of which in Book IV (dedicated to Galeotto Pico dalla Mirandola on the occasion of the death of Luigi Gonzaga) contains a lengthy evocation of the scene and of the reaction of Isabella ('Elisa'):

> But how, then, does it leave hapless Elisa?
> Hers is the grief which every grief increases,
> Such that no human language can describe it.
> Before her eyes now she must watch expiring
> (Oh, cruel fate) her most beloved consort.
> No sooner, miserable creature, seeing
> That dearest spirit from his body parted,
> She feels immediately all her forces
> Ebbing away: abandoned and defeated
> On the cold body of her husband falling.
> There, a long while, she stays in frozen stillness
> As though she were an image carved in marble,
> Until, some little natural warmth returning
> To her faint members, and her mind recovered,
> So had her grief grief's outlet still prevented
> That neither could she weep nor one word utter. [354]

353. *Ibid*, p.129.
354. Gerolamo Muzio, *Egloghe*, Venice, 1555, p.76 R.
Ma dove hor lascio l'infelice Elisa?
Dolor è'l suo, ch'ogni dolor avanza,
Tal, che ritrar no'l puote lingua humana.
Ella morir si vede inanzi à gli occhi
(O duro fato) il suo sposo diletto.
Et tosto ch'ebbe visto la meschina
Ch'era de l'alma amata il corpo sciolto,
Così subitamente ogni virtute
Perder sentissi: E abbandonata & vinta
Cadde sul freddo corpo del marito.
Ne quindi per gran spatio più si mosse,
Che fatto havrebbe una marmorea image,
Poi che, tornato à le smarrite membra
Il calor natural, fè in se ritorno,
Si le havea'l duol del duol chiusa la strada,
Che ne pianger potea, ne dir parola.
That Vespasiano was familiar with the Eclogues is corroborated in a sonnet dedicated to the river Sebeto, which ran through his land at Fondi, in which he quotes almost verbatim from another of the Eclogues (Book II, p.41 R) which refers, in almost precisely similar terms to this 'humble' river.

We need not concern ourselves here with the literary quality of this work. It is worth noting, however, that the second line: "Dolor è'l suo ch'ogni dolor avanza" so closely resembles the final line of Vespasiano's 'Over a Portrait': "E quel martir, ch'ogni martire avanza" that it is hard to believe that the association of Muzio's poem was not present in Vespasiano's mind when he wrote his own. There are other reasons for believing that this was the case.

In 1983, the French psychoanalyst André Green published 'The Dead Mother'[355]. Like many of the mental conditions with which Green concerned himself, this paper investigates a complex discoverable in 'many persons who are well adapted to social and external reality [but who] harbour what I have termed private madness.'[356] A significant aim of the study was to compensate lack of attention to the maternal imago in the Freudian and Lacanian accounts of Oedipal formation. So as to keep clear of the internal controversies of psychoanalytic discourse (which are irrelevant to our present enquiry) and to present a coherent (even if, for this reason, an oversimplified) account of the theory, what follows is based entirely upon Green's text, overlooking the fact that Green was drawing upon an extensive range of earlier work.

Fundamental to all psychoanalysis is the understanding that every human subject must make, at an early age, a transition from total absorption in, and physical and emotional dependence on, a protecting and nourishing mother, towards an independent confrontation of the external world and its objects. The residue of this 'weaning' process is the experience of a non-specific 'lack' which can be compensated in the subsequent formation of satisfying emotional relationships or, alternatively, sublimated in the many forms of human self-expression which constitute the institutions of civilized culture. In those cases, however, where the transition is brought about prematurely or abruptly through a change, inexplicable to the child, in the mother's attitude, a withdrawal, on her side, of motherly love and attention, the 'normative' pattern of development is distorted. Though physically still living, the mother is replaced in the psychic life of the child by the image of a 'dead mother', internalised and drained of any emotional charge ('decathected'), absorbing or displacing the lively and constructive narcissism around which a secure sense of identity should have been created. It is common in subjects afflicted with this condition that they feel their right to exist, as well as the meaning of their existence, to have been taken from them.

The structural phenomena which we have been describing do not, it should be stressed, occur within the conscious experience of the subject but the subject is, nonetheless, conscious of some of their effects. For this, if for no other reason, such subjects can, most of the time, perform remarkably well socially, intellectually or creatively. The 'hole' which is occupied by the dead mother is masked by 'a piece of cognitive fabric' or 'a patched breast' (Green is emphatic that the breast here is a metaphor), so that what has been denied internally is projected into the outside world in a sublimated form:

> It is evident that one is witnessing an attempt to master the traumatic situation. But this attempt is doomed to fail. Not that it fails where it has displaced the theatre of operations. These precocious idealized sublimations are the outcome of premature and probably precipitated psychical formations, but I see no reason, apart from bending to normative ideology, to contest their authenticity. Their failure lies elsewhere. The sublimations reveal their incapacity to play a stabilizing role in the psychical economy, because the subject remains vulnerable on a particular point, which is his love life.[357]

355. First published in English in André Green, On Private Madness, London, 1986. Green was, at one time, strongly under the influence of Jacques Lacan though he later became critical of many aspects of Lacan's theory and conduct.
356. Green, Op. Cit., p.15.
357. Ibid., p.153.

The formation of satisfactory relationships is blocked, in these subjects, because the loving impulse, though not destroyed, is 'buried' along with the dead mother: "...his love is still mortgaged to the dead mother. The subject is rich but he can give nothing away in spite of his generosity, for he does not reap enjoyment from it." and "the patient has the feeling that a malediction weighs upon him, that there is no end to his mother's dying, and that it holds him prisoner." At the heart of this subject, there is a cold core which "burns like ice" but

> ....behind the dead mother complex, behind the blank mourning for the mother, one catches a glimpse of the mad passion of which she is, and remains, the object, that renders mourning an impossible experience. The subject's entire structure aims at a fundamental fantasy: to nourish the dead mother, to maintain her perpetually embalmed.[358]

This inevitably skimpy and superficial account of an essay which is rich on every page with significant detail and insight is certainly not intended to provide a basis upon which, at a range of four hundred years and on the scantiest of real evidence, to attempt a clinical diagnosis in the case of Vespasiano Gonzaga. To do so would, in any case, be to overlook the entirely different circumstances in which the transactions between an aristocratic mother and her child would have been conducted in the sixteenth century. Such mothers did not, for instance, breast feed their babies[359]. Though it is easy to recognise, in Green's description, patterns of thought and behaviour which we have encountered at many points of our observation of Vespasiano in this and preceeding chapters, there can be no way of knowing whether their origin was analogous to the cases of Green's patients. Green's description does, however, resonate suggestively with several features of Vespasiano's poems, sufficiently so to justify a second look at the poems themselves from the perspective which, if only on the level of metaphor, the notion of the dead mother has opened up.

In the first place, the mood of the poems appears remarkably close to that of Green's patients: the cold core, the lack of meaning or explanation and the intermittently visible 'mad passion' as well as the resort to intellectual formations in what Green calls a 'compulsion to think' are features which point to a similar affective state. More specifically, the object of desire in Vespasiano's poems is represented either as forbidden (first sonnet), dangerous (Sorrow of Aristeus) or inanimate (projected onto external forms in the second sonnet or, in the other long poem, the portrait). In all but the first sonnet, 'she' is inattentive, unable or unwilling to hear or to understand him: "If she but knew...." in the second sonnet, "She, nothing hearing, ..., nothing replies" or, in Sorrow of Aristeus, "....who clearly sees love's pain appear/In Aristeus' brow, only replies/An echo."

Two of the poems present, explicitly, the thought that his existence and 'hers' are bound together and mutually dependent: "at least allow me/My life in her, hers that she lives in me", "If she but knew that by them I exist" (where 'them' is the myriad forms in which she appears) while the confusion of hope and fear in 'Over a Portrait' threatens to untie "my spirit's fragile bond". Even in 'Sorrow of Aristeus', the final verse introduces a desire for annihilation, frustrated by the force of his 'mad passion'. Here, we seem to find represented the twin themes, in Green's account, of identification, the sacrifice of the patients' identity to the internalized dead mother and the necessity to maintain her perpetually embalmed.

358. Ibid., p.162.
359. See, for instance, Margaret L. King: "La Donna del Rinascimento" in E. Garin (ed.) L'Uomo del Rinascimento, Rome-Bari, 2000, p.278.

If it docs no more, then, André Green's model of the dead mother complex has given us a way of reading Vespasiano's poems in which many things that seemed obscure, inappropriate or unfocussed can now be seen as making some sort of sense. We cannot, of course, know whether Isabella Colonna did, in reality, suffer the sort of depression or shock at the death of her husband (or for some other cause) which would lead to her withdrawal of lively maternal affection in the way that precipitated the symptoms which Green observed in his patients. One can only say that it would not be incompatible with the known facts. In the same way, there is no hard evidence of Vespasiano's constitutional inability to form satisfactory erotic relationships but only a strong inference; many other conditions might, in any case, have produced a similar result. This is probably as far as one can go. Almost:

We have noted already that the mythical figure of Aristeus was difficult to relate to the manifest content of Vespasiano's poem. His likely source for the myth would have been Virgil, in Book IV of the Georgics, where it appears as a part of his disquisition on bee-keeping. Here, in the prose translation of H. Rushton Fairclough[360], is how Virgil's narrative begins:

> Aristeus the shepherd, quitting Tempe by the Peneus, when - so runs the tale - his bees were lost through sickness and hunger, sorrowfully stopped beside the sacred fount at the stream's head, and with many plaints called on his mother thus: "O mother, mother Cyrene, that dwellest in this flood's depths, why, from the gods' glorious line - if indeed, as thou sayest, Thymbraean Apollo is my father - didst thou give me birth, to be hated of the fates? Or whither is thy love for me banished? Why didst thou bid me hope for Heaven? Lo, even this very crown of my mortal life, which the skilful tending of crops and cattle had scarce wrought out for me for all my endeavour - though thou art my mother, I resign. Nay, come, and with thine own hand tear up my fruitful woods; lay the hostile flame to my stalls, destroy my crops, burn my seedlings, and swing the stout axe against my vines, if such loathing for my honour hath seized thee."

Did Vespasiano intend that his readers would be familiar with Virgil's lines and would know that Aristeus' outcry is addressed to his mother? Probably not.

Virgil's poem continues, in a marvelous flow of imagery, with the nymphs, gathered in Cyrene's "bower beneath the river's depths", "rehearsing the countless loves of the gods" when Aristeus' cry is heard and his mother, "smitten with strange dread", has the rivers part asunder so that Aristeus can enter "his mother's home, a realm of waters, at the lakes locked in caverns, and the echoing groves" where, having cheered him with a good omen from "Ocean, universal father", she explains to him what he must do. On Cyrene's advice, Aristeus waits to ambush Proteus in his "vast cavern, hollowed in a mountain's side, whither many a wave is driven by the wind, then parts into receding ripples" and, as evening comes on, Proteus comes home to rest while "the seals lay them down to sleep, here and there along the shore." Seizing his opportunity, Aristeus "burst upon him with a loud cry and surprised him in fetters as he lies". Despite his transformation into "all wondrous shapes - into flame and hideous beast and flowing river", Proteus, who knows all that has been, all that is and all that will be, has no choice but to reveal to Aristeus the cause of his troubles.

360. Virgil, with an English translation by H. Rushton Fairclough, London and New York, 1920, Vol 1, p.219.

It is Orpheus who is seeking revenge upon Aristeus "and wildly he rages for the loss of his bride. She, in truth, hastening headlong along the river, if only she might escape thee, saw not the monstrous serpent". Orpheus, who "solacing love's anguish with his hollow shell, sang of thee, sweet wife - of thee, to himself on the lonely shore; of thee as day drew nigh, of thee as day declined. Even the jaws of Taenarus, the lofty portals of Dis, he entered, and the grove that is murky with black terror, and came to the dead, and the king of terrors, and the hearts that know not how to soften at human prayers". Retracing his steps "and the regained Eurydice was nearing the upper world, following behind", Orpheus had only not to look back "when a sudden frenzy seized Orpheus, unwary in his love, frenzy meet for pardon, did Hell know how to pardon!" As she slips back, Eurydice calls out: "What madness, Orpheus, what dreadful madness hath ruined my unhappy self and thee? Lo, again the cruel Fates call me back and sleep veils my swimming eyes." And so, "like smoke mingling with thin air", Eurydice vanishes and nothing remains for Orpheus, after seven months' solitary lamentation, but to meet his own violent end at the hands of the Thracian devotees of Bacchus.

For Orpheus to be pacified, Aristeus must sacrifice four bulls and four heifers, leaving their bodies in the grove: "Anon, when the ninth Dawn displays her rising beams, thou shalt send unto Orpheus funeral dues of Lethe's poppies, shalt slay a black ewe and revisit the grove. Then to Eurydice, now appeased, thou shalt do worship with the slaughter of a calf." From the putrifying bodies of the sacrificial bulls and heifers, swarms of bees began to emerge "till at last on a tree-top they stream together, and hang in clusters from the bending boughs."

So, at the back of Vespasiano's mind as he wrote his own tortured verses, there lies this astonishing narrative of a search for the cause of Aristeus' misfortune and its expiation. It is fairly clear that Virgil had more in mind, when he wrote this passage, than to recount what he knew about the history of bee-keeping[361] and equally clear that, in his reading of it, Vespasiano took it on at the level of profound imaginative experience far removed from the shallow text book 'knowledge' of a literary dilettante. Much of Virgil's imagery reappears in Vespasiano's poem, displaced and, at times, mutilated (like the contents of a dream), but its substance is totally transformed. Where Virgil's narrative ends in resolution and the acceptance of Aristeus' (not too onerous) act of atonement, for Vespasiano, his appeal to the mother remains unheard and even the 'funeral dues of Lethe's poppies' are denied him. It is as though Virgil's poem was, for Vespasiano, the dream he longed to dream and his own, the cruel reawakening. In the same way that he could not inhabit the imaginative world of Petrarch, could not see 'beloved golden tresses', Vespasiano's poem records his sense of exclusion from the humanly supportive universe of classical mythology.

Behind the living, attentive and comforting mother Cyrene, there is, of course, her dead shadow, Eurydice, almost brought back into the upper world but drawn (or pushed?) back into the shadows due to the 'dreadful madness' of Orpheus - or is it Aristeus, or both? - who have condemned her by loving her. If Vespasiano had recognised, in Virgil's poetry, the makings of a dream in which his own suffering might, momentarily, appear to find a remedy, it was one in which the apparent remedy was no more than a 'patched breast' concealing the dead prisoner still guarded at the 'cold core' of his being.

361. Fairclough tells us in a footnote that the passage was substituted at the last minute, when Virgil's eulogy of C. Cornelius Gallus had to be dropped subsequent upon the latter's disgrace and suicide. It is possible, therefore, that Virgil made use of a poem already available in draft but written with another intention.

~9)

An Idyll for the Dead.
Disturbing agendas in
decorative & architectural
themes at Sabbioneta.
The consolation of a
looking-glass Arcadia.

192

Dr Dicks:
I understand, then, that the outbreak of a neurotic illness, from the point of view of a man's development, is something favourable?

Professor Jung:
That is so, and I am glad you bring up that idea. That is really my point of view. I am not altogether pessimistic about neurosis. In many cases we have to say: 'Thank heaven he could make up his mind to be neurotic'. Neurosis is really an attempt at self-cure, just as any physical disease is partly an attempt at self-cure. We cannot understand a disease as an ens per se *any more, as something detached which not so long ago it was believed to be. Modern medicine - internal medicine, for instance - conceives of disease as a system composed of a harmful factor and a healing factor. It is exactly the same with neurosis. It is an attempt of the self-regulating psychic system to restore the balance, in no way different from the function of dreams - only rather more forceful and drastic.* [362]

Approaching the close of this investigation, we should now be at the point where those things which, at the start, seemed elusive and indistinct would begin to take on recognisable outlines and where, if only provisionally, some sort of general conclusion might be expected. If that is a reasonable expectation then it must be admitted, regretfully, that by such a standard this work must remain unfinished; we are not going to arrive at a triumphant Q.E.D. To the central question of the book - Why, if not simply to represent his power and prestige, did Vespasiano Gonzaga spend so much time, energy (and money) on the project of Sabbioneta? - we seem as far away as when we started from a satisfactory answer. Already, our speculations are bordering upon the culpably far-fetched and we are fast running out of new material in which to seek for further insight. If we have found some pointers towards a more complete understanding of Vespasiano's complex thought processes, these have, as often as not, pointed in contradictory directions, suggesting further layers of ambiguity beyond the reach of systematic investigation. None of this should be considered surprising; we are concerned, after all, with the mental life of a highly intelligent but also a very complicated person whose responses to the circumstances in which he found himself could not be worked out in advance, according to a fixed array of convictions but which reflect, in each case, the tensions of a particular encounter.

While the original internal appearance of Vespasiano's two churches has been largely obliterated by subsequent interventions, the Corridor Grande, the ducal palace and the garden palace retain, in various degrees of preservation, their original painted decoration, and an account of Sabbioneta would clearly be incomplete without some consideration of the themes which are developed in these interiors. (The decoration of the theatre has been briefly discussed in Chapter 7).

362. C.G. Jung, Analytical Psychology, its Theory and Practice, London, 1968, p.189.

Stripped of its intended content, Vespasiano's collections of naturalia, his antique sculpture, coins and medals, the decoration of the Corridor Grande seems to emphasise rather than to mitigate the linear, repetitive character of the space. In the same way, and for the same reason that we have recognised in the repetition of (now empty) niches on the building's exterior as suggestive of a 'cathedral of modern knowledge', it is hardly surprising to find that the long interior walls of this room are arranged in terms of a thematic 'list' such as could be extended, without compositional hierarchy, so as to fill up their considerable length: on one side the secular virtues of good government and on the opposite side the spiritual virtues of Christianity. It is the architectural frame within which the figures are set which imparts unity and coherence to these surfaces[363]. At each end of the corridor, spectacular and evidently playful exercises in *trompe-l'oeil* open up fictive loggias into open urban space. Elegant, though perhaps uninspired, the decoration of the Corridor Grande is clearly subordinate to its architectural and programmatic intention.

    The most complete interior to have survived in the ducal palace is the small but symbolically (as well as physically) central space of Vespasiano's studiolo on the first floor, above the entrance. We have already noted (in Chapter 2) that this room, by its 4:9 proportional ratio, could be seen to reverberate in harmony with the similarly proportioned piazza on the main axis of which it is situated. In a frieze of low-relief medallions are represented eleven generations of Vespasiano's ancesters and their wives, concluding with his own son, Luigi and his second wife, Anna of Aragona. The large oval panel which occupies the centre of the vaulted ceiling contains an image of Apollo driving his chariot through the heavens. Such an image dominating the centre of an important room was by no means unconventional in renaissance practice. Frances Yates has shown[364] that the representation of certain deities in the ceiling of a room could carry a special, indeed, a magical significance during the Renaissance. She quotes Ficino:

> [Someone may construct] *"on the domed ceiling of the innermost cubicle of his house, where he mostly lives and sleeps, such a figure with the colours in it. And when he comes out of his house he will perceive, not so much the spectacle of individual things, but the figure of the universe and its colours." I understand this to mean a painting on the ceiling of a bedroom, a painting which is also still a figure of the world, with perhaps still the figures of the Three Graces, the three fortunate planets, Sol, Venus, Jupiter predominating, and their colours of blue, gold and green as the leading colours of the painting or fresco.*

363. The decoration of the Corridor Grande was evidently carried out on the basis of designs by the brothers Alessandro and Giovanni Alberti, who worked in Sabbioneta from July until December 1587, when, abruptly, they left. See Ugo Bazzotti: "La Galleria degli Antichi di Sabbioneta: Questione chronologiche, attributive e iconografiche" in Atti del Convegno, pp.375-392.
364. Frances A. Yates, Giordano Bruno and the Hermetic Tradition, London, 1971, p.75.

In this way the influence of benign planets would be 'drawn down' while the influence of Mars and Saturn would be avoided. Venus, also driving a chariot, occupies the ceiling of a small room on the ground floor of the garden palace at Sabbioneta and in both representations the colours blue, gold and green are conspicuous. Vespasiano did not, however, entirely avoid the influence of Mars in his studiolo since he, together with Mercury, is represented in subsidiary panels to either end of the dominating image. The painting of Apollo is not only conventional in terms of its iconography; it is, in any case, a direct copy from the image painted by Giulio Romano in the Palazzo Té at Mantua. In the original, however, the cyclical motion of the sun is evoked in the complementary figure of Luna, who enters the sky as Sol is about to leave it. In Vespasiano's ducal palace, Luna is not to be found in the same sky as Sol but at the centre of a ceiling of her own, in a room on the ground floor to the side of the main entrance, where the supposedly chaste Diana is captivated by the beauty of sleeping Endymion in the adjacent presence of Jupiter, Juno, Mars and Venus. Giulio Romano's serene image of celestial harmony is here disjointed and mutilated: from what we know already, Diana could carry associations with Vespasiano's eponymous and evidently unfaithful wife, or his inattentive mother (cold moon, did you not hear / That wild outpouring of his miseries?) or, more likely, both at once, emblematic of a personal cosmology which was far from serene.

Much of the decoration which survives elsewhere in the ducal palace would, if anything, tend to support the conventional interpretation of Vespasiano's intentions: the themes represented appear to stress its 'official' status: allegorical and historical allusions to princely virtues, the emperors Maximilian II and Rudolf II (not, it should be noted, Philip II), elephants restrained by the hand of Justice and a plethora of heraldic insignia. In the ducal palace, it is the authority of government which is most insistently underlined. In the garden palace, on the other hand, where the decoration dates from the last decade of Vespasiano's life, the selection of themes is evidently expressive of more personal concerns: "It is here", writes Umberto Maffezzoli[365] "that the personality of the Duke of Sabbioneta shines through, his cult of classical antiquity and his humanist ideals." More specifically personal concerns are also to be found 'shining through'. If the decoration of the rooms on the ground floor is now too incomplete to support any reliable thematic interpretation, that on the upper floor has been comparatively well preserved and ought to yield a coherent insight to the sort of imagery with which, in his private capacity, Vespasiano chose to surround himself. This upper floor consists of a linear sequence of spaces such that they can only be traversed in a single order. More than one writer has noted the evident informality of its plan: we quoted earlier the comment of a Frenchman that, "by their dimensions, their ornament and the small scope which they offer for practical life, [these rooms] must clearly have been intended for princesses"[366]. It is hardly likely, however, that either the planning or the decorative schemes were the result of carelessness on Vespasiano's part and (though this may, indeed, be fortuitous) there appears to be, in the succession of themes represented, a progression tantalizingly close to the progression around which the present work has been ordered: a progression which begins in the 'public' world and moves increasingly into a world which is personal and private.

365. Umberto Maffezzoli, Sabbioneta, cit., p.31.
366. C.Yriarte, "Sabbioneta, la Petite Athènes", in Gazette des Beaux Arts, XL, T.19, p.123.

Before looking in greater detail at the thematic material presented on the first floor of Vespasiano's garden palace, there are some points which should be borne in mind:

1) Unlike the architecture of Sabbioneta, which was realized under the very direct control of Vespasiano, and still more unlike the poetry which Vespasiano seems to have written almost without reference to an audience other than himself, the painted decoration of his palace, however precise the verbal instructions which he might have given, was inevitably mediated through the technical and imaginative resources of those who were employed to execute them. A number of different hands have been identified even in the scope of this compact suite of rooms and, though it seems likely that they were coordinated under the general direction of Bernardino Campi, the technical as well as the aesthetic quality to be found in different parts is highly variable.[367] If, in the rendering of generally well understood themes, their visual interpretation appears as conventionally Mannerist, we cannot assume that this was the form in which Vespasiano had personally imagined them. The painters did not necessarily paint the thought which motivated the choice of subject.

2) If Vespasiano had been asked to explain his choice of decorative themes, it is probable that he would have given an account no less blandly conventional than that which commentators are apt to put forward. The patterns of associative relations, revealed in a series of particular choices, and which might be discoverable by someone deliberately seeking to uncover them, did not necessarily exist upon the surface of Vespasiano's conscious reflection. Even if they had done so, it would hardly have been in these terms that the iconographic programmes were communicated to the painters.

3) From our investigation of his architecture and from our reading of Vespasiano's poetry, we should have learned to anticipate a high degree of 'over-determination' - a bewildering number and variety of thoughts collapsed into a single image or form. In the interpretation of his pictorial programme, as much as in that of his buildings or his poetic works, an important implication of this must be that there will be no single, exhaustive or sufficient reading such that all others must be rejected. We are under no obligation to exclude Vespasiano's 'cult of classical antiquity and his humanist ideals', his princely auto-celebration, his identification with the deities and heroes of ancient Rome or that of Sabbioneta with the city of Rome; on the contrary, we should allow that each of these and, no doubt, many others, is present, having arrived there through either conscious or unconscious processes. If this present work has sought to open up a space for a more intimate and personal reading of Vespasiano and his city, it has been, precisely, in order to challenge reductive explanations of whatever sort. (It must also be admitted, however, that much of what is available by way of explanation amounts to little more than a catalogue of contents, as though the meaning of the juxtaposition of these were self-evident.)

367. Probably the most thorough account of likely attributions is in Chiara Tellini Perina, Sabbioneta, Cit., pp.36 ff.

4)

In his reading of classical and contemporary literature, we have seen that Vespasiano was inclined to respond directly, to inhabit the poetic space of its imagery rather than its lexical interpretation. It is the 'raw' material itself, not its received understanding, that seems to have interested him and, like the material which appears in the formation of dreams, it is subject to displacements, distortions, affective inversions and substitutions such that the latent content of his poetry is scarcely visible upon its surface. To discover why Vespasiano might have been moved by a particular phrase or image, it is seldom sufficient to discover its overt meaning or even what was intended when that image of phrase was originally produced. As we have found before, it may well be at precisely those moments where what we can see appears to make no sense, that we may find a point of entry into Vespasiano's personal world.

Leaving the fine staircase at the first floor of the garden palace, the sequence of rooms begins with the so-called Saletta dei Cesari, the 'Little Room of the Caesars'. The decorative content of this room has been discussed in an earlier chapter where our interest was to measure Vespasiano's identification with the glorious heritage of Rome and its citizens. While, in this first room of the garden palace sequence, it is Vespasiano's life as a soldier which is presented, the second, the Sala dei Circhi, appears to celebrate his activity as a builder. Centrally, in the vaulted ceiling, his coat of arms, supported by a winged spirit, is flanked by two lions in heraldic pose and by two cranes clutching pebbles in their raised claws (the former evidently symbolic of strength, the latter of vigilance: if they were to fall asleep, the cranes would be woken by the falling of the pebbles[368]). The two longer walls carry images, respectively, of the Circus Maximus and the Circus Flaminius, apparently copied from reconstructions in Antonio Lafréry's *Speculum romanae magnificentiae* of 1570[369]. On the shorter walls are a semicircular archway, revealing an agrarian landscape and, opposite, a perruzian cityscape focussed (as we noted earlier) on a gateway structure which closely resembles Luca Fancelli's gateway at Gonzaga. In fourteen lunettes above these architectural images, the story is told of Philomen and Baucis, humble peasants who earned the favour of Jupiter and Mercury on account of their pious hospitality when these gods arrived in disguise. In Ovid's account (the only antique source of this myth) the scene is set in "a marsh, once a habitable land, but now water, the haunt of divers and coots" where, turned away by a thousand homes, the gods are taken in at last by the aged couple. After the gods have revealed their true identity, they lead their hosts to the top of a nearby hill from which

> ....they looked back and saw the whole country-side covered with water, only their own house remaining. And, while they wondered at this, while they wept for the fate of their neighbours, that old house of theirs, which had been small even for its two occupants, was changed into a temple. Marble columns took the place of the forked wooden supports; the straw grew yellow and became a golden roof; there were gates richly carved, a marble pavement covered the ground. [370]

368. Tellini Perina, Op. Cit., p.46.
369. Ibid. p.46.
370. Publius Ovidius Naso (Ovid), Metamorphoses, Book VIII, lines 624 ff. Trans. Frank Justus Miller, Cambridge Mass. 1999.

As a reward of humble piety, then, the derelict cottage in a swampy place becomes a gleaming temple; under the strong and vigilant protection of its duke, Sabbioneta (which, as Nizzolio stressed in his inaugral speech as director of the academy, had risen from a swampy and inhospitable place) can take its place amongst the wonders of ancient Rome. Except, of course, that it is not quite that simple: if, as one can imagine he might have done, Vespasiano chose the images of two roman circuses because he could give the painter a book from which to copy them, the city of Sabbioneta was there just outside the windows and it would have been easy enough to make a recognisable likeness of one of the buildings there, for instance, the ducal palace. The gateway represented may not, of course, be the one at Gonzaga since, in Vespasiano's day, there could have been others similar which have now disappeared. We do know, however, of Vespasiano's attachment to the emblematic 'Gonzaga' brackets which feature strongly in the painted gateway. Once again, we seem to have several thoughts collapsed into a single form: Sabbioneta both representing and represented by an architectural type powerfully associated with the Gonzaga dynasty. The humble piety of Philomen and Baucis can refer both to that of the builder of Sabbioneta and, more generally, to that of the family who saved their 'house' from the swamps and achieved glittering renown. We will return to a further reading of the images in this room when we know a little more about the sequence as a whole.

Moving on to the next room, we enter the Sala dei Miti, so-called on account of the five panels in the ceiling in which scenes from classical mythology are represented. In the centre is Philyra, seduced by Saturn in the form of a horse; the other four panels show Arachne's ill-fated weaving contest with Minerva, the fall of Icarus as he flies too close to the sun, Marsyas, flayed alive at the command of Apollo, with whom he had competed unsuccessfully in music and, finally, Phaeton plunging into the Po as he loses control of Apollo's chariot while his sisters are transformed into trees. (Fig. 9.1 & 9.2) Around the frieze are painted emblems of the Gonzaga along with their mottoes and, below these, winged figures carrying coats of arms. The juxtaposition of these five myths (on the quite reasonable assumption that their selection out of the enormous range of possible subjects was not fortuitous) has prompted some essays in the interpretation of their 'message'. Hanno-Walter Kruft suggests we should understand that: "Mortals are punished for their presumption when they try to compete with the gods, but the gods are free to associate with mortals as they please."[371] So tritely conventional a thought can hardly be wrong though, as we shall presently discover, it can only very approximately be related to the subjects depicted. In the same way, Chiara Tellini Perina, who aims to localise her interpretation in an historical context observes:

> The ideological connection between these myths is contained in their moral message (it should be remembered that the diffusion of Ovid's Metamorphoses took place during the sixteenth century through the medium of moralising popularisations) a warning against the reckless arrogance of those who challenge Heaven and the gods, and thus also political authority.[372]

This could find some support from the display of Gonzaga heraldry which complements the mythical decorations, but only at the cost of an over-simplified (and textually imprecise) reading of the five mythical subjects.

371. Hanno-Walter Kruft, Städte in Utopia, cit., p.44.
372. Op. Cit., p.47.

To start with the centrepiece: we have noted already that Vespasiano was orthodox in his choice of the 'influence' to be placed above the inner sanctum of his 'official' residence, his public persona located under an apollonian sign, while the little room, in his more private residence, in which a venereal influence was invoked, would not have surprised anyone familiar with this way of thinking. We have Carli's word for it[373] that Vespasiano had no particular attachment to astrology and there is no evidence (unless his architectural 'reference' to Achille Bocchi's Academy might be taken as such) that would link him with the hermetic tradition which is the central theme of Frances Yates' study from which we quoted. In placing his Sala dei Miti 'under Saturn', then, we should not suppose that Vespasiano was consciously attempting some species of destructive magic but we should not, therefore, dismiss the thought that ideas about planetary influences were amongst the many types of thought to which he had been exposed and which would therefore have been available within his field of mental association. We could, at least, understand that in allowing Saturn, in a bestial disguise, to dominate the composition of this ceiling, Vespasiano might have wanted to express a negative inference: not Jupiter, not Apollo, not Venus.

So much we might reasonably infer, looking at the Sala dei Miti through the eyes of an educated person of the late Renaissance but we need, also, to ask ourselves what it was about the mythology of the ancient world - evidently more than simply its association with a 'lost' culture which the Renaissance sought to recapture - by which it came to exert such a powerful hold upon the imaginations of comparatively modern individuals. (Why, indeed, the fundamental poetic themes of Antiquity are, even today, embedded in the language by which we designate the psychological conditions observable in ourselves.) Like the version of Christianity which the Renaissance inherited from the middle ages, in which, to all intents and purposes, the virgin Mary had come to occupy the position ascribed, in 'correct' theology, to the Holy Ghost (and like the folklore of every known civilization), classical mythology develops its themes around the eternal human triangle: father, mother and child. Unlike the medieval Christian religion, however, and in a much more highly developed form than is commonly to be discovered in folklore, the myths of classical Antiquity are comprehensive and unflinching in their exploration of every possible permutation, inversion, substitution and recombination, within this triad, of which the human psyche is capable. As, then, during the Renaissance, individuals such as Vespasiano Gonzaga sought an understanding and a means of expressing personal experience which the concepts of medieval Christianity and social convention were insufficient to comprehend, the imaginative world of classical myth could offer a vehicle which was distinct from, though not overtly incompatible with, the more rational aspirations of humanist culture. In the words of André Chastel:

> ...one cannot be satisfied with the arbitrary glosses of an Ovide moralisé. The idea is that through the histories of the gods is manifested a knowledge of the relations between man and the world, which one could not arrive at in any other way.
> [....] These representations [....] constituted in fact the common anthropology of the renaissance, an anthropology which tended obstinately to express itself in images.[374]

373. See Chapter One.
374. André Chastel, "The Arts during the Renaissance" in Chastel, A. et al, The Renaissance, essays in interpretation, London & New York, 1982, p.240.

Of the five mythological themes presented in the vault of the Sala dei Miti, that of Saturn and Philyra is the one which least convincingly lends itself to the moral or political interpretations such as we have quoted. It is not, in any case, among the myths narrated by Ovid in his Metamorphoses, (though he does refer to it, as we shall see, in passing) and cannot, therefore, have come to Vespasiano's attention through a 'moralising popularisation'. The only extant classical source of this myth is in the Fables of Hyginus (a contemporary and acquaintance of Ovid) of which a ninth-century manuscript was copied and edited at Basle in 1535. Hyginus' account of the myth is very brief:

> *When Saturn was hunting Jove throughout the earth, assuming the form of a steed he lay with Philyra, daughter of Ocean. By him she bore Chiron the Centaur, who is said to have been the first to invent the art of healing. After Philyra saw that she had borne a strange species [half man and half horse], she asked Jove to change her into another form, and she was transformed into the tree which is the linden.*[375]

Even for a pedantic humanist, it would be difficult to extract a moral interpretation from this brief narrative. Certainly, as Campi represents her, Philyra's expression exhibits no shame or distress at her seduction and her subsequent transformation into a linden tree (not represented) is a dispensation which she herself has requested when she discovers that she has given birth to the Centaur. But one cannot help wondering, in the light of our previous investigation of his poetry, whether Vespasiano might, at some level below conscious thought, have associated his mother's transformation into an inanimate thing with an idea that she had given birth to a freak.

In the terminology of psychoanalysis, the theme of Phylira and Saturn could be understood as a 'fantasy of the primal scene', a subconsciously reconstituted parental copulation. André Green, whose essay on the Dead Mother we noted in the last chapter, is at pains to stress (unlike Freud) that "what counts in the primal scene is not that one has witnessed it but precisely the contrary, namely that it has taken place in the absence of the subject."[376] He goes on to characterise six defensive positions commonly adopted in relation to fantasies of the primal scene by subjects affected by a 'dead mother complex'. These are:

1   hatred of both objects
2   interpretation of the scene as sadistic
3   the mother seen as a 'lewd monster'
4   alternating identification of the father as aggressor and healer
5   various forms of sublimation "Another solution: artistic creation, which is the support for a fantasy of autosatisfaction."
6   regressive negation of the entire fantasy; bad false breast, false self, false baby.

If the image of Phylira and Saturn could, without too much difficulty, be placed in the third of these categories, most, if not all of the other five could, as we shall see, shed light on other material depicted on the first floor of Vespasiano's garden palace.

375. Trans. and Ed., Mary Grant, The Myths of Hyginus, Lawrence, Kansas, 1960, No.CXXXVIII, p.114.
376. André Green, On Private Madness, cit. p.159.

The theme of transformation into trees (comparatively common in the mythology narrated by Ovid and Hyginus) suggests a possible link with the story of Phaeton shown in an adjoining panel. Hyginus' version of this myth is:

> *Phaeton, son of Sol and Clymene, who had secretly mounted his father's car, and had been borne too high above the earth, from fear fell into the river Eridanus [the Po]. When Jupiter struck him with a thunderbolt, everything started to burn. In order to have a reason for destroying the whole race of mortals, Jove pretended he wanted to put out the fire; he let loose the rivers everywhere, and all the human race perished except Deucalion and Pyrra. But the sisters of Phaeton, because they had yoked the horses without the orders of their father, were changed into poplar trees. [377]*

The story of Phaeton's descent into the Po and the associated origin of the Lombardy poplar is, not surprisingly, one in which the Gonzaga family took a certain personal pride; it was their own special myth and it is in this spirit that it crops up in Vespasiano's poetry:

> *We, by that stream where Phaethon fell headlong,*
> *With moats and walls, a great pile have begun,*
> *Against the wrath of Mars secure, to raise, [378]*

Through this connection, the Gonzaga could see the land which they possessed as a living theatre of the mythological world, in which their own actions were invested with the resonance of a more than individual human destiny. If Vespasiano's aim, in his Sala dei Miti, had been to submit his own life and actions to the impartial judgement of mythological Antiquity, it would have made sense to place the image of Phaeton in the centre of the vault. Its displacement to the side might seem to suggest a more complex motive.

In Ovid's much longer (and more poetically inventive) account, Phaeton's desire to drive the chariot of the sun originates in his wish to verify that he is, indeed, the son of Apollo. Apollo, unwillingly, allows his son to drive the chariot, having rashly promised to grant him any wish. Jove brings Phaeton down with a thunderbolt in order to stop the conflagration in which the whole world is being consumed as the chariot crashes towards earth (Apollo is bitterly resentful of Jove's intervention). In this version, the metamorphosis of the sisters into trees is connected, not to their disobedience, but to the grief of their mother. (Ovid does not refer specifically to poplar trees):

> *Then one day the eldest, Phaëthusa, when she would throw herself upon the grave [of Phaeton], complained that her feet had grown cold and stark; and when the fair Lampetia tried to come to her, she was held fast by sudden roots. A third, making to tear her hair, found her hands plucking at foliage. One complained that her ankles were encased in wood, another that her arms were changing to long branches. And while they look on those things in amazement bark closes round their loins, and, by degrees, their waists, breasts, shoulders, hands; and all that was free were their lips calling upon their mother. [379]*

377. *Hyginus, Fables, cit.. No.CLII A, p.123.*
378. *Noi presso al fiume, u'già cadde Fetonte,/Di fossi, e muri una perpetua mole/Contra l'ira di Marte intenti ergemo, from the sonnet to Bernardino Rota quoted by Affò, Vita di Vespasiano Gonzaga, cit., p.68.*
379. *Ovid, Metamorphoses, cit. p.85.*

As Ovid recounts this myth, the sisters' transformation into trees is clearly to be seen as a tragic event in that human contact between the mother and her daughters is inexorably severed. There is, however, no suggestion that either the sisters or their mother were suffering a punishment; simply, that the metamorphosis was the inescapable outcome of their common grief at the death of Phaeton. In many of Ovid's stories (e.g. Daphne), transformation into a tree is a way by which women can be rescued from unwanted amorous pursuit; Baucis and Philomen are turned into trees so that they can remain together after death. The metamorphosis is, in itself, affectively neutral and the same neutrality seems to characterise the spirit in which this trope was absorbed into the culture of the Renaissance. Ovid's text, quoted above, is clearly recalled in Francesco Colonna's *Hypnerotomachia Poliphili*:

> *[Jove's] divine and tremendous majesty was being celebrated by a chorous of seven nymphs dressed in white, with indications of solemn singing and reverent applause. They then transformed themselves into green trees of transparent emerald, covered with bright blue flowers, which bowed devoutly to the high god. The last one was entirely turned to a tree, her feet becoming roots; the next, all but her feet; the third, all but the part from the waist to the arms; and so on successively. But the tops of their virginal heads showed that the metamorphosis would happen to each in turn.*[380]

While the imagery remains strikingly close to the ovidian original, the affect is here entirely transformed. Colonna's illustration of this scene (Fig. 9.4) seems, in its visual interpretation of the subject, to have informed the painting at Sabbioneta, either directly or at second hand, via Gerolamo Genga's extraordinary adaptation in the Villa Imperiale at Pesaro, in which female figures, half transformed into trees, stand in a painted woodland whose foliage extends to form an entire covering to the room. We have already had reason to suggest that Vespasiano knew Genga's work, which is recalled by numerous details of the architecture and the decorative repertoire to be found at Sabbioneta. The clearly 'over-determined' theme of women transformed into trees, whatever the 'meanings' intended in the various sources from which Vespasiano may have recovered it, should also, perhaps, be seen in the context of Vespasiano's personal psychic experience, an experience of which we caught a glimpse in the second of the sonnets which we considered in the last chapter:

> *If, by the Tagus, driven by love's will,*
> *By field, or hill, or woodland's dark recesses,*
> *I see those fair cheeks and those lovely tresses,*
> *The light of those dear eyes that haunts me still.*
> *So firmly is the thought now taken hold,*
> *Hardly, by now, have I begun to list*
> *The myriad forms she takes before my eyes.*

380. Francesco Colonna, *Hypnerotomachia Poliphili*, cit., p.174.

As Phaeton plunges head-first into the Po, the horses of which he has lost control fall with him, occupying the centre of the composition. Their posture, tightly pulled-in hind legs emphasising the power of their rumps, is strongly reminiscent of the two horses (whose front parts are hidden) which draw Apollo's chariot across the sky in Vespasiano's *studiolo*; it is as though they had been frozen in their motion and turned through ninety degrees to hang, head down above the surface of the water. This may be no more than the careless copying of what was already a copy (though the brutal reversal here of that serene image copied in Vespasiano's 'official' residence is unlikely to have been accidental) but these three suspended horses are unmistakably the same as the three (two chestnut and a white one between) whose backsides are seen disappearing into a cloud in the painting of Daedalus and the fall of Icarus (also a fairly close derivative of Giulio Romano's original in the ducal palace at Mantua). The thematic content of the two paintings, as of the two myths, is, indeed, so closely parallel that, if the significance of the two stories were to be read simply in terms of their moral implication, one would be inclined to wonder why Vespasiano should have wanted to represent the same thing twice. In their differences, however, the two paintings reveal symmetrical, but contrasting structures:

1)   In the image of Phaeton, it is the sisters who are immobilised by their grief; in the Icarus painting, it is the father who watches helpless as his own invention leads to the destruction of his son.

2)   The horses which, in the painting of Icarus and Daedalus, follow their proper course through the sky, steering a path between Scorpio and Leo, appear in the scene of the fall of Phaeton devoid of force or purpose.

We shall find other indications of the nexus of symmetries, latent and manifest, which both link and differentiate the depicted themes of the Sala dei Miti.

Ovid's narrative of the myth of Daedalus and Icarus first introduces Daedalus as the architect entrusted with the construction of his labyrinth on the island of Crete:

> *Daedalus, a man famous for his skill in the builder's art, planned and performed the work. He confused the usual passages and deceived the eye by a conflicting maze of divers winding paths. Just as the watery Meander plays in the Phrygian fields, flows back on itself, beholds its own waves coming on their way, and sends its uncertain waters now towards their source and now towards the open sea: so Daedalus made those innumerable winding passages, and was himself scarce able to find his way back to the place of entry, so deceptive was the enclosure he had built.* [381]

It seems unlikely (though not impossible) that Alberti was thinking of this passage when he recommended that "it is better if the roads are not straight, but meandering gently like a river flowing now here, now there, from one bank to the other" [382], but one can imagine that Vespasiano might have recognised in this description of Daedalus' labyrinth an echo of his own, consciously deceptive planning of Sabbioneta.

381. *Ovid, Metamorphoses, cit.,
Book VIII, p.417.*
382. *L.B.Alberti, On the Art
of Building in Ten Books, cit.,
p.106. See Chapter Two.*

The purpose for which the labyrinth was built was, of course, to conceal the "strange hybrid monster-child", fruit of the adulterous liaison of Pasiphaë with a wild bull. Here, then, we might again discover a latent symmetry with the story of Saturn and Philyra and with the suggestion of Vespasiano's anxious identification. It was in order to escape from Crete, from Minos and his wife, that Daedalus, trapped by the sea, resorted to the invention of artificial flight; his son, over-excited by this novel experience, passed too near the sun, causing the disintegration of his wax-fastened wings while Daedalus, flying prudently, continued in search of his native land.

Apollo, the benign celestial influence of Vespasiano's studiolo, has appeared in the Sala dei Miti, as a reluctant accessory to the destruction of his son and as a natural force which consumes what comes too close. In the myth of Marsyas (Marsyas was a Satyr, another half-man half-beast associated with sexual hyper-activity), he appears as a vengeful and duplicitous rival. This is Hyginus' account:

> *Minerva is said to [have] been the first to make pipes from deer bones and to have come to the banquet of the gods to play. Juno and Venus made fun of her because she was gray-eyed and puffed out her cheeks, so when, mocked in her playing and called ugly, she came to the forest of Ida to a spring, as she played she viewed herself in the water, and saw that she was rightly mocked. Because of this she threw away the pipes and vowed that whoever picked them up would be punished severely. Marsyas, a shepherd, son of Oeagrus, one of the satyrs, found them, and by practising assiduously kept making sweeter sounds day by day, so that he challenged Apollo to play the lyre in a contest with him. When Apollo came there, they took the Muses as judges. Marsyas was departing as victor, when Apollo turned his lyre upside down, and played the same tune - a thing which Marsyas couldn't do with his pipes. And so Apollo defeated Marsyas, bound him to a tree, and turned him over to a Scythian who stripped his skin off limb by limb. He gave the rest of his body for burial to his pupil Olympus. From his blood the river Marsyas takes its name.* [383]

Here, for the first time, we seem to have the specific theme of punishment for seeking to compete with an olympian deity. Even in this case, however, the fate of Marsyas (himself a demi-god) was sealed at the moment when he picked up Minerva's pipe, having no knowledge of the consequences which would follow from this apparently innocent act. If there is a moral to this fable, it can only be that the ferocity of the gods is random and inescapable. The vindictive cruelty of Minerva links this with the last painting of the series, depicting the weaving contest of Minerva with Arachne. If Marsyas, who has become the rival of a male deity, suffers a fate which, in the terminology of psychoanalysis, would fall easily into the broad category of 'castration' then the myth of Arachne evokes the mirror image of the same anxiety: Arachne, in rivalry with a virginal female deity, is transformed into a spider. On the subject of spiders, Sigmund Freud has this to say:

> *According to Abraham (1922) a spider in a dream is a symbol of the mother; but it means the phallic mother, whom one fears, so that the fear of the spider expresses the horror of incest with the mother and the abhorrence felt towards female genitals. You know perhaps that the mythological figure of the Medusa's head is to be traced back to the same motive of castration-fear.* [384]

383. Hyginus, Fables, cit., No.CLXV, p.128.
384. Sigmund Freud, New Introductory Lectures on Psycho-analysis, trans. W.J.H.Sprott, London, 1946, p.37.

There is a sexual connotation, also, in the repeated theme of horses, explicit in the disguised figure of Saturn but clearly implicit in the emphasis given to the powerful backsides and huge testicles seen to propel Apollo's chariot in the Icarus painting and implicitly reversed in the 'suspended' horses which accompany Phaeton's fall. If recent forensic evidence is correct and if Vespasiano's young son, Luigi, did, indeed, die from congenital syphilis, then the fall of Icarus (while his architect father continues his journey) could have carried a very direct associative charge. The anxieties which seem to be suggested in the other images are more difficult to locate biographically but are by no means inconsistent with what we do know of Vespasiano's personal life or with our reading of his poetry.

In his account of the myth of Arachne, Ovid stresses the contrast between the respective points of view of gods and mortals: Minerva's tapestry depicts the twelve principal deities with the attributes for which they are worshipped while, in the corners, are scenes showing the dreadful fate of those who dare to compete with them. Arachne, meanwhile, weaves the stories in which the gods, by treachery and disguise, had ravished and ruined countless innocent young women (the case of Philyra and Saturn is specifically mentioned here[385]). This axis of symmetry, which appears to operate on a structural rather than a moral plane, draws together the last two of the paintings in this room with the first, the seduction of Philyra. In a sense, also, the contrast between the gods' and human morality is a fundamental structure in the content of the cycle as a whole. We need not suppose that Vespasiano who, so far as we can tell, thought of himself as a moderately orthodox Christian, believed in the deities and the myths of ancient paganism as their creators might have done, but we need not assume, on the other hand, that he (or many of his contemporaries) could see in the poetic world of classical mythology nothing more than a set of exemplars upon which to construct precepts of moral behaviour. If his interest, in the decoration of the Sala dei Miti, had been no more than to exhort himself or his visitors to a stoical acceptance of the evident injustice which rules human affairs, he could have done so by examples (plenty of which exist in classical literature) which clearly manifest such dignified resignation. Instead, Vespasiano chose to compile a cycle of images whose cumulative effect is one of stark horror and a sense of outrage at the destructive operation of forces beyond human or rational control. At this mid-point of his upper floor sequence in the garden palace, then, Vespasiano chose to decorate the walls of this room with emblems of his worldly success while in the five panels overhead we might, perhaps, feel that we are presented with a description of the psychic world which he inhabited. It is a world in which femininity is either lubricious, inaccessible or threatening, in which fathers must watch the destruction of their sons, powerless to intervene, in which the gods deceive and cheat while the (literally, unbridled) virile energy of horses careers unrestrained or hangs impotently disabled; where the concourse of women with beasts begets monsters.

385. Ovid, Metamorphoses, cit.,
Book VI, p.297.

The Sala dei Miti is traversed diagonally, breaking the regular alignment of the first three rooms and suggesting a point of transition. If each of the first three rooms could be seen as containing a static representation, a 'snapshot' self-portrait in relation to three aspects of Vespasiano's mental life, the two rooms which follow appear to present us with a narrative. The next space to be entered is, in fact, little more than a lobby, from which it is possible to proceed immediately to the last room in the sequence while the so-called Sala di Enea is laid off to the left. Here, beneath a vaulted ceiling in which winged putti playfully carry the emblems of Mercury (in the centre), Pluto, Jove, Neptune and Bacchus, alternated with monochrome figures of Fortitude, Justice, Prudence and Temperance while the interstices filled with an encyclopedic 'natural history' of known and fabled animal species, the wall frescoes illustrate scenes from the first six books of Virgil's Aeneid. (Fig. 9.3)

Exceptionally, in the case of the Sala di Enea, we are fortunate in that a scholarly and well-considered analysis of its decorative programme is available in a paper by Susanne Grötz[386]. In this study, the eight scenes are identified (running clockwise) as:

1)   Laocoön struggling with the serpents,
2)   the entry of the wooden horse into Troy,
3)   Troy in flames,
4)   the flight of Aeneas,
5)   Aeneas setting sail,
6)   Aeneas and his mother Venus at Carthage,
7)   Aeneas with Dido at Carthage,
8)   Aeneas and Sybil at the entrance to Hades.

386. Susanne Grötz, "La Saletta di Enea ed il Mito della Città Ideale" In Atti del Convegno, cit., pp.153-174.

Previous commentators[387] had supposed the final scene to represent Aeneas and Dido seeking shelter from the storm in a cave, the occasion of Aeneas' seduction by the Carthaginian queen. As though this were the conclusion of the hero's quest. Grötz points out that no other virgilian cycle painted during the renaissance is at all similar to this one at Sabbioneta which must, therefore, be examined in terms of its allegorical meaning. Her reading of the Sabbioneta cycle is based upon a detailed study of the original virgilian text set within the framework of Cristoforo Landino's *Disputationes Camaldulenses*, a fifteenth-century analysis of Books I - VI of the Aeneid by which the stages depicted in the frescoes can be found to correspond with stages in the purification of the human spirit. The Trojan scenes thus come to denote the uncontrolled bodily passions of youth; the flight and embarkation, the beginnings of wisdom; the Carthaginian episodes, the learning of self control and good government while the final scene is the dedication of the purified spirit to the contemplative life. It seems probable that Vespasiano was indeed familiar with Landino's commentary and likely that he would have approved of this sort of interpretation. Grötz's thesis becomes less persuasive, however, when she wants to argue that the descent of Aeneas to Hades is a reference to the foundation of Rome, which is there prophesied. It is not Aeneas himself who is destined to build the first city of Rome but his descendant Romulus; Anchises' prophetic speech does not culminate in this event, touching upon it only in passing:

> *Illustrious Rome will bound her power with earth,*
> *Her spirit with Olympus. She'll enclose*
> *Her seven hills with one great city wall,*
> *Fortunate in the men she breeds...*[388]

and it is with 'the men she breeds' that the prophecy carries on for another hundred and fifty lines. As we have seen before, the reduction of Vespasiano's intentions to an identification with the first builder of Rome can only be supported by a reduced reading of the evidence. Since, in the present work, we are inclined to approach Vespasiano from a different direction, we can look, in any case, for different indications in the paintings and in the text which might account for his selection of these particular subjects.

The correspondence of the painted scenes in the Sala di Enea with the virgilian text is remarkably close, so that the source of each can be located in just a few lines of the poem; background detail refers to material either immediately before or after the principal source. Laocoön's hopeless struggle with the two sea-serpents which first devour his two sons and then overpower his armed resistance - "Like a slashed bull escaping from an altar, The fumbled axe shrugged off" - before they go on to coil up demurely at the feet of Minerva, powerful image though it is, has no obvious place in the narrative scheme of the other paintings. Grötz is obliged to admit that the story of Laocoön does not figure in Landino's allegorical commentary and must content herself with the observation that this story was a generally popular theme of renaissance art.

387. e.g. Tellini Perina, Sabbioneta, cit., p.56.
388. Virgilius Maro, Publius, The Aeneid, trans. Robert Fitzgerald, London, 1992, Book VI, line 1049, p.187.

It was, of course, Laocoön who had earlier attempted to dissuade the
Trojans from accepting the greek 'gift' of the wooden horse. The pictured episode
begins as Laocoön is about to put the knife to "a massive bull" in sacrifice to Neptune,
so that the simile of the "slashed bull escaping from an altar" takes on a double (or
perhaps a triple) resonance. It was a massive bull that fathered the "strange hybrid
monster-child", born of Pasiphaë which had to be concealed in the labyrinth on
Crete. This image is possibly reminiscent of André Green's fourth 'defensive position'
in relation to fantasies of the primal scene: alternating identification of the father as
aggressor and healer so that we might see, in the image of Laocoön's destruction, the
destruction of the 'good' father by his bestial counterpart. What a way to begin the
'narrative' of Vespasiano's life!

In the two images which follow, an enormous and life-like trojan horse
is seen, first, on the point of 'violating' the city whose wall has been willingly breached
by the Trojans and, afterwards, within the city as Troy collapses in fire and devastation
under the Greek assault:

> So we breached the walls
> And laid the city open. Everyone
> Pitched in to get the figure underpinned
> With rollers, hempen lines around the neck.
> Deadly, pregnant with enemies, the horse
> Crawled upward to the breach.

And then:

> Greeks are the masters in our burning city.
> Tall as a cliff, set in the heart of town,
> Their horse pours out armed men. [389]

If the struggle of Laocoön and his sons can be understood as a 'family
scene', then the two images representing the 'rape' of Troy stand framed, in this
sequence, between this and another version of the theme of 'family'. Aeneas escapes
from the conflagration of his home city, carrying his 'good' father on his shoulders:

> over my breadth of shoulder
> And bent neck, I spread out a lion skin
> For tawny cloak and stooped to take his weight.
> The little Iulus put his hand in mine
> And came with shorter steps beside his father.
> My wife fell in behind.

Soon after this, in Virgil's narrative, the wife becomes a 'dead mother':

> Alas,
> Creusa, taken from us by grim fate, did she
> Linger or stray, or sink in weariness?
> There is no telling. Never would she be
> Restored to us. Never did I look back
> Or think to look for her, lost as she was, [390]

389. Ibid., Book II, lines 313
and 440, pp.43 and 45.
390. Ibid., Book II, lines 936
and 959, pp.58 and 59.

When Aeneas does go back looking for Creusa, he finds only "her sad wraith" who tells him that he cannot take her with him: "It was not so ordained". The passage has echoes of Virgil's description of Euridice's withdrawal to Hades, quoted in the last chapter, but, unlike Orpheus, Aeneas had not even looked back.

With this she left me weeping
Wishing that I could say so many things,
And faded on the tenuous air. Three times
I tried to put my arms around her neck,
Three times enfolded nothing, as the wraith
Slipped through my fingers, bodiless as wind,
Or like a flitting dream. [391]

In the next painting, Aeneas sets sail, an exile in search of a new homeland. Virgil has, in this instance, nothing at all to say about the embarkation, merely noting that it took place, so that it is not entirely clear why such a scene should have been included in the cycle. Vespasiano could, of course, have been thinking of his own embarkation, at the age of fifteen, when he set off to serve as page-boy to Charles V, at an unknown foreign destination and feeling, surely, as lonely and apprehensive as the hero of the Aeneid when he "drew away from our old country,/ our quiet harbours, and the coastal plain/ Where Troy had been."

Facing the Trojan scenes, on the third wall of the Sala di Enea, two Carthaginian episodes from Book I are represented. In the first of these, Venus, who is Aeneas' mother but is disguised as a huntress, reassures him that he has not, as he believed, lost all his ships and companions in a storm and that he should "Go on then, where the path leads, go ahead!" The lines which follow have a familiar ring about them:

On this she turned away. Rose-pink and fair
Her nape shone, her ambrosial hair exhaled
Divine perfume, her gown rippled full length,
And by her stride she showed herself a goddess.
Knowing her for his mother, he called out
To the figure fleeting away: "You! Cruel, too!
Why tease your son so often with disguises?
Why may we not join hands and speak and hear
The simple truth?

Not many lines later, and in the next painting, Dido is seen

Amid her people, cheering on the toil
Of a kingdom in the making. At the door
Of the goddess' shrine, under the temple dome,
All hedged about with guards on her high throne,
She took her seat. Then she began to give them
Judgements and rulings, [392]

391. *Ibid., Book II, line 1026, p.61.*
392. *Ibid., Book I, lines 552 and 686, pp.18 and 21.*

When Aeneas steps into this scene, he is concealed in a cloud which Venus has made around him and his companion. The painting shows the moment that the cloud clears and Dido sets eyes, for the first time, upon the object of her subsequent passion. Aeneas is, of course, readily seduced by the "kingdom in the making" - as Vespasiano might have felt himself to have been - and by its queen. It requires a special embassy from Mercury to remind him that his destiny lies elsewhere and that he must go down to Hades in order to find his father.

Which is what Aeneas is doing, accompanied by "the sybil feared by men", sword in hand and protected by the golden bough, in the last picture of the cycle. It is worth noting, also, that the temple in which the Sybil is found (and which appears in the background of the picture) is said by Virgil, in the same passage, to have been constructed and decorated by Daedalus and (in this decorative cycle within a decorative cycle?) included a scene which we have encountered before:

> *Here the brutish act appeared: Pasiphaë*
> *Being covered by the bull in the cow's place,*
> *Then her mixed breed, her child of double form,*
> *The minotaur, get of unholy lust.*
> *Here too, that puzzle of the house of Minos,*
> *The maze none could untangle…*[393]

The emergence of this reference, so close to the manifest content of two scenes depicted in Vespasiano's garden palace, could lend weight to a suspicion which has been expressed earlier, that our prince was obsessively troubled with the fear that he was a 'child of double form'.

The theme of descent into the world of the dead is reiterated in the short passageway which by-passes the Sala di Enea. Four scenes from the myth of Orpheus are depicted here, evidently based, this time, upon Ovid's version of the story: Orpheus in Hades, Orpheus with Pluto, Orpheus enchanting the wild animals with his music and Orpheus torn to pieces by the Bacchantes. The last scene depicted as one leaves this small chamber shows the poet's dismembered body floating on the river while the Bacchantes are turned into trees. (Fig. 9.4) In Ovid's version, there is no mention of Aristeus and the second loss of Eurydice is quite briefly passed over. The grief-stricken poet turns to homosexuality and it is with tales of aberrant human sexual behaviour that he regales the wild beasts. After his death at the hands of Bacchus' unruly followers, Orpheus returns to the underworld:

> *The poet's shade fled beneath the earth, and recognized all the places he had seen before; and seeking through the blessed fields, found Eurydice and caught her in his eager arms. Here now side by side they walk; now Orpheus follows her as she precedes, now goes before her, now may in safety look back upon his Eurydice.*[394]

393. Ibid., Book VI, line 37, p.160.
394. Ovid, Metamorphoses, cit., Book XI, p.125.

Nothing in the relentlessly sombre content of the preceding rooms can seem to have prepared the visitor for the experience which follows. The Sala degli Specchi is so called because the central panels of the ceiling and of the end walls were originally filled with mirrors; even without these, the effect of this, the largest apartment in the garden palace, is one of sparkling magnificence and one can imagine that it was the scene of brilliant receptions. (Fig. 9.5) On each of its long walls, framed by corinthian pilasters which mark out the intervals of the windows, two large panels are filled with elegantly painted landscape scenes which have conventionally been given the titles of *l'imbarco* (the embarkation), *la caccia* (the hunt), *il soggiorno agreste*, (the stroll in the countryside) and *la passaggiata*, (a country excursion) (for French visitors, this last is labelled 'la baignarde', a bathing scene). Hanno-Walter Kruft rightly reminds us that it was Vitruvius himself who recommended the decoration of rooms with scenes of pastoral landscape : "....and their walks, on account of the great length, they [the Greeks] decorated with a variety of landscapes, copying the characteristics of definite spots. In these paintings there are harbours, promontories, sea-shores, rivers, fountains, straits, fanes, groves, mountains, flocks, shepherds;" and pictures designed in the grand style, heroic events, etc.[395] Vitruvius then, incidentally, goes on to condemn the fantastic and "untruthful" images which had become fashionable in his "days of bad taste", by which he meant the style of 'grotesque' decoration which Vespasiano and his contemporaries also deployed without evident compunction.

One could still wonder, however, why, at the culmination of so unflinchingly serious a sequence of iconographic programmes (serious, whether by the reading which has been suggested here or by that which is more conventionally offered), Vespasiano should have chosen, at this point, to abandon themes of consequence in favour of an elegant but shallow hedonism. Certainly, the mood which the Sala degli Specchi seems to evoke is one which could hardly be more remote from that of his poetry, of the things he said or of the way that he appears to have conducted his life. Extrovert, vital and sensuous, the feeling created by the 'pastoral' decoration of the Sala degli Specchi is much more nearly reflected in a sonnet written by Vespasiano's father, Luigi Gonzaga:

> *Now that Love's beams are all around extending*
> *And the whole Earth is smiling, gracious and fair,*
> *And the grim icy waste, now, everywhere,*
> *From mountain heights in swollen streams descending.*
> *Now spreads Aurora's coral, softly blending*
> *Celestial nimbus in the dewy air,*
> *Day opens joyfully serene, and there*
> *Stops and inflames each fleeting heart, attending.*
> *The love-lorn beasts with longing howls lament,*
> *And in the open fields, twittering birds*
> *Tell of desire's peremptory command.*
> *Lilies and pearls, Love's painted ornament*
> *Purple and rose, embracing, I speak words*
> *To fill the air with sweetness, and the land.*[396]

395. Hanno-Walter Kruft, Städte in Utopia, cit., p.45. The passage to which he refers is in Book VII, Cap.V, 2.
396. Quoted in Irene Affò, Vita di Luigi Gonzaga & Vita di Vespasiano Gonzaga, cit., p.141.
Or che 'l raggio d'Amor per tutto splende
E fa la Terra graziosa intorno,
Il dianzi orrido ghiaccio d'ogn' intorno
Da più alti monti furioso scende.
E de'più fin corai l'Aurora stende
Celeste nembo rugiadoso, e adorno,
Apre soave, e dilettoso giorno
Che I cor fugaci avvolge, arreta, e incende.
Quinci ulular le fiere, che amor strinse,
S'odon garrir gli augelli in campo aprico,
E sospirar cui gran desio fa guerra.
Le rare perle, e i gigli, che depinse
Di rose Amor, e d'ostro, abbraccio, e dico
Parole d'addolcir l'aria, e la terra.

Vespasiano, who was certainly familiar with his father's poetry (he quoted from it in his own, as we have previously noted), might well have wished to emulate, in the decoration of his Sala degli Specchi, the state of mind which this sonnet so strongly evokes, even though (or even because) it was a mood which he himself can seldom have inhabited.

Pt 4 ~9

Unlike the characters depicted elsewhere in the garden palace, those that appear in the 'pastoral' scenes of the Sala degli Specchi are in the dress of Vespasiano's day, suggesting a contemporary, rather than an ancient literary source if there was any. In each of the scenes, there are figures larger and more prominent than one would expect if they were to be seen merely as 'local colour' to enliven the landscapes. Also, in each scene, an apparently similar female figure is to be seen, wearing (when she wears anything at all) a blue dress. In *l'imbarco*, she stands in conversation with some men while, close by, a ship is in port, evidently about to set sail. If one were looking for a source in Luigi Gonzaga's poetry in which the content of any of these paintings might have a direct visual counterpart, it would be found in the sonnet which Luigi wrote to his intended bride, Isabella Colonna, during the difficult time at which, although contracted to be married, the couple was beset by obstacles (including rival bids for her hand from the Colonna clan, Ippolito de' Medici, until he was made a cardinal, and Vespasiano's subsequent guardian, Don Ferrante Gonzaga.) On the Pope's orders, Isabella had to be 'examined' to test her determination to marry Luigi while he went to argue his case with lawyers at Bologna, where the Emperor, Charles V awaited coronation by Pope Clement VII. The sonnet expresses il Rodomonte's understandable anxiety:

If this your troubled ship seems far away,
Which only now seemed safely home in port,
By angry fortune's vengeance now is caught
Bound in the wayward sea's enforced delay;
And if, of what remains, some little way
Is still to go, Lady, be not distraught.
Till happy landfall now the time is short
That rich and worthy cargo will repay.
Learn from Briseis who faithfully endured
The hardest days, and carried in her womb
Noble Achilles' seed, so true her love,
Or from that other Greek who, what she wove
By day, each night unravelled on the loom,
So, every honour shall be your reward. [397]

If we imagine that the ship in port is not about to set sail but, equally credible, that it has just arrived, one could, perhaps, see the lady in blue as Isabella, in the part of Penelope, beset by suitors as Luigi/Odysseus arrives just in time with his 'rich and worthy cargo'. In the conventions of chivalric literature, blue was the colour of fidelity. [398]

212

397. Quoted in Ibid., p.143.
Se quella vostra travagliata barca,
Che or or vi parve in si sicuro porto,
Fortuna irata la respinge a torto
In l'alto mar troppo gravata, e carca;
Non vi turbata Donna, se ancor varca
Il poco che vi resta, perchè scorto
Tengo il bel lido, ove farà di corto
Di ricca, e onesta merce lieve, e scarca.
Ragion è se imitaste I duri giorni
Di quella Greca, a cui 'l gran seme increbbe
D'Achille, si del primo amor le calse,
Ch' or imitate l' altra, a cui più valse
Torre a la notte quel, che 'l giorno accrebbe,
Acciò ch' ogni valor vi fregi, e adorni.
398. See Huizinga, The Waning of the Middle Ages, cit., p.116.

Vespasiano can hardly even have seen his father; as soon as his mother was pregnant, Luigi had set off back from Fondi to Lombardy where he appears to have been busy hunting and refereeing duels while awaiting the emperor's call to go and fight the Turks. Instead, he was sent by the pope to enforce a take-over of Ancona (on the pretext of its defence against the Infidel), only returning to Fondi shortly before the incident at Vicovaro in which he lost his life. For the rest of his life, Vespasiano could only reconstruct an image of il Rodomonte from what his mother and his aunt Giulia told him and from the fulsomely laudatory accounts of poets and admirers by which Luigi was raised to almost mythical status as the paragon of aristocratic manhood. Amongst these panegyrics was the Eclogue written upon the death of Luigi by Gerolamo Muzio, undoubtedly known to Vespasiano and from which we quoted in the last chapter. Luigi's prowess as a huntsman was noted in his day; when he accompanied Charles V to the court of king Henry VIII, Luigi "earned the praise, and the warmest recognition from Charles, and from Henry" as a result of his performance in Windsor Great Park.[399] Muzio's poem picks up the theme:

> And he it was the bear's rapacious claw
> Faced without fear, and stood before its charges
> Giving no ground to the wild bristling boar.
> There, where Alceo turned, the place was guarded,
> Free from the scourge of predatory beasts.
> So skilful was he, and so great his courage,
> As far preeminent above all others
> As lofty pine-tree over lowly scrub.[400]

Vespasiano, unlike the majority of his kinsmen, seems to have had no particular enthusiasm for hunting. While the correspondence of his cousins at Mantua is full of references to favourite dogs and falcons, detailed instructions to game-keepers, plans for hunting expeditions[401], there seems to be no indication that Vespasiano had any such preoccupations although, no doubt, he would participate in such activities where the social situation demanded that he should. He did establish a hunting park at Bòzzolo where, if necessary, he could entertain his guests. The hunting scene in the Sala degli Specchi could well, therefore, have commemorated not Vespasiano's, but his father's exploits though it is less easy to imagine that Isabella, like the lady in blue, would have been actively involved.

399. Affò, Vita di Luigi Gonzaga, cit., p.52.
400. Gerolamo Muzio, Egloghe, cit., p.77V.
Altro non fu, che de l'unghiute branche
Non temesse de l'orso; & ch'à gli assalti
Del setoso cinghiar non desse luoco.
Ovunque Alceo volgeasi era sicuro
Per tutto intorno da noïose fiere.
Perchè con tal valor, con si bell'arti
Alto sorgea fra gli altri, come suole
Fra l'humili vermene eccelso Abete.
401. See, for instance, Giancarlo Malacarne, Le Cacce del Principe, cit.

In the two scenes painted on the wall opposite, (Fig. 9.6) it is far from clear what is the nature of the activities represented. That which is known as *il soggiorno agreste* shows a traveller on horseback in a wooded place, accompanied by two male figures on foot while two female figures, one the lady in blue, also on foot, come to meet them. In the scene which is (unaccountably) known as *la passaggiata*, a naked male figure is seated beside a river while, in front of him, stands the lady no longer in blue, though her blue gown floats behind her from her shoulder and another female figure, clothed, who might be the same as the companion in the previous picture. Close to this group lies a dog which, like the blue dress, could be an emblem of fidelity. Amongst the many strange features of these two scenes, the strangest is the casual nudity of the two principal figures; the clothed figures, as we have noted, are in the dress of the time but it is simply not believable that, in the late sixteenth century, people would have publicly taken off their clothes in order to enjoy themselves in the countryside. A similar violation of accepted social mores in the painting attributed to Giorgione, "Le Concert Champêtre" in the Louvre, has generated a voluminous, though inconclusive literature,[402] in the light of which it is, to say the least, odd that the fresco at Sabbioneta has been so uncritically taken at its retrospective face value. Either, then, the scene is entirely fanciful or we are missing something. Following closely after the passage about hunting, Muzio's poem continues:

> Oh, Tyrrhenia, thrice, even four times favoured
> By a propitious star, above all others,
> Not destined for that dark forgetfulness.
> You, happy first, amongst the sorrowing spirits
> At that mire whither every soul is summoned
> To the grim transit of the stygian ferry,
> Come now to meet you, find your dearest friend;
> Embracing, naked shade and naked shadow
> Among pale spirits, on that gloomy pathway,
> You'll be to him a guide and dear companion.
> And now to the dense thickets, hidden places
> Of flickering souls, towards the shadowy myrtles
> Guiding your steps, amongst these you'll discover
> Some solace on this long and sightless journey.
> At last, these fields of tears, this path of shadow
> Now left behind you, a clear sky will open
> You'll find yourself where a new sun is shining,
> And where new stars appear in a new heaven.
> There, a broad plain, in pristine verdure painted
> Is ringed with pleasant hills and smiling valleys.
> There, between shrubs, fresh herbiage and flowers
> Runs a clear river, in its course divided
> In rivulets amongst the verdant borders;
> Going by ample, gracious meanders
> Parting the land through all this happy country.
> Where among leafy groves of branching laurel
> Over the living water's gentle murmur
> Is heard the rustic pipe and singing voices:
> And there are scenes of graceful happy dancing,
> Festival games and youthful exercises.[403]

402. This literature is comprehensively reviewed by Francoise Bardon in Le Concert Champêtre, Première Partie, Paris, 1995, and a post-structuralist reading of the painting in the Seconde Partie which leaves its most puzzling aspect as obscure as ever.

403.
*O fuora l'altre per tre volte, &
quattro*
*Fortunata Tirrhenia à tanta
agnoscia*
Non riserbata da benigna stella.
Tu prima lieta tra le afflite genti
*A la palude, ov'ogni anima
arriva,*
*A'i tristi guadi del nocchier di
stige,*
*Ti farai'ncontra al dilettoso
amico;*
*Et nuda ombra abbracciando
l'ombra ignuda*
*Per lo buio camin tra l'alme
smorte*
*Cara à lui diverrai compagna,
& guida.*
*Quindi à le folte selve, à i luoghi
occulti*
*De l'alme accese, & de gli
ombrosi mirti*
*Drizzando il pie tra quelli alcun
riposo*
*Prendera de la lunga, & cieca
via.*
*Lasciati appresso I lagrimosi
campi*
*E'l camin tenebroso, ad aere
aperto*
Vedrassi giunto, la've novo Sole,
*Novo ciel apparisce, & nove
stelle.*
*Quivi ampio pian di
verdeggiante smalto*
Cignon ameni colli, & liete valle.
*Donde fra varie piante, & herbe
, & fiori*
Chiaro fiume, scorrendo si divide
Tra'l fresco verde per diversi rivi;
Et va con dolci, & spatiosi giri
Tutto partendo quel felice suolo.
*Dove infra boschi di fronduti
allori*
Al dolce mormorio de l'onde vive
*S'ode versi cantar, sondar
zampogne:*
Et far si vede gratiosi balli,
*Festosi giuochi, & giovenili
prove.*

The thoughts expressed in this passage are by no means original; many of them are borrowed directly from Book VI of the Aeneid. In certain details, however, there seems to be a close correlation between Muzio's text and the painted scenes in the Sala degli Specchi. There is a meeting, in woodland, with a 'dearest friend', there are the 'naked shade and naked shadow' and there is the dominant image of the river. There is, of course, nothing in the Eclogue about a lady in blue, nor any reference to the idea of fidelity. These are themes which Vespasiano has imported from other associative sources, so that it would be wrong to assume that the paintings are direct 'illustrations' of any single text. The themes of reunion which we discovered in Ovid's version of the Orpheus myth, of Aeneas' meeting with his father in Hades, of Odysseus' safe homecoming and the fidelity of Penelope, of Luigi Gonzaga's intrepid hunting exploits ("festival games and youthful exercises"), are conflated and overlaid in this cycle of four 'pastoral' scenes so as to construct an entirely new poetic interpretation, a version that was entirely personal to Vespasiano.

It has been conjectured that while Bernardino Campi was responsible for the landscape painting in these four panels, figures were painted in by another artist. If this had been done using less permanent pigments, it could account for the ghostly transparency of many of the minor (though not the major) figures, an effect which, in the present condition of the frescoes, certainly contributes in a very strange way to the unworldly effect of the paintings.

The realisation that, on entering this glittering apartment with its tranquil images of rustic pleasure, one is entering the world of departed spirits, that these are not the landscapes of an earthly Arcadia but the Elysian Fields, would, in all probability, have been as disturbing to Vespasiano's guests as it might be to ourselves. The visitor has, of course been prepared for it in the content of the two preceding rooms: the scenes from the Aeneid which culminate in Aeneas' descent to Hades reiterated in the myth of Orpheus. But the shock lies not so much in the subject-matter itself as in the affect which it has been made to carry: the underworld is emphatically a happy place. One need not suppose that Vespasiano - even if he was, himself, conscious of another interpretation - had any particular intention that this interior (or any of the others) should be taken at other than its face value; like his poems, the significance of these rooms seems to be directed, not to the outside world, but to Vespasiano's personal interior life. The clues which could lead us to this interpretation are clues only because modern investigations of the human psyche have enabled us to recognise them as such.

We prefaced this chapter with a remark by C.G.Jung, stressing the idea that neurosis contains within it an effort at self-cure; that the symptoms of mental disturbance can, and should, be regarded as favourable. Might one suppose, then, that in this culmination of the sequence of rooms on the upper floor of his garden palace, Vespasiano presented to himself the resolution of his internal conflicts? Do we see a reunion of his father and his mother (under their benign aspects), in a space apart, safe from the destructive tensions which drive the imagery of the Sala dei Miti? Hardly surprising, in that case, that the affect should be so confusingly serene.

Over each window, in the Sala degli Specchi, there is a monochrome
plaster relief in which a scene from Roman history records an example of outstanding
personal courage: Horatio Cocles, Mutius Scaevola (again) along with Attilius
Regulus, Decius Murus, Marcus Curius and Papirius Maso. These episodes might
appear strangely incongruous in a room seemingly dedicated to arcadian imagery;
their shallow relief seems to project them into the real, rather than the fictive space
of the room while their monochromy further detaches them from the fictive world
of the paintings. The three lines which follow those we have just quoted from Muzio
may supply an explanation:

> *Hither descend to stay, peacefully resting,*
> *Those who by virtue, worthy of high honour*
> *For some short time have dwelt among the living:*[404]

The thought is, again, borrowed from Book VI of the Aeneid, that
only outstanding mortals are admitted to the Elysian Fields and, in these terms, the
presence of the scenes depicted in relief could make perfect sense.

It is unfortunate that no one has yet made the effort to reinstate the
mirrors from whose magical effect the Sala degli Specchi has taken its name. The
production of mirrors in flat and comparatively large pieces, such that they could
be employed as an architectural device, was a technical innovation only achieved in
1675 by Louis Lucas de Néhou, and precipitated a widespread vogue for mirrored
interiors through the eighteenth century. Because the experience of such rooms has
become familiar, it is easy to forget that the technology for producing them did not
exist in Vespasiano's time. It seems likely that the mirrors at Sabbioneta were specchi
d'acciaio, plates of metal coated with an alloy of copper and tin whose manufacture
was patented at Venice in 1572. Neither perfectly flat nor able to remain untarnished
for any extended period, such mirrors, like those also made in Venice from glass,
could hardly produce the literal illusion of extended space which we associate with
the baroque interiors of a later century. Insofar as they were seen as having any
architectural potential, this was generally restricted to the field of practical jokes;
writing, also, in 1572, Leonardo Fioravanti has this to say:

> *This art, therefore, gives great pleasure in many ways. Without it, it would be*
> *difficult for women to make up their faces or arrange their hair. But anyone*
> *who sees a monkey or an imp look at itself in a mirror will be delighted to*
> *see the affection which they show to the one they see reflected. But it seems to*
> *me, in fact, that mirrors are a very bad thing to have in the house; because*
> *a beautiful woman, seeing herself, will fall into the sin of vainglory: and one*
> *who is ugly will sin equally in her mental disturbance: and for this reason*
> *mirrors are a bad thing to have in the house: the more so, since these days it*
> *is not just women but men, too, who want to see their reflection. And because*
> *of this, there are so many masters in the world of this art who devote the most*
> *subtle thought to the invention of grotesque mirrors whose diverse effects are*
> *to be seen. I remember once having seen in the glorious City of the Kingdom*
> *of Naples, a fine gentleman, who had a mirror made with such artifice that*
> *a person who stood in front of it to look at himself would see more than a*
> *dozen figures or shadows coming out of it, striking terror in those who saw*
> *their reflections, the most monstrous thing I have ever seen in this art. [....]*
> *While it might seem that a mirror would be a fine ornament in a room: and*
> *for this they are greatly admired, those who admire them the most are Ladies,*
> *and infants; because these have lighter brains, and because of this lightness,*
> *the curiosity of mirrors appeals to them.*[405]

404.
Quivi discende al placido
soggiorno
Chiunque per virtu di laude
degno
Per alcun tempo è stato tra
viventi:
405. *Leonardo Fioravanti, Dello*
Speccio di Scientia Universale,
Venice, 1572, p.62R. The book
is a comprehensive review of
the arts and sciences, in which
Architecture comes after the art
of domesticating wild animals.
Francis Bacon evidently had a
mirror dedicated to a practical
joke in his house of Gorhambery,
St Albans. (See John Aubrey, ed.
John Buchanon-Brown, Brief
Lives, Harmondsworth, 2000,
p.33.)

It seems clear, then, that at the time that Vespasiano decorated his Sala degli Specchi, there was no established tradition for the architectural deployment of mirrors on a large scale. If (to paraphrase Vespasiano's assessment of his vice-regency at Navarra, quoted earlier) he was not the first to see an architectural potential in mirrors, he was not second to many. But it is likely, also, that, given the technical, as well as the cultural limitations of the product available to him, Vespasiano had in mind something very different from the sparkling fragmentation of optical space so much enjoyed in the eighteenth century. At best, technically and as perceived in the popular imagination of his time, his mirrors would reveal a shadowy and mysteriously populated world, uncanny, perhaps, rather than monstrous but, nonetheless, decidedly 'other'. One is reminded of the conversation held at Casale:

> ....*but yet I think that according to your meaning and the bare words, it may stand with reason, that there are not more dead men, but rather more living, because Plato was wont to say, that during this present life, we are as dead men, and that our bodies are our owne sepulchres, meaning to inferre thereby, that we begin to live, when we dye. Whereupon, according to this construction, we that are living must be accompted dead, and those that are dead, must be thought as living, the which graunted, most true it is, that ther are in number more living men, then dead.*

Epilogue

From our investigation of the 'love' poetry which he wrote, we have gained the impression that Vespasiano was trying to reach an understanding of his own psychic condition, a condition which, nevertheless, he felt himself powerless to change. In the cycle of paintings which we have just considered (and which dates from a later phase of Vespasiano's life), a similar condition is indicated but, in this case, the series ends with a poetic resolution of his conflict. The city of Sabbioneta was under construction during virtually the whole of Vespasiano's adult life, so that one should not expect to find in it (even if architecture, like poetry and painting, were able to carry such specific psychological content) the expression of a single, definitive thought. Sabbioneta was, on the contrary, the receptacle into which Vespasiano poured the whole of his complex, evolving and often contradictory impulses. If it is possible, in the architecture of Sabbioneta, to discover a sense of 'resolution', we might still have discovered no more than that 'aesthetic finality' which resides in any piece of architecture which has been well worked out. It is in the nature of architecture, whatever the personal mental state of the architect, to strive towards such a condition. Beyond a purely formal resolution, conspicuous in parts and conspicuously absent in others, there is, however, at Sabbioneta, a sense of 'completeness' about the place which we noted in the Introduction. It seems that Vespasiano regarded the city in which he died as, to all intents and purposes, finished. In seeking to account for the way in which Vespasiano could have regarded his city as 'finished', we would not be looking for perfection in its formal configuration or detail so much as for a narrative or psychological completeness.

The myth of Philomen and Baucis, which occupies the upper part of Pt 4 ~9 the 'architectural' room in the garden palace sequence, might suggest that Vespasiano wanted to see Sabbioneta as a 'home' for the reception of the immortals, a home which would be transformed, through their occupancy, into a shrine tended, thereafter, by its mortal householders. A psychic project such as this would be consistent with André Green's observation of the subject's desire "to nourish the dead mother, to maintain her perpetually embalmed." More specifically perhaps, in the case of Sabbioneta, a 'home' in which the father/mother/child triangle, reintegrated, would exist without the fear of violation: a city safe within its walls, never to be violated as Troy had been, depicted in conflagration on the wall of the Sala di Enea. A home was, after all, something of which, as a child, Vespasiano had been largely deprived.

In each of Sabbioneta's principal urban spaces, there is a trio of representational structures, an arrangement for which there is no suggestion to be found in any of the architectural treatises. In the Piazza Ducale, there is the ducal palace, suggestive of 'paternal' authority, the Palazzo della Ragione, the protected and disciplined subject whose diminutive architectural scale renders it almost literally child-like, and the church of Santa Maria Assunta (the Virgin assumed into heaven - another dead mother?). In the Piazza d'Armi, the trio is formed by the 'paternal' rocca, the distinctly 'feminine' garden palace (where, in an inner chamber, the painted ceiling 'draws down' venereal influence) and the Corridor Grande, the 'cathedral of modern knowledge', a room only to be reached by a bridge linking it to the Sala degli Specchi, site of a parental reunion.

The spatial relationship of Sabbioneta's two other principal monuments - the church of the Incoronata and the theatre - to the two major urban spaces is strikingly similar; both are partially visible but withdrawn a similar distance into a subsidiary perspective space. Clearly, by this device, the sense that a variety of further representational structures is distributed outside of the main urban spaces has been effectively produced and there is every reason to suppose that this effect was intentional. Francesco di Giorgio, whom we quoted in Chapter 2, thought that a theatre should be located a little distant from the principal monuments of the city since this would encourage people to approach it with curiosity; something of this thought may have been in Vespasiano's mind also. But if the motivation of Sabbioneta's labyrinthine quality was evidently overdetermined, one could, at least, allow that the idea of Daedalus' cunning construction, whose purpose was to conceal a half-human monster, would have a place in the latent content of Vespasiano's cunningly constructed architectural dream. And if the church of the Incoronata - Vespasiano's mausoleum and also, perhaps, his hiding-place - is an incompletely felt presence in relation to the ducal piazza, the embodiment of Sabbioneta's political configuration, then the improbably accidental symmetry of the theatre's location in relation to the space in which Vespasiano's dynastic consciousness was most forcefully exhibited could suggest that this, the metaphorical space of his public appearance was intended, like his tomb, as an incompletely felt and, perhaps, in some sense, a critical presence.

The project of Sabbioneta might, then, be seen in terms of Vespasiano's need, over the course of his life, to construct, on the scale of a small city what was constructed in microcosm in the upper floor of the garden palace: a space (one might, indeed, call it a theatre) in which to act out the progress and, perhaps, the eventual resolution of his 'private madness'. And if, even today, one can sense in Sabbioneta a mirage-like quality, the metaphor might recall the 'looking-glass world' created in the Sala degli Specchi. In the space of Sabbioneta every image seems to refract into the after-image of its contrary: the present into the past, the distant into the close-up, the ordinary into the monumental, the ideal into the contingent. The apparent simplicity of its architectural components belies an extraordinary work of condensation.

If we have achieved anything through this investigation, it can only be that we have added to the already long list of possible explanations for the project of Sabbioneta. To the expression of personal power and prestige, the construction of a 'new Rome', a Utopia or an 'ideal city', city as 'theatre', an exercise in precocious picturesque urban design or a nostalgic retreat from the historical realities of its time, we have added a few more. In the first chapter, we were able to see Sabbioneta as a critique of Italy's lack of leadership and self-reliance while, in the second, we seemed to find a critical amendment to the prescriptions of the trattatisti. The third and fourth chapters enabled us to see Sabbioneta as the focus for an ambition and a creativity frustrated by the changing realities of modern politics and warfare. Then, in Chapter 5, we discovered the notion of Sabbioneta constructed around the image of an ideal academy, an academy evidently linked with contemporary efforts to transcend the religious divisions which threatened the very foundations of society; and we saw the emergence of a new psychological, scientific and historical self-consciousness, expressed in the rampant eclecticism of Sabbioneta's architectural references. Chapter 7 explored the idea of Sabbioneta as some sort of talismanic repository of the magical force of Vespasiano's ancestors, but we found, also, that it could be read as a template for the institution of a revived Imperium. Finally, through the study of Vespasiano's poetry and of the mythological themes which he deployed in his garden palace, we caught a glimpse of motives more intimate and more closely bound up with the circumstances of his early life, suggesting that Sabbioneta could be seen as an Elysium, a place of reconciliation where the tormented (or tormenting) spirits of Vespasiano's mother and father could be preserved in peace.

If the city of Sabbioneta remains cryptic, we have discovered, at least, that it is so because it was 'overdetermined' in the mind of a lonely, highly self-conscious and intelligent, idealistic and psychically troubled human being. And if, as we are told, Vespasiano's dying words were: "ora sono guarito" (now I am cured), it was a cure achieved with very little outside help and through a quite unusual form of personal endeavour. In the first chapter we saw a convoy of wagons, carrying the family's furniture to Luigi Carrafa's properties in Naples and the triumphal arch, intended to celebrate Carrafa's investiture as second duke of Sabbioneta, finished only because it was already started. For the citizens of Sabbioneta who had, literally, inhabited Vespasiano's externalised mental world, this may have been a cruel reawakening into the harsh realities of normal life, but it seems that, for Vespasiano, in the end, the looking-glass space of his dream life had - just about - held firm.

~

Figures.

In 1588, Leone Leoni's bronze figure of Vespasiano was placed "outside his palace, beside the marble stair, to the left, coming out of the palace" according to the diary of Niccolo de Dondi. It was removed, upon his death, to its present position in Vespasiano's funeral monument in the church of the Incoronata.

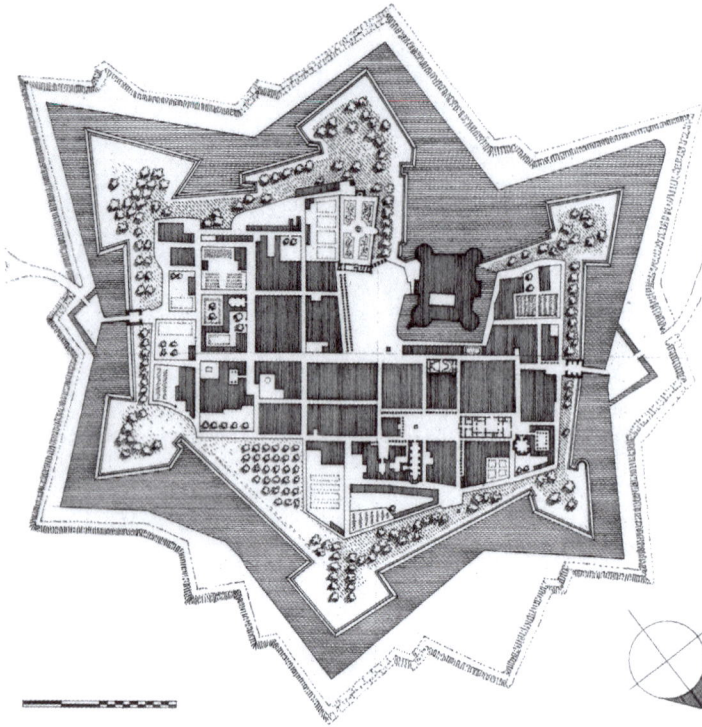

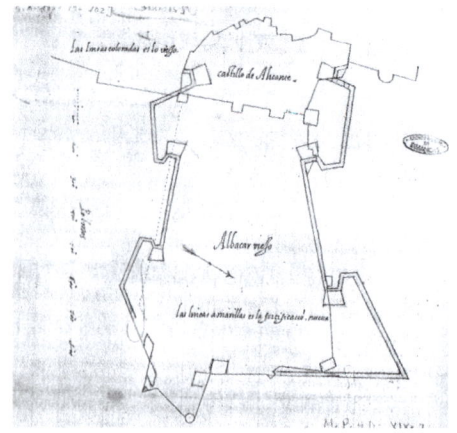

Reconstructed plan of Sabbioneta and its defensive system prior to
interventions of the eighteenth and nineteenth centuries.

*Drawn according to a convention which distinguishes between
the space of domestic or private life (shown as hatching) and that of conceptually
public experience (shown as 'white' space, whether internal or external), this image
of Sabbioneta is intended to convey something of the richness and variety of urban
conditions that was compressed into the modest footprint of its defensive enclosure.
The general form of the Rocca can be retrieved from early maps, though its internal
arrangement is unknown. Clearly, this structure, surviving from an earlier settlement,
was not incorporated into the new order as (in Alberti's words) a 'well-guarded back
door to the city' able, therefore, to function as an independent unit; though it might have
dominated by virtue of its size, its position is by no means dominant. The systematic
closure of linear views through the city and the labyrinthine quality of its street pattern,
have been noted, variously interpreted, by many commentators.*

*This drawing to show a proposed
extension of the fortifications at Alicante was
sent by Vespasiano Gonzaga to Philip II and is
one of the few known to be from his hand, which
have been preserved. Though its purpose was
to inform rather than to seduce and it is clearly
the sort of drawing that an engineer would do
in those circumstances, precise, economical and
matter-of-fact, it shows, nevertheless, a complete
grasp of the conceptual requirements of an
architectural drawing, an understanding of scale
and of relationships in space. None of Vespasiano's
buildings at Sabbioneta depends upon carved
ornament, which might have required an artist's
drawing skill; their architecture is of the sort that
could be sufficiently described with drawings no
more elaborate than this.*

Key: 1, Porta Imperiale. 2, Vespasiano's Academy. 3, Church of the Carmelites. 4, Captain's House. 5, Corridor Grande. 6, Garden Palace. 7, Garden. 8, Rocca. 9, Column of Minerva. 10, Theatre. 11, Lieutenant's House. 12, Palazzo della Ragione. 13, Synagogue. 14, Church of San Rocco. 15, Church of Santa Maria Assunta. 16, Ducal Palace. 17, Church of the Incoronata. 18, Library. 19, Porta Vittoria. Hatched areas are open arcades at ground level. Circled corners indicate extant setting-out stones.

This plan, based upon indications from a number of early plans of Sabbioneta, is, to a certain extent, conjectural. The precise location of the mint, thought to have been in the area of Porta Imperiale, is unknown. The highlighted 'representational' structures stand ambiguously in relation to the city's domestic blocks; generally free at least one corner they are, nevertheless, clearly subsumed within the order of urban spaces: legible as autonomous entities but forming a part, also, of larger elevational compositions. Open arcades are deployed sparingly and to maximize a sense of generous luxury at important viewpoints, particularly within and looking out of the main piazza. The distribution of 'cippi' the corner-stones by means of which the blocks were laid out, is indicative of the scope of new construction undertaken during Vespasiano's lifetime.

2.3

2.4

Types of bastion illustrated in
Pietro Cataneo's I Quattro Primi
Libri di Architettura (1553).

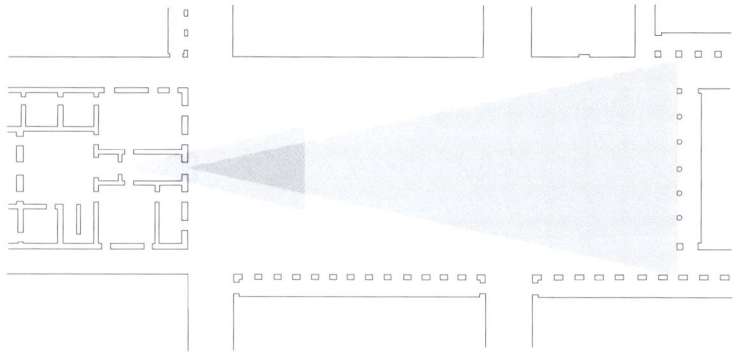

Plan of the first floor of Vespasiano's ducal
palace and of the piazza ducale.

Plan of the bastions
at Sabbioneta.

Emblem from Jacob Cats' Silenus Alcibiadis
(1618) in which the 'answering' vibration
of two equally tuned lutes denotes a condition
of mutual love.

*Though some look more
'aggressive' than others, no particularly powerful
argument favoured one type of bastion above any
other. One must suppose that Vespasiano played
so many variations at Sabbioneta from a desire
to collect the complete set. It seems that sections of
older walls were incorporated into the first round
of re-building, which may partially account for
the apparently haphazard form of Sabbioneta's
defences.*

*The 'consonance' of Vespasiano's studiolo with the piazza outside
seems too close to have been accidental. The streets respectively to the north and south
of the ducal palace are of slightly unequal width (a difference of 75 cm), so that the
piazza is not perfectly symmetrical about the centre-line of the palace; if the narrower
of the two streets were replicated on the north side, the correspondence would have been
almost perfect. Rather than following Alberti's prescription of a double square for the
plan of a 'forum', Vespasiano has taken from Alberti's musically derived theory the
idea of a 4:9 proportion, applying it in a way which is probably without precedent in
renaissance planning. Of the four major rooms, which surround the studiolo, two have
a proportion of 1:1, one of 2:3 and one of 4:9.*

Via dell'Accademia.

The 'Captain's House'.

View into Sabbioneta from the
Porta Vittoria.

The Servite church of
the Incoronata.

The Teatro all'Antico (1589)
by Vincenzo Scamozzi.

The Palazzo della Ragione and, to the left, the church of
Santa Maria Assunta.

*A palette of painted plaster,
brick and sparingly used stone was deployed at
Sabbioneta to make an architecture which called
for no special skills of drawing or ornamental
sculpture.*

*These 'representational' structures simultaneously
reveal and dissimulate their three-dimensional autonomy, allowing
the void space of the city to be read both as figure and as ground.
The 'ideal' form of the Incoronata emerges only partially from the
fabric of conventual buildings, the theatre slips sideways out of the
picture and the Palazzo della Ragione, placed with taller buildings
in the background, can be seen both as free-standing pavilion and as
bounding element to the ducal piazza.*

3.0   4.0

A fortified city with a harbour from the Treatise of
Francesco di Giorgio Martini.

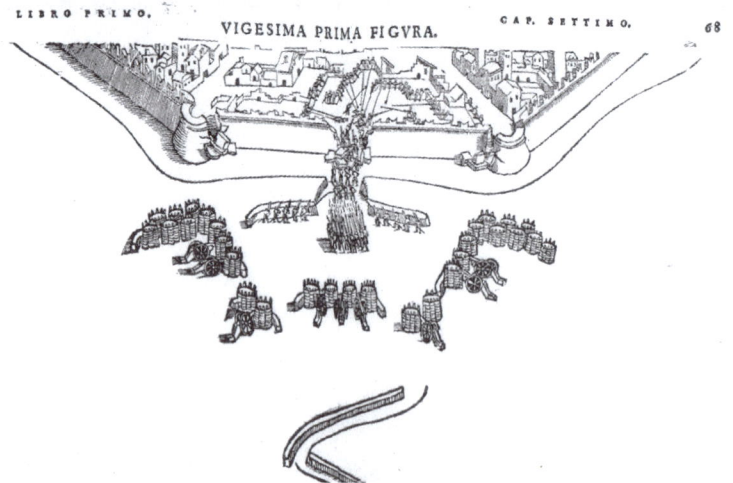

LIBRO PRIMO.   VIGESIMA PRIMA FIGVRA.   CAP. SETTIMO.   68

The successful breaching of obsolete fortification from the
Treatise of Gerolamo Cataneo.

*That Sabbioneta should have
become an object capable of being imagined as a
dukedom was both a political and an architectural
achievement.*

*Francesco di Giorgio's drawing is one of the very few extant
illustrations to show the appearance of the sort of city described in an architectural
treatise. For all the evident splendour of the city's internal appointments, its
fortifications are strikingly similar to those whose comparatively easy destruction
is the subject of Cataneo's illustration. Though seemingly without aesthetic intent,
Cataneo's perspective is more nearly credible than that of the artist.*

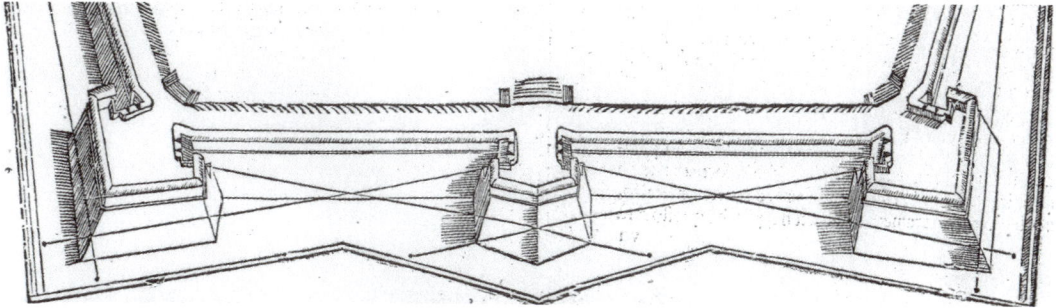

Bastions and the firing-lines which dictate their form from the Treatise of Gerolamo Cataneo.

Giorgio Vasari, detail from the Siege of Pisa, Palazzo della Signoria, Florence.

Tabulated formulae for the deployment of troops from Catane's fourth book.

Vasari's dramatic illustration brings together the three modes of warfare practised in his day: to the right, the aristocratic mode of cavalry; in the centre, the expendable bulk of the infantry and to the left, the new, technical activity of the bombardiers. The reduction of warfare to the 'scientific' application of calculable precept was a development which undoubtedly ran counter to the heroic aspirations which still animated the nobility of sixteenth century Europe, but it was the area in which, whether he liked it or not, Vespasiano Gonzaga became a noted expert.

Unknown artist, Portrait of Giulia Gonzaga, Galleria Borghese, Rome.

The castello at Fondi, home of Giulia Gonzaga, before her move to Naples in 1535, birthplace and home of Vespasiano until he was four years old. This imposing military structure was defensive not only against local rivals but also against the frequent raids by Turkish and Algerian pirates. On one of these occasions, Giulia, together with Vespasiano and his mother are said to have escaped through the back door.

This painting, now in the civic museum at Como, has been definitively identified as a portrait of Vespasiano Gonzaga; the scar on his upper lip (received at the siege of Ostia, 1556) and the emblem of a winged thunderbolt, etched onto his breastplate, leave little room for doubt as to the subject. The painting is dated 1559 making its conventional attribution to Antonis Mor is somewhat problematic. (Mor was still in Spain at the time that Vespasiano went to Flanders in that year). Other artists working at that time, specifically in Lombardy, would have been capable of executing a portrait in this manner.

The beauty of Vespasiano's high-minded aunt was legendary. Situated on the via Appia about halfway from Rome to Naples, her court at Fondi was a sought-after venue for distinguished visitors. While staying at Fondi, cardinal Ippolito de' Medici died by poisoning though Giulia was not, it seems, implicated in the scandal.

Figures   5.2

231

The wooden cornice now attached to
the garden palace.

Half-elevations of the lieutenant's house, Vignola's project for Palazzo Bocchi and Vespasiano's
ducal palace with attic storey and corner obelisks reconstructed.

*An open loggia is substituted
for the battered base of Vignola's design, but this
latter motif reappears on the adjacent elevation of
the lieutenant's house. The architectural detail at
Sabbioneta is generally simplified but if the wooden
cornice of the garden palace belonged originally to
the ducal palace, the resemblance of this elevation
to Vignola's would have been striking.*

View of ducal palace with the lieutenant's
house next door.

"Bernardino Campi painting the portrait of Sofonisba Anguissola" by Sofonisba Anguissola. Museo Nazionale, Siena.

The Uffizi, Florence (1560-71) by Giorgio Vasari.

The Antiquarium in the archducal Residenz at Munich (started 1569) probably based upon suggestions by Jacopo Strada.

The 'Corridor Grande' at Sabbioneta, general view (probably finished 1584)

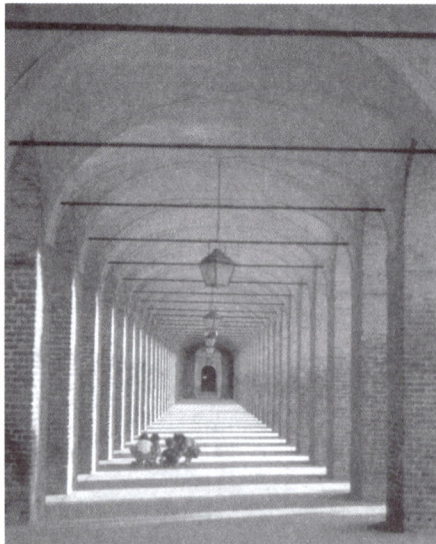

While Campi turns to look at his sitter, she, in her painting of his painting, looks out at the viewer. A curiously involuted record of her relationship with her first instructor and evidence of a sophisticated interest in the artistic transactions of representation and recognition.

The 'Corridor Grande' at Sabbioneta, ground floor arcade, (probably finished 1584)

Project for a palazzo del Podesta by
Sebastiano Serlio (Book VI).

Part elevation of the Corridor
Grande at Sabbioneta.

Urban perspective by Sebastiano Serlio
(Florence, Uffizi).

Villa Imperiale, Pesaro, (about 1530),
by Gerolamo Genga.

*Vespasiano's Corridor Grande seems to quote
elements from Serlio's urban perspective which may, in turn, have
been derived from Genga's Villa Imperiale but both could refer
independently to Genga's original. If the quite close correspondence
of Vespasiano's facade to Serlio's project for a Palazzo del Podesta is
more than accidental, it would provide confirmation that Vespasiano
had seen the manuscript of Serlio's Book VI in the possession of
Jacopo Strada.*

5.6

5.7

Vienna, Stefandom,
(1399 -1446).

Munich, Antiquarium,
detail.

End window of the southern wing of the Servite
convent of the Incoronata.

Sabbioneta, Corridor Grande, Detail.

Drawing for a tragic stage setting by Baldassare Peruzzi
(Florence, Uffizi).

In each case, the occupied (or implicitly occupied) niche substitutes a structure of thematic content for a literal architectural structure, whose place it usurps. Though different in style, the interior of Strada's Antiquarium resembles, in many respects, the equally overcrowded interior of the Stefansdom (which Strada would have known well, having worked often in that city). Though architecturally austere by comparison with either, Vespasiano's Corridor Grande suggests, even with its niches unoccupied, a structured content standing in the space of the architectural structure. If the 'summa' of knowledge is no longer to be theological, it's ordering nevertheless appropriates that of the theological 'built order of knowledge' represented in the architecture of a Gothic cathedral.

The 'gothic' window at the end of what was originally the 'public' library of Sabbioneta has attracted no critical attention. A window of the same general form is to be seen at the other end of the same wing, evidence that this was not a later insertion. A somewhat similar window appears in Peruzzi's drawing. Peruzzi also worked on contextually 'gothic' proposals for the facade of San Petronio in Bologna but the self-conscious use of such an archaic motif is distinctly odd in the context of Sabbioneta. The rotation of the ionic capitals - evidently a deliberate blunder - adds to the impression of ironic detachment in Vespasiano's design.

Left to right: Vespasiano and his ancestors: Luigi 'il Rodomonte' Gonzaga (1500-1532),Vespasiano's father, Gianfrancesco Gonzaga (1443-1496), founder of the Sabbioneta and Bozzolo branch of the family and Lodovico Gonzaga (1414-1478), second Marquess of Mantua.

Only these four survive of the ten wooden equestrian figures, which were originally placed 'one behind the other along the walls' of the principal salone of Vespasiano's palace. At the same time leader and follower in the dynasty, Vespasiano, who 'came after' his ancestors was, in another sense, driven by them.

The surviving tower from an earlier defensive structure at Revere.

Luca Fancelli's gateway tower at Gonzaga.

The tower at Rivarolo of 1461, probably by Fancelli's colleague, Giovanni di Padova.

The Castello at Mantua.

Luca Fancelli's facade of the palace at Revere (begun 1450).

The sixteenth century gateway at Corte Spinosa, which Giulio Romano would have seen.

A fancellian gateway frescoed in the 'Sala dei Circi' in the garden palace at Sabbioneta.

The walled-in ghibelline crenellation, which crowns the palace, refers to ancestral precedent but fails in relation to the classicising ambition of the facade as a whole. The machicolation of the tower (or others like it) seems to have suggested an alternative point of departure.

Vespasiano, like Giulio Romano, was evidently aware of these solutions to the problem of a 'crowning' intended to recall machicolation.

The 'imbarcadero' at Corte Spinosa, near Mantua, believed to be by Giulio Romano or his school.

The outer gateway at Casatico.

The inner gateway at Casatico, both evidently executed to suggestions from Giulio Romano.

It is clear that Giulio had understood not only the expressive potential of the fancellian brackets but also their derivation. His client, the son of Giulio's friend Baldassare Castiglione, would have been likely to appreciate the double-take in this distinctly 'literary' set of allusions.

The bracketed cornice of the ducal palace at Sabbioneta.

The more emphatically 'machicolated' cornice of the Corridor Grands at Sabbioneta.

The gateway towers at Rivarolo, probably built by Vespasiano's father, Luigi il Rodomonte.

Vespasiano's tower at Commessaggio.

Opposite the Corridor Grande stood the Rocca, likely to have resembled the Rivarolo towers, so that the reference would have been contextually explicit. At Commessaggio, fancellian blind crenellations return the evolution of this motif to its origin.

South lateral wall in the theatre at Sabbioneta.
The Castel Sant'Angelo, Rome, as it appeared
in Vespasiano's day, encrusted with medieval
structures. The triumphal arch in which it is
framed bears a dedication to the emperor,
Rudolf II. In the scene to the right, crumbling
ruins are shown in a semi-rural setting while
'tourists' are depicted in contemporary dress.

The fifteenth century
church of Santa Maria
Assunta at Fondi, (birthplace
of Vespasiano Gonzaga.)

The parish church of Santa
Maria Assunta at Sabbioneta.

On the north lateral wall, the Campidoglio at
Rome, whose architectural systemization had
been started, with Michelangelo's new facade
to the palace of the Conservators (inaccurate,
but recognizable), the access ramp and central
pavement and some of the sculptures in
position.

The elevated link, which joined the garden palace
to the rocca at Sabbioneta.

Detail of 'archaic' columns of
the palazzo della ragione.

*The roman structures which
Vespasiano chose to represent in his theatre refer
neither to the splendour of the ancient city (as, for
instance, the Collosseum would have done) nor to
the grandiose ambition of the emerging papal city
(as the new components of the Vatican or St. Peter's
would) but, more specifically, to the 'constitutional'
imperium of the Antonines.*

*There were, no doubt, many reasons for Vespasiano
to recall so strongly, in his parish church at Sabbioneta, the design
of the parish church of his birthplace but the effect is to reinforce the
impression that Sabbioneta had a history. The diagonal brickwork of
the small corridor (visible in roman ruins where the original facing is
lost) could also suggest that Vespasiano wanted this 'fragment' to look
like an antique ruin. The columns of the ground floor of the palazzo
della ragione appear to have been re-cycled from an earlier structure.*

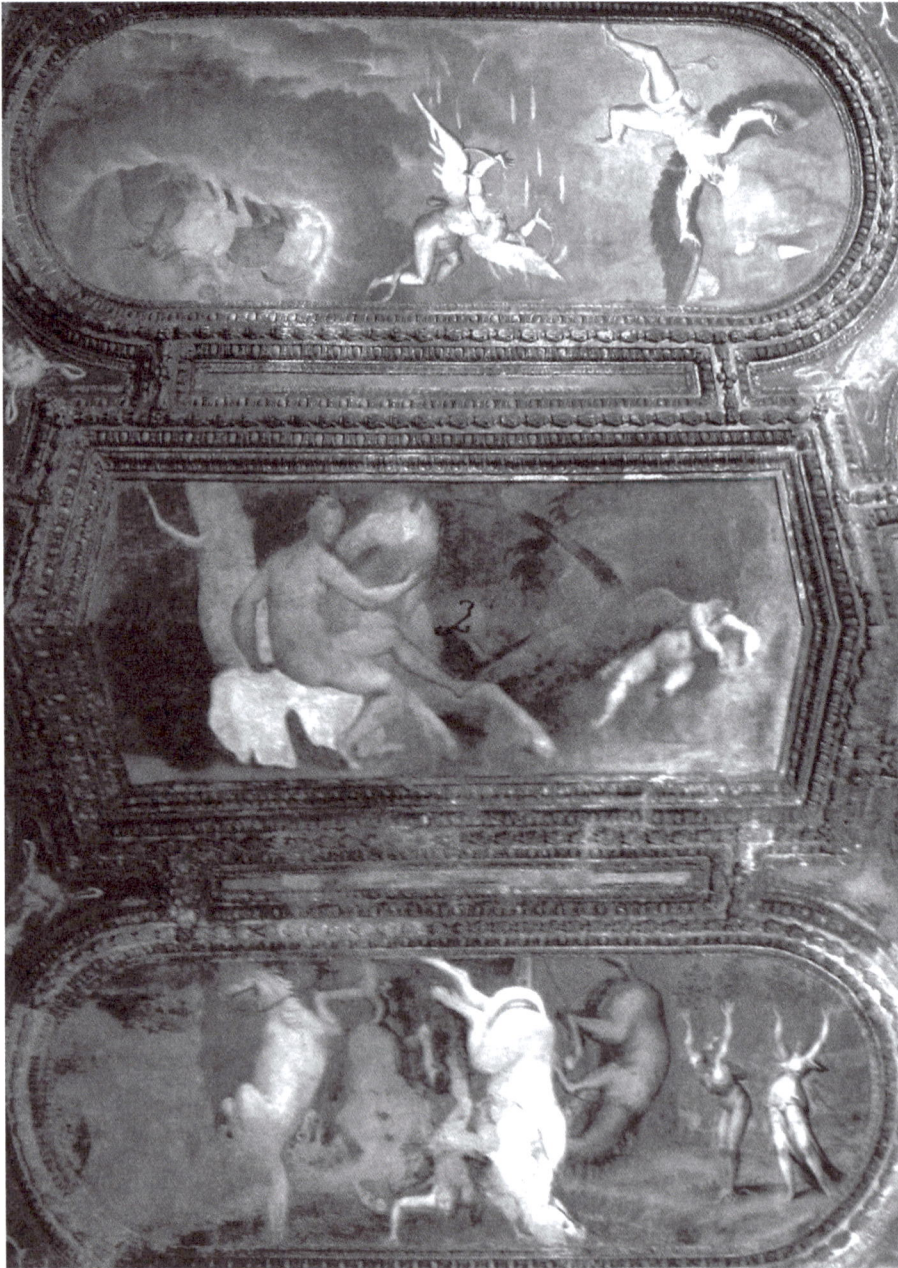

Central part of the ceiling in the Sala dei Miti,
Garden Palace, Sabbioneta.

In the 'primal scene', which forms the centrepiece of this psychic self-portrait, Phylira exhibits neither modesty nor remorse at her concourse with Saturn in the guise of a horse. The scene is framed with the images of falling (Icarus above and Phaeton below) in which Daedalus the father (above) and Phaeton's sisters (below) are impotent spectators. The same horses, which, in the scene above, propel Apollo on his relentless course across the sky, appear, in the lower image, devoid of strength or purpose. Phylira, when she found that she had given birth to a half-monster, was turned to a linden tree; Phaeton's sisters are turning into poplars. It was Daedalus who built the labyrinth in which to conceal another half-monster, the Minotaur who was sired by a bull. A complex pattern of symmetries, inversions and substitutions serves both to link and to differentiate the content of these images.

Scenes in the Salaletta di Enea, in the Garden Palace, Sabbioneta... The Trojan Horse is taken into the city whose wall the Trojans have themselves breached.

Aeneas with his disguised mother, Venus.

End panels of the ceiling of the Sala dei Miti, Garden Palace, Sabbioneta.

At the two ends of the central image, Marsyas flayed alive at the command of Apollo (above) and Arachne about to be transformed by Minerva into a spider (below). Though both images represent the results of unsuccessful competition with a deity, it seems, in the context of the imagery of the ceiling as a whole, unconvincing to account for these subjects purely in terms of the 'moral' which could be drawn from them. The theme of castration is close to the surface in the image of Marsyas (another half-man, half-beast) while a similar anxiety is associated with spiders (Arachne's web is barely visible in the window to the left). Latent symmetries, here again, belie the ostensibly moral interpretation of the cycle.

Out of eight scenes from Virgil's Aeneid, which are depicted in this room, two are concerned with the Trojan horse, suggesting that this image had a special imporatnce for Vespasiano. Horses are an important theme also in the Sala dei Miti, where their sexual association seemed to be prominent. There is little about this Trojan horse to suggest that it is made of wood; on the contrary, it is not only life-like but seemingly charged with furious energy. The horse violates a city, which had willingly breached its own defences, just as a horse (Saturn in disguise) violates Phylira, who has clearly offered no resistance. While his men are hunting the deer, which have conveniently presented themselves, and while Dido awaits his arrival at her court in Carthage, Aeneas is baffled by the disguise of his mother, who appears to him in the form of a huntress.

9.3

Nymphs transformed into trees as they pay homage to Jupiter, from the Hypnerotomachia Poliphili of Francesco Colonna, (circa 1499).

The recurrent ovidian theme of women turned into trees links the Orpheus legend to that of Phylira and of Phaeton depicted in the Sala dei Miti. The apparently inscrutable image in the Hypnerotomachia seems to refer in some way to Ovid's account of the metamorphosis of Phaeton's sisters, though its meaning (is there is one) as well as its affect, is evidently unrelated to that story; but the image could well have been a visual source for the frescoes at Sabbioneta. In the field of Vespasiano's subconscious associations, the myth of Orpheus was closely related to that of Aristeus (the self-identified subject of Vespasiano's poem) so that the trope of a poet torn to pieces by women could carry a specifically personal resonance.

Scene from the Corridoio di Orfeo in the Garden Palace, Sabbioneta. The dismembered body of Orpheus, torn to pieces by the Maenads, floats, along with his lute, on the river Hebrus. The serpent, about to bite his head as it is washed up on the shore of Lesbos, is turned to stone, while his crazed assassins are transformed into oak trees.

The Sala degli Specchi in the Garden Palace, Sabbioneta.

Il Soggiorno Agreste.

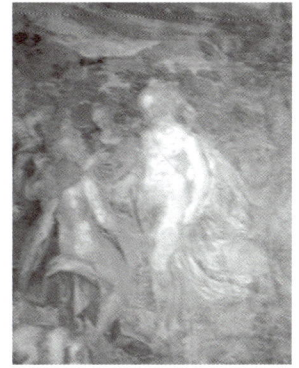

Detail of La Passaggiata.

Detail of l'imbarco (visible to the left of the picture above).

Detail of La Passaggiata.

The blank panels of the ceiling and end wall contained mirrors, creating a highly ambiguous relation of 'real' to illusory space, while the monochrome relief panels over the windows belong clearly to the order of the room. La Caccia, a hunting scene is the further of the visible frescos. There is no way of telling whether the scene below depicts an arrival or a departure, but the lady in blue appears to be the same figure who also appears in La Sosta and in La Passaggiata, suggesting that these are not just incidental scenes of rural life.

Possibly, but not necessarily, the transparent, ghostly quality of the figures in the lower picture could have been the result of over-painting. But the mood and the content of the other scenes cannot be convincingly described as 'everyday'.

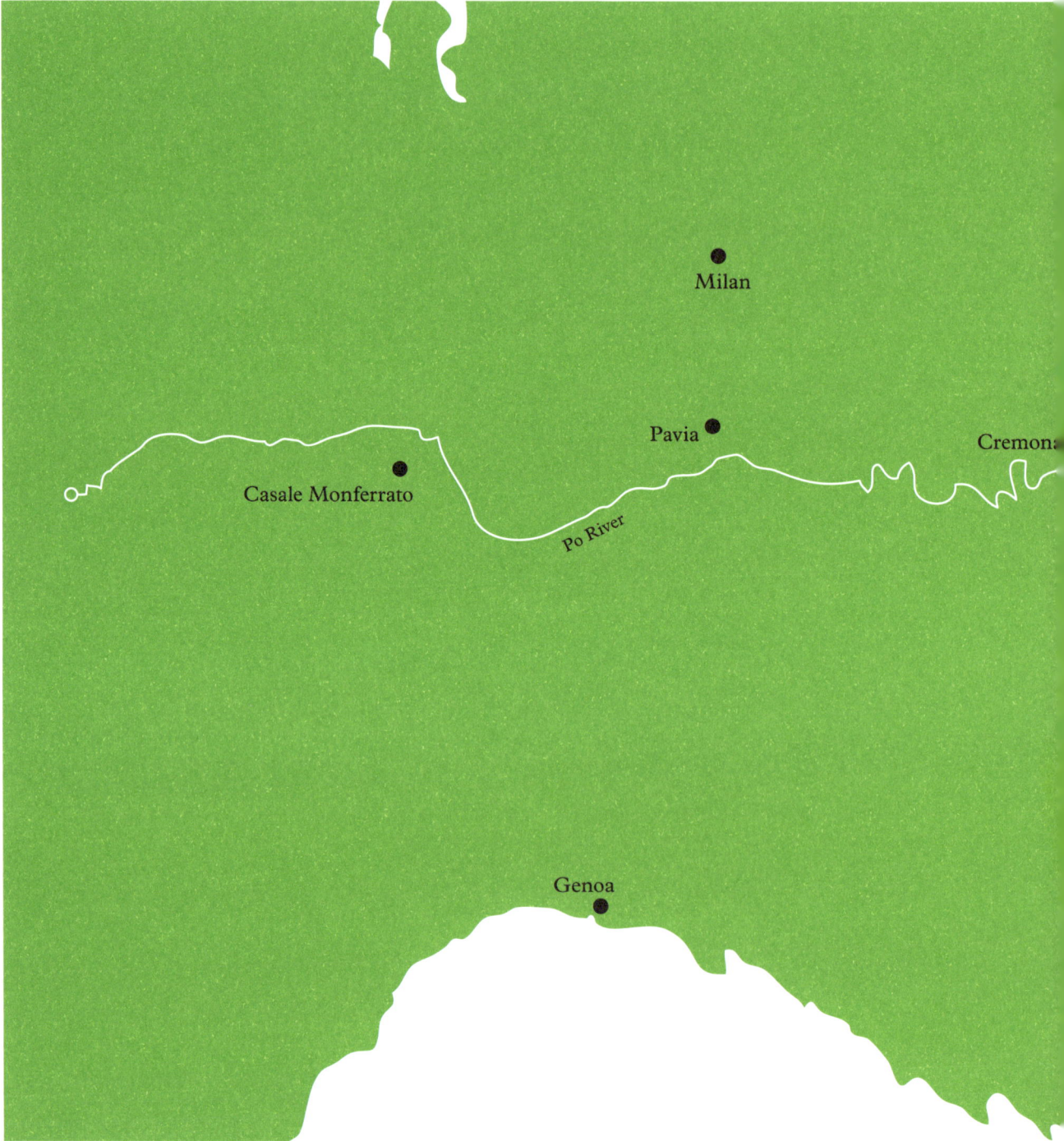

Milan

Pavia

Cremona

Casale Monferrato

Po River

Genoa

Map of Northern Italy with key locations
along the Po River.

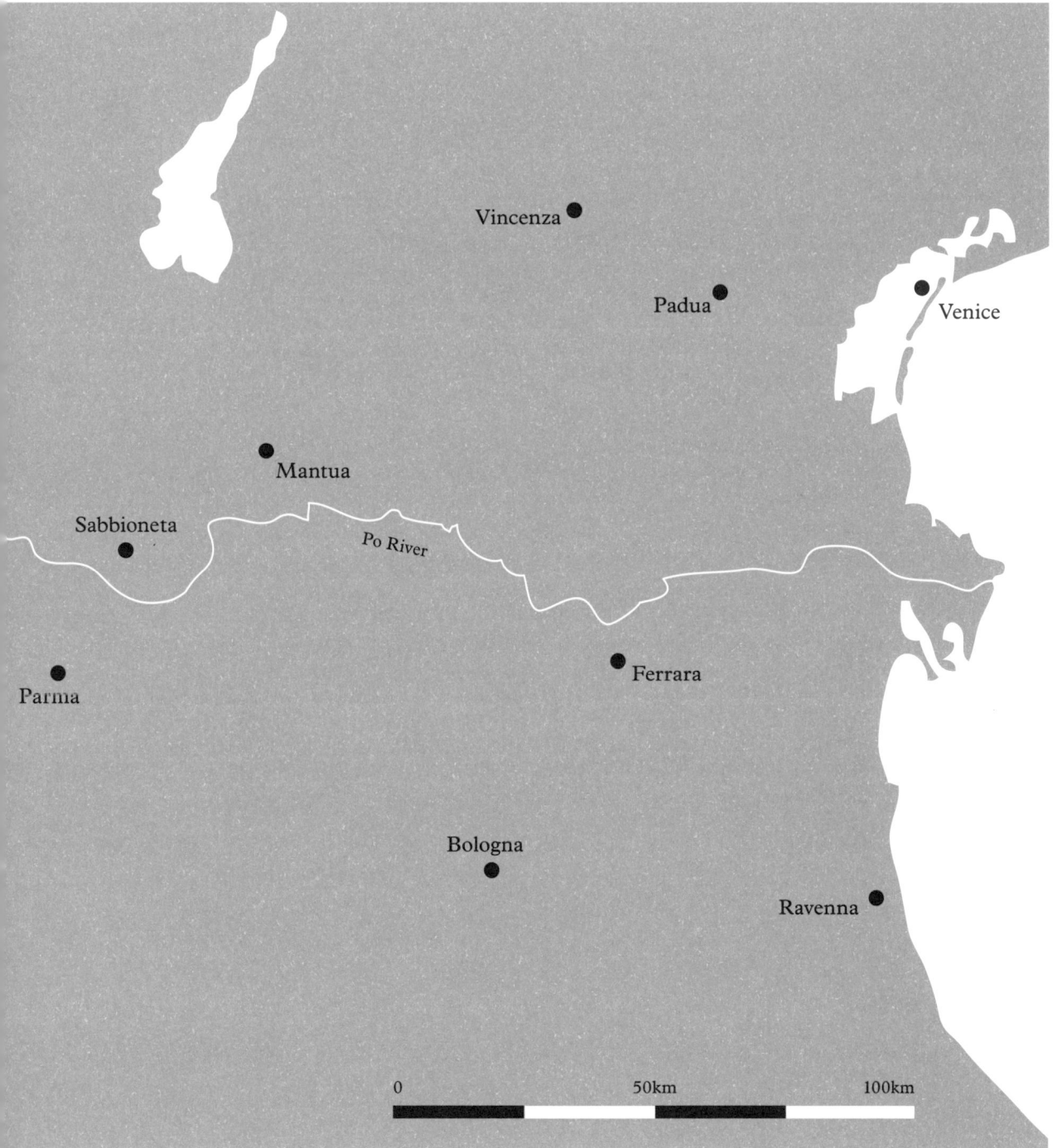

Vincenza

Padua

Venice

Mantua

Sabbioneta

Po River

Parma

Ferrara

Bologna

Ravenna

0   50km   100km

Affò, I.
Vita di Luigi Gonzaga & Vita di Vespasiano Gonzaga, etc.
Parma, 1780.

Affò, I.
Vita di Monsignore Bernardino Baldi, Primo Abate di Guastalla
Parma, 1783.

Alberti, L.B.
On the Art of Building in Ten Books, trans. J.Rykwert, N.Leach and R.Tavernor
Cambridge Mass and London, 1992.

Amadè, L.S.
Il Duca di Sabbioneta - Guerre e amori di un Europeo del XVI Secolo
Milan, 1990.

Amadè, L.S.
"Alla Scoperta di Sabbioneta" in
Sabbioneta Una stella e una pianura
Milan, 1985.

Argan, G.C.
The Renaissance City, trans. S.E.Bassnett
New York, 1969.

Ariosto, L.
Orlando Furioso, trans. B.Reynolds
London, 1977.

Arrighi, B.
Storia di Mantova
Brescia, 1974.

Baldi, B.
Vite inediti di Matematici
Urbino, 1707.

Baldi, B.
La descrizione del palazzo ducale
Florence, 1889.

Baldi, B.
Raccolta di poemi didascalici
Milan, 1813.

Bardon, F.
Le Concert Champêtre
Paris, First Part 1995, Second Part 1996.

Bazzotti, U.
"La Galleria degli Antichi di Sabbioneta: Questioni cronologiche, attributive e iconografiche" in Various,
Vespasiano Gonzaga e il Ducato di Sabbioneta: atti del convegno
Mantua, 1993.

Bazzotti, U.
"Nobilis Cicatrix - Un Nuovo Ritratto e una nota impresa di Vespasiano Gonzaga" in *Civiltà Mantovana*, 12, 1986.

Benevolo, L.
The Architecture of the Renaissance, trans. J. Landry
London, 1978.

Benevolo, L.
Storia della città
Roma-Bari, 1993.

Berzaghi, R.
"La 'Galleria delle città' nel Palazzo Grande di Sabbioneta" in *Civiltà Mantovana* Nos. 65-66 (1977)

Bocchi, A.
Symbolicae Quaestiones, (first published 1555)
London and New York, 1979.

Boase, T.S.R.
Giorgio Vasari, The Man and the Book
Princeton N.J. and Guildford Surrey, 1979.

Bologni, B.M.
Memorie Storiche dei commune di Rivarolo Fuori, Piadena, Calvatone o Città di Vegra e del Vico Bebriaco
Cremona, 1986.

Braudel, F.
The Mediterranean and the mediterranean world in the age of Philip II, trans. Siân Reynolds
London and Los Angeles, 1995.

Burckhardt, J.
The Architecture of the Italian Renaissance, trans. J. Palmes, ed. P. Murray
London, 1985.

Buzzi, T.
"Il 'Teatro all'Antica' di V. Scamozzi" in
Dedalo VIII, 1927-1928.

Buzzi, T.
"I palazzi di Sabbioneta" in *Dedalo*,
1928-1929.

Campagnari, R. & Ferrari, A.
"Quattrocento e cinquecento in
una residenza signorile: La Corte
Castiglione a Casàtico" in Various, *Corti
e Dimore del Contado Mantovano*
Firenze, 1969.

Campagnari, R. & Ferrari, A.
"Accenti aulici in una fattoria del pieno
Rinascimento: La Spinosa"
in Various, *Corti e Dimore del Contado
Mantovano*
Firenze, 1969.

Carli, A.
Vespasiano Gonzaga Duca di Sabbioneta
Florence, 1878.

Caroli, F.
L'Anima e il Volto
Milan, 1998.

Carpeggiani, P.
Sabbioneta
Sabbioneta, 1989.

Carpeggiani, Pietro,
"Un documento dell'architettura
di Giulio Romano: La Villa Zani di
Villimpenta" in Various, *Corti e Dimore
del Contado Mantovano*
Firenze, 1969.

Cataneo, Gerolamo,
Dell'Arte Militare Libri Tre
Venice, 1571.

Cataneo, P.
I Quattro Primi Libri di Architettura
(First published 1554)
New Jersey, 1964.

Cervantes, M. de,
Don Quixote, trans. J.M. Cohen
Harmondsworth, 1950.

Chambers & Martineau (eds.)
Splendours of the Gonzaga
V & A London, 1981.

Chastel, A. Et al.
The Renaissance, essays in interpretation
London and New York, 1982.

Cieri Via, C.
"Collezionismo e Memoria alla Corte
di Vespasiano Gonzaga: Dalla Galleria
degli Antenati alla Galleria degli
Antichi" in Various, *Vespasiano Gonzaga
e il Ducato di Sabbioneta: atti del convegno*
Mantua, 1993.

Conforti, C.
Giorgio Vasari Architetto
Milan, 1993.

Colonna, F.
Hypnerotomachia Poliphili, trans. and ed.
Joscelyn Godwin,
London 1999.

Croce, B.
"Un Angolo di Napoli" in *Scritti di
Storia, Letteraria e Politica*
Bari, 1919.

d'Alberto, L.
"La Chiesa dell'Incoronata" in *Civiltà
Mantovana* IV n.21, 1969.

dall'Acqua, M.
"Il Principe e la sua Primogenita" in
Various, *Vespasiano Gonzaga e il Ducato
di Sabbioneta: atti del convegno*
Mantova, 1993.

dal Prato, P.
"Una Concezione di Luca Fancelli: Il
Palazzo di San Martino Gusnago"
in Various, *Corti e Dimore del Contado
Mantovano*
Firenze, 1969.

Dean, T. & Lowe, K.J.P.
*Crime, Society and the Law in Renaissance
Italy*
Cambridge, 1994.

de Wolfe, I.
Special 'Townscape' issue of
Architectural Review Vol. 131 No. 784
London, 1962.

De Zanchi, B.
Del Modo di Fortificar la Città
Venice, 1560.

Dillon, E.
Glass
London, 1907.

Dondi, Niccolo di
"Estratti del Diario delle cose avvenute in Sabbioneta dal 1580 al 1600" in G.Müller, *Raccolta di Cronisti e Documenti Storici Lombardi Inediti*
Milan, 1857.

Elam, C.
'Sabbioneta' in *AA Files 18*
London, 1989.

Evans, R.J.W.
Rudolf II and his World
Oxford, 1973.

Falbe, L.C.
Sabbioneta: a Drama in three Acts
London, 1907.

Ferrari, D.
"Vespasiano e I Gonzaga di Mantova" in Various, *Vespasiano Gonzaga e il Ducato di Sabbioneta: atti del convegno.....*
Mantova, 1993.

Filarete
Treatise on Architecture, trans J.R. Spencer
Newhaven & London, 1965.

Fioravanti, L.
Dello Specchio di Scientia Universale
Venice, 1572.

Forster, K.W.
"From 'Rocca' to 'Civitas': Urban Planning at Sabbioneta" in *L'Arte*, Fasc.5, March, 1959.

Forster, K.W.
"Stagecraft and Statecraft: The Architectural Integration of Public Life and Theatrical Spectacle in Scamozzi's Theatre at Sabbioneta" in *Oppositions IX*,
New York, 1977.

Freud, S.
The Interpretation of Dreams, trans. J. Strachey,
London, 1991.

Freud, S.
New Introductory Lectures on Psycho-analysis, trans. W.J.H.Sprott,
London, 1946.

Frommel, C.L.
"Serlio e la scuoal romana" in Various, *Sebastiano Serlio, Sesto Seminario*
Milan, 1989.

Frommel, S.
Sebastiano Serlio Architetto
Milan, 1998.

Gallerati, M.
Architettura Scala Urbana
Florence, 1979.

Garin, E. (Ed.)
L'uomo del Rinascimento
Rome-Bari, 1988.

Garin, E.
La Cultura Filosofica del Rinascimento Italiano
Milan, 2001.

Gazzola, P.
"Sabbioneta. Proposte per la rinascita della città" in *Civiltà Mantovana II*, No.7 (1967)

Ghisi Mutti, V.E.
"La Centuriazione del Territorio di Mantova" in *Civiltà Mantovana VIII*, No. 46, (1974)

Gombrich, E.H. et al.
Giulio Romano
Milan, 1989.

Gonzaga, Scipione.
Autobiography ed. Dante Della Terza
Modena, 1987.

Green, André.
On Private Madness (first published in French, 1983)
London, 1986.

Grötz, S.
"La SS Incoronata, mausoleo di
Vespasiano Gonzaga" in *Civiltà
Mantovana*, 3rd series, No.9 (1993).

Grötz, S.
"La Saletta di Enea ed il Mito della
Città Ideale" in Various, *Vespasiano
Gonzaga e il Ducato di Sabbioneta: atti del
convegno.....*
Mantova, 1993.

Guazzo, S.
Civile Conversation tr. Pettie & Young,
Ed. Sir E. Sullivan, Bart.
London & New York, 1925.

Hale, J.R.
Renaissance War Studies
London, 1983.

Hale, J.R.
*Renaissance Fortification - Art or
Engineering?*
London & New York, 1977.

Hale, J.R.
*The Civilization of Europe in the
Renaissance*
London, 1993.

Hay, D.
*The Italian Renaissance in its Historical
Background*
Cambridge, 1977.

Heer, F.
The Holy Roman Empire trans. J.
Sondheimer
London, 1968.

Hollingsworth, M.
Patronage in Sixteenth Century Italy
London, 1996.

Huizinger, J.
The Waning of the Middle Ages, trans.
F. Hopman
Harmondsworth, 1965.

Hyginus,
The Myths of Hyginus, trans. And ed.
Mary Grant
Lawrence, Kansas, 1960.

Jansen, D.J.
"Jacopo Strada et la commerce d'art" in
La Revue de l'art 77, (1987).

Jansen, D.J.
*Jacopo Strada (1515 - 1588): Antiquario
della Sacra Cesarea Maestà*
Delft, 1982.

Jansen, D.J.
"Jacopo Strada editore del Settimo
Libro" in Various: *Sebastiano Serlio, Sesto
Seminario*
Milan, 1989.

Jenkins, H. (ed.)
The Arden Shakespeare: Hamlet
London & New York, 1982.

Jung, C.G.
*Analytical Psychology: its Theory and
Practice*
London and Henley, 1968.

Jusserand, J.J.
"A Duke and his City. Vespasiano
Gonzaga, duke of Sabbioneta" in *The
School for Ambassadors and other essays*
London 1924.

Kamen, H.
Philip of Spain
New Haven and London, 1997.

Koenigsberger, H.G. & Mosse, L.
Europe in the Sixteenth Century
London, 1968.

Kristeller, P.O.
Renaissance Thought and its Sources
New York, 1979.

Kruft, H.W.
Städte in Utopia
Munich, 1989.

Kruft, H.W.
*A History of Architectural Theory from
Vitruvius to the Present*
London & New York, 1994.

Lacan, J.
*The Four Fundamental Principles of
Psycho-analysis* trans. A. Sheridan
Harmondsworth, 1979.

Lantieri, G.
Del Modo di Fare le Fortificatione
Venice, 1558.

Larivaille, P. (tr. Pra, R.)
La Vita Quotidiana in Italia ai Tempi di Machiavelli
Milan, 1995.

Lemprière, J.
Lemprière's Classical Dictionary Writ Large
London, Boston, Melbourne & Henley, 1984.

Levin, H.
The Question of Hamlet
New York, 1959.

Lievsay, J.L.
Stefano Guazzo and the English Renaissance
North Carolina, 1961.

Liva, A.
"Gli Statuti della Comunità di Sabbioneta e la successiva legislazione di Vespasiano Gonzaga" in Various, *Vespasiano Gonzaga e il Ducato di Sabbioneta: atti del convegno.....*
Mantova, 1993.

Livy (Titus Livius)
The History of Rome from its Foundation, trans. A. De Sélincourt.
London, 1971.

Lotz, W.
Studies in Italian Renaissance Architecture
London & Cambridge Mass. 1977.

Lynch, J.
Spain Under the Habsburgs
Oxford, 1965.

Machiavelli, N.
The Prince, trans. Bondanella, P & Musa, M.
Oxford, 1984.

Maffezzoli, U.
Sabbioneta, piccola reggia padana
Modena, 1994.

Malacarne, G.
"Gli Stemme di Vespasiano Gongaga dal Ramo Cadetto di Sabbioneta" in Various, *Vespasiano Gonzaga e il Ducato di Sabbioneta: atti del convegno.....*
Mantova, 1993.

Malacarne, G.
Le Cacce del Principe
Modena, 1998.

Marani, E.
Sabbioneta e Vespasiano Gonzaga
Sabbioneta, 1977.

Marani, E. & Perina, C.
Mantova: Le Arti Vol III
Mantova, 1965.

Marchini, R., & Rossi, E.
"La Corte della 'Grangia' a Villa Pasquali: Residenza suburbana di Vespasiano Gonzaga" *Civiltà Mantovana* No. 107. Nov. 1998.

Marlier, G.
Anthonis Mor Van Dashorst
Brussels, 1934.

Martini, F. Di Giorgio
Trattato di Architettura civile e militare, ed. Corrado Maltese,
Milan, 1967.

Masson, G.
Italian Villas and Palaces
London, 1966.

Michelangelo
Poèmes French and Italian version, trans. and ed. P. Leyris,
Paris, 1983.

Minturno, A.
L'Arte Poetica
Venice, 1563.

Montanari, M.
La fame e l'abbondanza: Storia dell'alimentazione in Europa
Roma-Bari, 1997.

Muir, K.
Shakespeare's Sources
London, 1961.

Muzio, Gerolamo,
Egloghe
Venice, 1550.

Nizolius, M.
De Veris Principiis ed. Quirinius Breen,
Rome, 1956.

Nulli, S.A.
Giulia Gonzaga
Milan, 1938.

Orazi, A.M.
Jacopo Barozzi da Vignola, 1528-1550
Rome, 1982.

Ovid, (Publius Ovidius Naso)
Opere di P. Ovidio Nasone, trans.
Dorrucci, L. Vol 1.
Firenze, 1879.

Ovid,
Metamorphoses, trans. Frank Justus
Miller,
Cambridge Mass., 1999.

Pacioli, L. (With commentary by
Giuseppina Masotti Biggiogero)
De Divina Proportione
Milan, 1956.

Palvarini, M.R. & Perogalli, C.
Castelli dei Gonzaga
Milan, 1983.

Paolucci, A.
I Gonzaga e l'Antico
Rome, 1988.

Paolucci, A. & Maffezzoli, U.
Sabbioneta: il Teatro all'Antica
Modena, 1993.

Patrizi, G.
"Vespasiano Gonzaga e la Forma
del Vivere Cortegiano" in Various,
*Vespasiano Gonzaga e il Ducato di
Sabbioneta: atti del convegno.....*
Mantova, 1993.

Perlingieri, I.S.
*Sofonisba Anguissola, The First Great
Woman Artist of the Renaissance*
New York, 1994.

Petrarch, F.
*Petrarch's Lyric Poems: The Rime sparse
and Other Lyrics* ed. R.M. Durling,
Cambridge Mass and London, 1976.

Pevsner, N.
A History of Building Types
London, 1976.

Pilati, R.
"I Feudi Gonzagheschi nel Regno
di Napoli" in Various, *Vespasiano
Gonzaga e il Ducato di Sabbioneta: atti del
convegno.....*
Mantova, 1993.

Pinelli, A. & Rossi, O.
*Genga Architetto, aspetti della cultura
urbinate del primo 500*
Rome, 1971.

Pinessi, O.
*Sofonisba Anguissola - Un "pittore" alla
corte di Filippo II*
Milan, 1998.

Pinotti, G.
Un Principe del Rinasciamento
Sabbioneta, 1996.

Prescott, W.H.
History of the Reign of Philip II
London, 1855.

Puerari, A.
Sabbioneta Ed. Domus,
Milan, 1955.

Racheli, A.
Memorie Storiche del dottor A.R. (First
published Casalmaggiore, 1849.)
Bologna, 1979.

Rainerio, A.F.
Cento Sonetti
Milan, 1553.

Rosenau, H.
The Ideal City
London & New York, 1983.

Rowe, C. & Satkowski, L.
*Italian Architecture of the Sixteenth
Century*
New York, 2002.

Ruscelli, G. (Ed.)
Precetti della Militia Moderna, Tanto per Mare, Quanto per Terra
Venice, 1572.

Sanvito, P.
"Collezionismo Imperialregio
e Collezionismo a Sabbioneta:
L'influenza del Modello Asburgico" in
Various, *Vespasiano Gonzaga e il Ducato di Sabbioneta: atti del convegno.....*
Mantova, 1993.

See Watson, E.
Achille Bocchi and the Emblem Book as Symbolic Form
Cambridge, 1993.

Shakespeare, W.
The Works of William Shakespeare
London, 1947.

Sitwell, O.
Winters of Content
London, 1950.

Spenser, E.
The Works of Edmund Spenser
London, 1850.

Tafuri, M.
"Ipotesi sulla religiosità di Sebastiano Serlio" in Various: *Sebastiano Serlio, Sesto Seminario*
Milan, 1989.

Tamalio, R.
"Vespasiano Gonzaga al servizio del Re di Spagna in Spagna" in Various,
Vespasiano Gonzaga e il Ducato di Sabbioneta: atti del convegno.....
Mantova, 1993.

Tasso, Torquato.
Jerusalem Delivered English prose version, trans. and ed. Ralph Nash.
Detroit 1987.

Tellini Perina, C.
Sabbioneta
Milan, 1993.

Trevor-Roper, H.
Princes and Artists
London & New York, 1991.

Valdès, Juan de
Alfabeto Cristiano (first pub. Venice, 1545) with introduction by B. Croce
Rome, 1938.

Various.
Vespasiano Gonzaga e il Ducato di Sabbioneta: atti del convegno ....
Bazzotti, U., Ferrari, D., Mozzarelli, D. (Eds.)
Mantova, 1993.

Various.
Sabbioneta una stella e una pianura
Milan, 1985.

Various.
"Sabbioneta dopo Vespasiano" in *Civiltà Mantovana* n.s., No. 13, 1986.

Various.
Sofonisba Anguissola e le sue Sorelle
Cremona, 1994.

Various.
Sebastiano Serlio, Sesto Seminario, ed. C. Thoenes
Milan, 1989.

Varisco, T.
"La Ricostruzione della scena del teatro Olimpico di Sabbioneta" in *Civiltà Mantovana* No. 1 (1966)

Vasari, G.
Le Vite dei piu celebre Pittori, Scultori e Architetti
Florence 1925.

Vasic Vantovec, C.
Luca Fancelli - architetto, Epistolario Gonzaghesco
Florence, 1979.

Ventura, L.
Vespasiano Gonzaga Colonna 1531 1591 - mostra iconografica
Modena 1991.

Ventura, L.
"Vespasiano e I Gonzaga" in Various,
Vespasiano Gonzaga e il Ducato di Sabbioneta: atti del convegno.....
Mantova, 1993.

Virgil (Publius Virgilius Maro),
Works with trans. by Rushton
Fairclough, H., Vol.1.
London & New York, 1920.

Virgil,
The Aeneid, tr. R. Fitzgerald,
London, 1992.

Vitruvius
The Ten Books on Architecture trans.
M. Hicky Morgan
New York, 1960.

Villard de Honnecourt
Disegni eds. A. Erlande-Brandenburg, R.
Pernoud, J. Gimpel and R. Bechmann.
trans. C. Formis
Milan, 1988.

Wittkower, R.
*Architectural Principles in the Age of
Humanism*
London, 1949.

Von Simson, O.
The Gothic Cathedral
London, 1956.

Woodward, W.H.
*Vittorino da Feltre & other Humanist
Educators*
Cambridge, 1897.

Wurm, H.
Baldassare Peruzzi
Tübingen, 1984.

Yates, Frances A.
The Rosicrucian Enlightenment
London and Boston, 1972.

Yates, Frances A.
*Giordano Bruno and the Hermetic
Tradition*
London, 1964.

Yriarte
"Sabbioneta, la petite Athènes" in
Gazette des Beaux Arts XL t.19. 1898.

255